XCMD'S FOR HYPERCARD

Gary Bond

To Mark, Best Wishes!
Dan Winkler

Mark, Let's work together for a better Hypercard! Gary Bond 8/11/88

Happy XCMDing! Sioux

MIS:
PRESS

MANAGEMENT INFORMATION SOURCE, INC.

COPYRIGHT

DEDICATION

To my mother Helen and my stepfather Richard.

ACKNOWLEDGMENTS

Thanks **Scot Kamins** for being my friend and mentor and for your continuing guidance and support during this project. Your words of wisdom and rebuke were always taken in the spirit they were intended. In fact, I couldn't have done it without you.

A special thanks also goes to Sioux Lacy, who spent many of her free hours converting the Pascal code and examples in this book into C. Sioux's one of the best programmers on the HyperCard development team and is herself the author of several terrific XCMD's and HyperCard stacks.

Swami Phil Wyman helped review the book in its early stages. His comments and suggestions brought balance and harmony. David Leffler's patience and kind words helped me juggle the responsibilities of working on HyperCard while simultaneously writing this book.

And finally, a very special thanks goes to Dan Winkler, friend and mentor. His foresight and ingenuity made this book possible.

TABLE OF CONTENTS

DISK ORDER FORM
ON LAST PAGE
OF BOOK

FOREWORD

You know, people often ask me if HyperCard can help them with some particular little task they have in mind, such as simulating wind tunnel experiments on their proposed design for a diesel-powered egg-beater or, more typically, analyzing old gum wrappers to distinguish the real ones from the clever forgeries. I am always happy to tell them that through a remarkable coincidence, they have independently struck upon precisely what I had in mind when I designed XCMD's. XCMD's, I tell them, will allow HyperCard to do anything the Mac can do, including what they have in mind, even though, through a regrettable oversight, that particular functionality was not actually built into the product. Usually we agree that there must be tens of other people, at least, out there in the world interested in similar issues involving the relationship between aerodynamics, internal combustion, handwriting analysis, and vegetarian cooking, and I point out that only one of them has to write the appropriate XCMD and then all of them can use it, thus generally advancing the state of human knowledge in their important field and possibly earning a small fortune in the process. On rare occasions, they ask me if I would like to assist in their noble endeavor, and I am unfortunately forced to decline, explaining that I am myself hard at work on an XCMD that will allow HyperCard to pilot the space shuttle to the moon since I know that it is only a matter of time now before NASA calls asking for just such an item. Well then, they ask, how can one learn more about these marvelous XCMD's that could lead to the creation of the world's first fuel-efficient, counterfeit-proof, vegetable-based, flying gum wrapper? All you have to do is turn the page....

Dan Winkler
Cupertino, CA
April 1988

INTRODUCTION

This book contains a complete, step-by-step approach to the creation and use of HyperCard's external commands and functions—commonly referred to as XCMD's and XFCN's. XCMD's and XFCN's let you create new HyperTalk commands and functions.

In this book, you will learn what XCMD's and XFCN's are, how to call them from HyperTalk, and where they fit into the inheritance path. You'll become familiar with the XCMD interface and glue routines (pre-programmed procedures and functions) and how to create your own glue routines. You'll learn how to pass data to and from your XCMD's and XFCN's, how to access HyperCard's internal data structures, and how to use the call-back interface. You'll learn what to avoid when creating an XCMD or XFCN, and you'll pick up a few tips and tricks along the way.

If you are relatively new to Macintosh programming, you'll find that HyperCard's external commands and functions provide an excellent medium in which to develop and hone your programming skills. While this book isn't intended to be about Macintosh programming, it does contain a significant amount of source code and development information that can be an enormous aid in your early programming efforts.

What You Need to Know

You should have a passing acquaintance with Volumes 1-5 of *Inside Macintosh,* and you should possess a good understanding of HyperTalk—HyperCard's built-in programming language. You should also know one high-level language—preferably Pascal or C.

How This Book is Organized

MPW Pascal (Macintosh Programmers Workshop—available from APDA) was chosen as the primary language for the examples in this book due to its widespread use among Macintosh programmers. Below each Pascal example, you will find a section that shows the equivalent information in LightspeedC™ (from Think Technologies, Inc.).

What Each Chapter Contains

Chapter 1—"Designing XCMD's and XFCN's"—includes information about what XCMD's and XFCN's are and how to use them; how XCMD's can be used to communicate with the outside word; the syntax and inheritance of XCMD's and XFCN's, and more. This chapter provides the information you'll need when designing an XCMD or XFCN.

Chapter 2—"Understanding XCMD's and XFCN's"—covers XCMD's and XFCN's in detail. Topics include parameter passing, error trapping, the call-back interface, using HyperTalk commands from within your XCMD's and XFCN's, pitfalls, and more. This chapter provides the information you'll need when coding an XCMD or XFCN.

Chapter 3—"Accessing HyperCard's Internal Structures"—covers the external inter-face and the tools you'll need when creating an XCMD or XFCN. Each of the built-in glue routines is explained in detail, and a section on creating your own glue routines is included. In addition, the chapter contains information on accessing some of HyperCard's internal data structures.

Chapter 4—"Creating Your First XCMD"—takes you from beginning to end in the creation of an XCMD. Consideration is given to Apple's Human Interface Guidelines and to maintaining the elegance and ease of use of the HyperTalk programming language.

Chapter 5—"Debugging and Related Information"—pays special attention to removing bugs from your XCMD's and XFCN's. Common mistakes are pointed out, and possible solutions are suggested. This chapter also offers various tips and tricks for getting the most out of your XCMD's and XFCN's.

Chapter 6—"Ready-to-Use XCMD's and XFCN's"—includes program listings for 20 XCMD's and XFCN's. Included are XCMD's for adding menus to HyperCard, performing file operations such as deleting and renaming files, printing the contents of individual fields, making HyperCard talk, copying resources from one stack to another, and more. Source listings are shown in both Pascal and C.

Several appendices and a glossary complete the book.

If You Can't Wait to Get Started...

Everyone should read Chapter 1 and Chapter 2. Chapter 1 contains basic information you'll need to know before designing an XCMD or XFCN, and Chapter 2 contains specific information you'll need to know before coding an XCMD or XFCN.

If, after reading Chapters 1 and 2, you can't wait to get started building your first XCMD, skip to Chapter 4—"Creating Your First XCMD." If you skip ahead, you may need to occasionally refer to Chapter 3—"Accessing HyperCard's Internal Structures"—to understand a few of the routines used in the example XCMD in Chapter 4.

Conventions Used Throughout This Book

The following conventions and syntatical descriptions are used throughout this book:

HyperCard

Words and terms shown in bold type are defined in the glossary.

HyperTalk Code Type

All HyperTalk commands and scripts appear in the above font. Most text appearing in this font can be typed directly into the message box or typed into any HyperCard script.

Pascal Code

All Pascal program listings appear in this font. Any text in this font can be typed directly into your Pascal compiler (with the proper modifications).

C Code

All C program listings appear in this font. Any text in this font can be typed directly into your C compiler (with the proper modifications).

{Pascal Comment}

Comments appear within curly brackets in the Pascal source code.

Note: While most comments may be optionally eliminated, this is not true for MPW Pascal's compile and link directives (see "Special Treatment of Compile and Link Directives" below).

```
/* C Comment */
```

In the C source code, comments are enclosed by right slashes and asterisks.

For the C Programmer

Sections with the heading "For the C Programmer" provide information or source listings for the C programmer. Source code found in this section is written for the LightspeedC Compiler and may require minor modifications when used with other C compilers.

Special Treatment of Compile and Link Definitions

Pascal source listings in this book contain the information necessary to compile and link the code that follows. Notice that the information appears within a Pascal comment block, such as in the following:

```
(*
© 1988 by Gary Bond
All Rights Reserved

DeleteFile — a HyperCard XCMD that deletes the specified file

Form: DeleteFile filename

Example: DeleteFile "HD:MyFolder:MyFile"

Note: Pathnames are allowed and are necessary if the file is not on the root level
```

continued...

...from previous page

To compile and link this file using MPW Pascal, select the following lines and press the ENTER key

pascal DeleteFile.p
link -o "HD:HyperCard:Home" -rt XCMD=1612 -sn Main=DeleteFile DeleteFile.p.o ∂
{MPW}Libraries:Interface.o -m ENTRYPOINT ∂
{MPW}PLibraries:PasLib.o -m ENTRYPOINT

*)

The lines that follow "To compile and link this file using MPW..." contain the information needed to compile and link the source files shown in this book, using the MPW Pascal compiler. To compile and link a file, follow these steps:

1. Change the destination pathname (HD:HyperCard:Home) of the compiled/linked file.

2. Change the resource number (XCMD=1612) of the compiled/linked file.

3. Drag-select the lines and press the Enter key.

Changing the Pathname of the Destination File

You'll find the pathname on the second line following the "link -o" directive ("HD:HyperCard:Home"). The pathname shown in the previous example would attach the compiled XCMD "DeleteFile" to the home stack found in the folder "HyperCard" on the disk volume "HD." To change the pathname, first decide where you want the compiled file to appear; then, replace "HD:HyperCard:Home" with your own pathname (the quotes are necessary).

> **Note:** if you specify a stack that has no resource fork, the MPW compiler will change the file type from 'STAK' to 'APPL', which will cause the Finder to believe that your stack is now an application. It will also prevent HyperCard from opening the stack. Use ResEdit to change the file type back to 'STAK'. (To avoid the problem altogether, always provide a pathname to a stack with an existing resource fork.)

Changing the Resource Number

Following the pathname is the directive "-rt XCMD=1612". The number following the equal sign (1612) is the number that will be assigned to the newly created resource. You may want to change this number if it duplicates an existing resource number in the destination stack.

> **Note:** The XCMD's and XFCN's appearing in this book are numbered sequentially starting at 1500.

Selecting the Correct Lines

To make sure you are selecting the correct lines when compiling and linking the XCMD's and XFCN's shown in the book, look for this note:

To compile and link this file using MPW Pascal, select the following lines and press the ENTER key

---

The lines following the note are the lines to drag-select before pressing the Enter key (those lines will change with each XCMD or XFCN). Following are the lines you would select for the example previously shown:

```
pascal DeleteFile.p
link -o "HD:HyperCard:Home" -rt XCMD=1612 -sn Main=DeleteFile DeleteFile.p.o ∂
{MPW}Libraries:Interface.o -m ENTRYPOINT ∂
{MPW}PLibraries:PasLib.o -m ENTRYPOINT
```

Borrowing Code from Other XCMD's

Bill Atkinson once said, "I don't remember what goes at the beginning of a [Macintosh] program, I just copy it [from another program]."

As you create your own XCMD's and XFCN's, you may find it useful to copy part of the source code from another XCMD or XFCN to save time. Chapter 3 includes the minimum source code necessary to create the basic structure of an XCMD or XFCN. Enter this code into a source file, save it, and then treat it as a template. When you need to create a new XCMD or XFCN, copy the file and customize it.

What is APDA?

Throughout the book, you'll find references to APDA. APDA is short for Apple Programmer's and Developer's Association—an Apple users group licensed by Apple to distribute Apple products. There is a yearly membership fee of about $20. You can write to APDA directly at the following address:

Apple Programmer's and Developer's Association
290 SW 43rd Street
Renton, Washington 98055

Note: Copyrighted code in this book cannot be sold commercially by users, but it can be freely used for personal programming purposes.

CHAPTER 1

DESIGNING XCMD'S AND XFCN'S

Programming the Macintosh has never been an easy task. When the Macintosh was first introduced, programmers complained that in addition to the huge volume of information they had to digest, they couldn't use a Macintosh to program a Macintosh (in those days, you had to use Apple's **Lisa computer** to write and compile code for the Macintosh). Given the price of the Lisa (more than $10,000), it was a little bit like using gold for pop tops on soft drink cans. It took a considerable amount of time to write a full-blown Macintosh program—that is, until the introduction of HyperCard.

HyperCard is a development tool that can help programmers shorten the development process by making interface design issues (a large part of any Macintosh programming effort) almost trivial. With HyperCard, it's easy to create a mock-up of your program in just a few hours. In many cases you'll want to use HyperCard to create your entire program. Even with all of HyperCard's features, however, there remains a need to extend HyperCard's abilities—to push the limits ever farther.

EXPANDING HYPERCARD

HyperCard's built-in programming language—HyperTalk—goes a long way toward being the "language for the rest of us." While HyperTalk is one of the most versatile languages around, however, it doesn't do everything. Fortunately, Dan Winkler—the designer and programmer of HyperTalk—realized that no matter what he put into HyperTalk or how easy he made it to use, he could not please everyone, so he added something very special: the ability for any Macintosh programmer to expand HyperTalk using what he called the **external interface**.

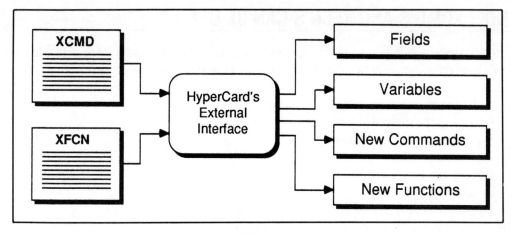

Figure 1.1

The external interface lets you communicate with HyperCard's internal structures.

The external interface provides the means for you to rewrite or create new HyperTalk language commands (XCMD's) and functions (XFCN's). The external interface allows you to work *inside* HyperCard *while it is running*. This environment is different from what most programmers are accustomed to.

The concept is similar to what you might experience during a normal work day. When you get to work, you must function efficiently inside the working environment. You must solve problems, respond to input, give output when asked, and conduct yourself in an orderly manner so as not to disturb the basic operation of the workplace. This is true of XCMD's and XFCN's as they operate inside HyperCard. It can be a confusing and volatile environment in which to work (in Chapter 2, you'll learn what precautions you can take to protect your code and HyperCard).

Once created, XCMD's and XFCN's are executed like any other HyperTalk command or function. For example, you won't find the flash command in any lexicon of HyperCard's built-in commands—it is an XCMD.

HOW XCMD'S AND XFCN'S CAN BE USED

XCMD's and XFCN's have a wide range of uses. Your imagination is the only real limit to what you can do with an XCMD or XFCN. Following are a few possibilities:

- Adding menus to HyperCard's menu bar
- Accessing the toolbox
- Replacing HyperCard's menu bar
- Deleting disk files
- Printing the contents of a field
- Ejecting a disk
- Copying resources from one stack to another
- Animating objects in real time
- Sorting the contents of a field
- Returning the summed contents of a field
- Changing the sound volume
- Creating popup menus
- Determining the type of Macintosh you are running on
- Making HyperCard talk
- Protecting proprietary algorithms
- Improving speed in mathematical operations

XCMD's and the Outside World

XCMD's and XFCN's can do many things a normal Macintosh application can do, including sending and receiving raw serial data and sending and receiving packets over the LocalTalk (AppleTalk) and Ethernet networks.

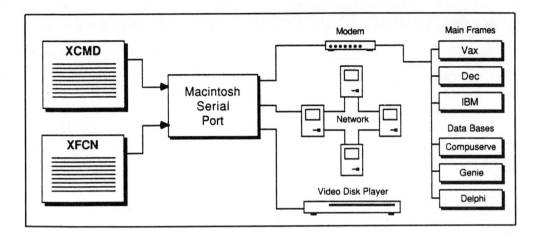

Figure 1.2

XCMD's and XFCN's can talk to many devices through the serial port.

With serial communications capability, an XCMD could interface HyperCard to any modem and, therefore, to any mainframe computer or database in the world. For example, it would be relatively simple to create a stack that emulates the front end to Compuserve, Delphi, or Genie (given the addition of a serial XCMD), or you could hook HyperCard up to a VAX, DEC, or IBM mainframe. You could even build a complete telecommunications package using HyperCard and a few XCMD's.

Using HyperCard as a Controller

The serial port and, therefore, HyperCard (with the use of an XCMD or two) is capable of transmitting as well as receiving control codes and data. Given this capability, HyperCard could be used to drive equipment such as a telescope. You could click on a transparent button covering the picture of a planet and have your motorized telescope align itself with the appropriate position in the heavens.

Note: Telescope control was the reason the programming language FORTH was originally designed. Though it isn't as simple as throwing together some paint, a button, and an XCMD, you can use HyperCard and your Macintosh to accomplish a similar task.

Following are a few ideas for interfacing XCMD's and XFCN's with the outside world:

- Weather equipment
- Automated factory production lines
- Video Disks and other video equipment
- Remote-controlled cars and trains
- Compact disks
- Serial I/O controllers
- EPROM burners and other electronic equipment
- Scientific Equipment
- Telephones, modems, and other communications equipment
- Medical and laboratory equipment
- Biofeedback devices
- Other computers
- MIDI equipment and other musical devices
- Voice recognition devices

Home Control of Lights and Appliances

If you own an ultrasonic, [BSR]-type home controller, you might think about creating an XCMD that would allow HyperCard to control your home. For example, you could turn your lights and appliances on and off with the click of a button. You might even create a kind of slide switch control to dim your lights.

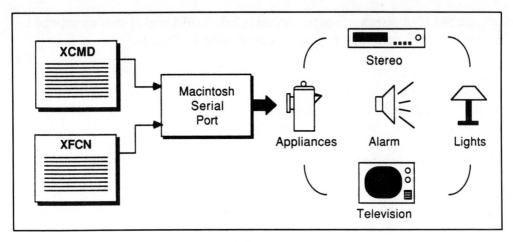

Figure 1.3

XCMD's and XFCN's can control your home appliances by sending special control codes through the serial port of your Macintosh.

If you want to fully automate the control of your home, you could create a stack that, when programmed properly, might automatically start and stop the coffee pot, cook a roast to perfection, dim the lights, regulate the temperature, watch for the mail or even wake you in the morning using the gentle sound of your stereo. While you're away, you might set the stack to turn your lights and TV on and off at random intervals to deter burglars.

Executing HyperTalk Expressions with XCMD's

XCMD's and XFCN's can be used to execute and evaluate HyperTalk commands and expressions.

Using the SendCardMessage, SendHCMessage, and EvalExpr glue routines covered in Chapter 3, you can perform many tasks, including the following:

• Get the name of a stack
• Send a message to an object
• Ask for a password
• Open, read, and write text files
• Do time/date conversions
• Execute menu items
• Edit a script
• Use HyperTalk's find, search, and sort capabilities
• Play a sound
• Move from card to card or stack to stack
• Perform visual effects
• Get the number of cards
• Check the status and position of the mouse
• Perform floating point calculations
• Get and set any HyperCard property

WHAT LANGUAGE TO USE WHEN CREATING AN XCMD

Virtually any language that can create a code resource can be used to create XCMD's and XFCN's, including Pascal, C, and even assembly language.

Regardless of the language you choose, you'll need Volumes 1-5 of *Inside Macintosh* (Addison Weseley). Remember to refer to Volume 4 first because it covers material specific to the 128K ROM (Macintosh Plus or later). Volume 5 contains information on the Macintosh II and color Quickdraw.

You may also find it helpful to refer to Scott Knaster's books, *How To Write Macintosh Software* (Hayden Books) and *Macintosh Programming Secrets* (Addison Wesley). In addition, Stephen Chernicoff wrote an excellent series entitled *Macintosh Revealed* (Hayden Books). Knaster's and Chernicoff's books are clear and powerful teaching tools for learning to program the Macintosh and should not be overlooked.

MAINTAINING THE ELEGANCE OF HYPERTALK

HyperTalk is an elegant, easy-to-use, and easy-to-learn language. Because of those qualities, HyperTalk is being taught as a first computer language in many schools. Because XCMD's and XFCN's are extensions of HyperTalk, you should take the time to carefully design the parameters to your commands and functions so that they maintain HyperTalk's elegance and ease of use.

For example, to get the time in HyperTalk, you could type the time into the message box. It's easy and intuitive. If instead you had to type "the hours:the minutes:the seconds" into the message box, it would be difficult and clumsy. Try to keep the parameters to your commands and functions as simple and intuitive as possible.

Following are some examples of XCMD's and XFCN's that you can understand by looking at them:

- SUM(field 1)
- ARRANGE(card field 1, ascending, text)
- ADDMENU MenuName, MenuNumber, MenuItems
- EJECTDISK 1
- SETGLOBAL value,name1,name2,name3
- TALKSTRING "The string to be spoken"

HUMAN INTERFACE GUIDELINES

When the Apple engineers developed the Macintosh, they also created what they called a **standard user interface** and required all Macintosh developers to use that interface when creating a Macintosh application. The theory was that if all Macintosh software behaved in about the same way, it would take users less time to learn each new application.

At first, developers deviated, and many new interfaces were introduced. Ultimately, however, it was the *user* who decided that Apple's standard user interface should stay. Over time, and with a fair number of modifications, that user interface has been formalized into a book. Today, applications that deviate from Apple's **Human Interface Guidelines** are virtually shunned in the marketplace.

Even if you're not a professional developer, it is a good idea to get a copy of the *Human Interface Guidelines* (Addison Wesely) and read them. The guidelines contain much useful (and often eye-opening) information.

XCMD'S AND FOREIGN COUNTRIES

If you are going to distribute your XCMD's or XFCN's outside of your own country, before you send them, it is a good idea to make sure they will work in the countries they are destined to arrive in. *Inside Macintosh* Volume 1 has a section entitled "Int'l Utilities." You should read this section thoroughly, especially if your XCMD or XFCN is going to do any kind of string comparisons (as would be necessary in an XCMD that sorts the contents of a field or that checks the validity of parameters passed to it).

Using the international utilities routines costs nothing and can save you and your users a lot of grief. Because HyperCard already uses the international utilities package in its date and time conversions, you need only worry about the string comparison and metric conversion parts of the package. Pay particular attention to the functions IUMetric, IUCompString, IUMagString, IUEqualString, and IUMagIDString.

THE INHERITANCE OF XCMD'S AND XFCN'S

Before you can design an XCMD or XFCN, you must understand both how XCMD's and XFCN's are called from HyperTalk and how and where they operate within the normal **inheritance path** of HyperCard.

The inheritance path is the route along which a **message** travels on its way to HyperCard. Messages are originated either by the user or by HyperCard. All messages then traverse the inheritance path until they reach HyperCard. A mouse message, for example, will first be sent to the button, field, or card under the pointer. If there's no **handler** for the message at that level, the message passes to the current card (if sent to a button or field), then to the current background, then to the current stack, and so on (see Figure 1.4).

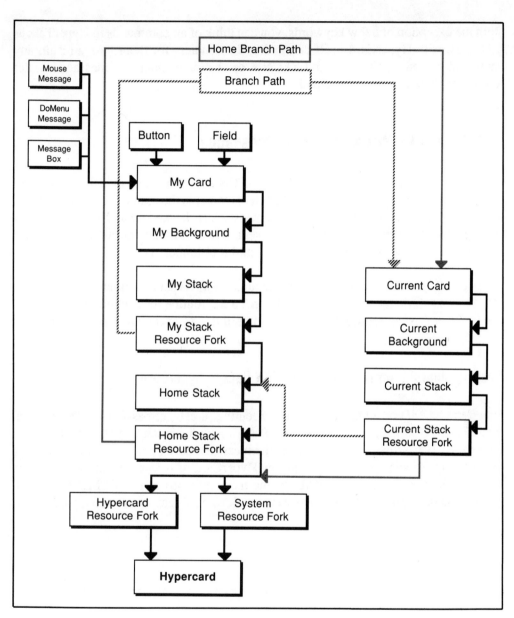

Figure 1.4

The complete inheritance path for HyperCard

With the exception of a few keywords, you can think of all commands in HyperTalk as messages, with HyperCard itself containing the handlers for them. As a result, any command, including XCMD's and XFCN's, can be intercepted by a message handler anywhere along the inheritance path.

XCMD's and XFCN's Also Sent as Messages

The names and parameters of XCMD's and XFCN's are sent along the inheritance path like any other message. If no message handler is found in the current card, background, or stack script, the **resource fork** of the current stack is checked for an XCMD or XFCN that corresponds to the name of the message sent. If none is found, the message continues along the inheritance path (see Figure 1.4) until it ultimately reaches HyperCard.

If an XCMD or XFCN *is* found in the resource fork, HyperTalk treats the XCMD or XFCN as a subroutine and executes a Jump To Subroutine instruction to the external code. Control is not returned to HyperCard until the XCMD or XFCN is finished.

Passing Control from Your XCMD or XFCN Back to HyperCard

When the XCMD or XFCN is finished executing, it can set passFlag in the external interface to be either TRUE or FALSE. PassFlag works much like HyperTalk's Pass command. If passFlag is set to TRUE, the message and its parameters will continue along the inheritance path until it reaches HyperCard or is intercepted by a message handler. If passFlag is set to FALSE, the message stops at the XCMD or XFCN, proceeding no farther along the inheritance path. You'll learn more about passFlag in Chapter 2.

HINTS AND TIPS

- When a message is passed to a branch stack, HyperCard first finishes the inheritance path for the current stack including that stack's resource fork. If the home stack happens to be the current stack, the XCMD's and XFCN's of the home stack get executed only once—not twice as you might expect.

- HyperTalk performs no internal checking to see if the message you send is valid. If it falls through to HyperCard, and HyperCard doesn't have a built-in handler for the message, HyperCard displays an error dialog informing the user that it can't under stand the message.

- You can't use global variables or string literals ('this is a string literal') when using versions of MPW C less than or equal to version 2.0.2. The global variables and string literals manipulate the A5 register and can cause HyperCard to crash (Light-speedC by Think Technologies treats global variables and string literals differently than does MPW C. It is possible to use global variables from LightspeedC).

- To make your XCMD's and XFCN's truly international in scope, see the separate document entitled "Script Manager Compatibility," which describes the use of the Script Manager now being shipped with new versions of the system (the Script Manager allows for full compatibility even in countries like Japan that use two-byte characters).

- By using XCMD's and XFCN's to conceal your proprietary algorithms, you gain both speed and privacy.

SUMMARY

In this chapter, you learned some of the many things you can do with XCMD's and XFCN's. You learned about their place in the inheritance path, how they are called, and how they pass control back to HyperCard. Also, you learned that it is a good idea to make your XCMD's and XFCN's compatible with other countries even if you don't plan on using them outside of your own country. You also learned that XCMD's and XFCN's can be created in almost any programming language, though you might find it easier to work in Pascal because many of the Macintosh ROM routines expect to be called from Pascal.

When designing an XCMD or XFCN, it is important to keep the Human Interface Guidelines in mind. An XCMD or XFCN should never attempt to redefine or ignore these guidelines.

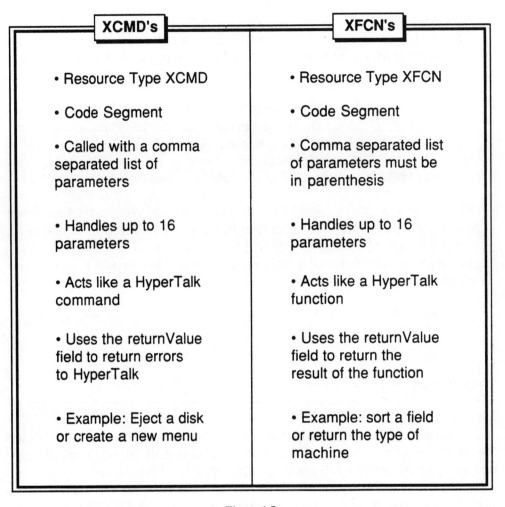

XCMD's

- Resource Type XCMD

- Code Segment

- Called with a comma separated list of parameters

- Handles up to 16 parameters

- Acts like a HyperTalk command

- Uses the returnValue field to return errors to HyperTalk

- Example: Eject a disk or create a new menu

XFCN's

- Resource Type XFCN

- Code Segment

- Comma separated list of parameters must be in parenthesis

- Handles up to 16 parameters

- Acts like a HyperTalk function

- Uses the returnValue field to return the result of the function

- Example: sort a field or return the type of machine

Figure 1.5

Summary of differences and similarities between XCMD's and XFCN's

CHAPTER 2

UNDERSTANDING XCMD'S
AND XFCN'S

This two-part chapter contains information on creating XCMD's and XFCN's. The first part presents information on XCMD's, and the second part presents information on XFCN's. Because XCMD's and XFCN's are so closely related, much of the information in the section on XCMD's also applies to the section on XFCN's.

PART ONE: XCMD'S

An XCMD is a Macintosh **code segment** that—like a Desk Accessory—includes no header bytes. XCMD's are not stand-alone applications; they are separately compiled **resources** you can attach to the resource fork of your HyperCard application file or any HyperCard stack.

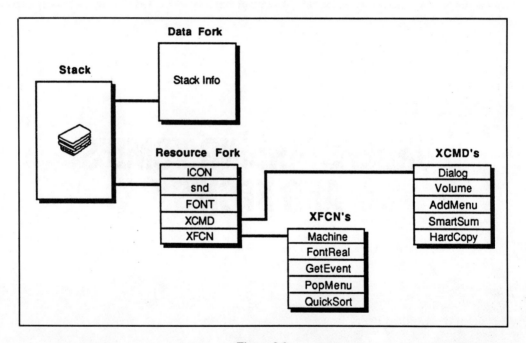

Figure 2.1

XCMD's and XFCN's can be attached to the resource fork of any HyperCard stack.

XCMD's attached to the Home stack or directly to HyperCard can be used by any HyperCard stack; XCMD's attached to any other stack can only be used by that stack.

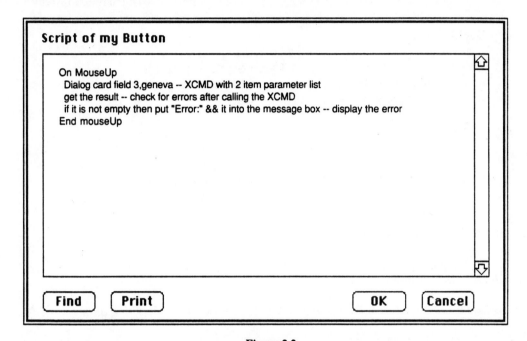

Figure 2.2

How you might use a typical XCMD from within a HyperTalk handler.

A Typical XCMD

The name of the XCMD shown below is Volume; it adjusts the sound volume level of your computer. Volume takes an integer in the range 0-7 (corresponding to the sound levels of the Control Panel) as its only parameter.

The following example shows how you might use the Volume XCMD to control a musical passage:

```
on PlayMyTune
    Volume 5 -- set initial volume a little loud
    play "harpsichord" ce ee ge ee fe de eq ce ee ge ee
    wait until the sound is "done" -- else volume changes too fast
    Volume 2 -- play last 3 notes a little softer
    play "harpsichord" fe de cq
end PlayMyTune
```

Following is the Volume XCMD (in MPW Pascal format):

```
{$R-} {MPW compiler directive}
(*
  © 1988 by Gary Bond
  All Rights Reserved

  Volume -- a HyperCard XCMD that sets the speaker volume ignoring parameter RAM

  Form: Volume number 0-7

  Example: Volume 5

  Note:  A volume of 0 will turn the sound off completely while a volume of 7 will make
  it as loud as it will go. Values outside the range 0-7 produce an error.
  _____
  To compile and link this file using MPW Pascal, select the following lines and press
  the ENTER key
  _____

  pascal Volume.p
  link -o "HD:HyperCard:Home" -rt XCMD=1500 -sn Main=Volume Volume.p.o ∂
  {MPW}Libraries:Interface.o -m ENTRYPOINT

*)
```

continued...

...from previous page

```
{$S Volume } { Segment name must be the same as the command name. }

UNIT DummyUnit;

INTERFACE

USES MemTypes, QuickDraw, OSIntf, ToolIntf, HyperXCmd; {library includes go here}

PROCEDURE ENTRYPOINT(paramPtr: XCmdPtr);

IMPLEMENTATION

TYPE Str31 = String[31];  {needed by many of the glue routines}

PROCEDURE Volume(paramPtr: XCmdPtr); FORWARD; {forward declaration}

PROCEDURE ENTRYPOINT(paramPtr: XCmdPtr); {main procedure}
  BEGIN
    Volume(paramPtr);
  END; {Entrypoint}

  PROCEDURE Volume(paramPtr: XCmdPtr); {begin XCMD Volume procedure}

  CONST  paramErr = 1;
         maxParams = 1;
         rangeErr = 2;
         minSndLvl = 0;
         maxSndLvl = 7;

  VAR  str:     Str255;
       sndLvl: Integer;

{$I XCmdGlue.inc } {include the glue routines}

  PROCEDURE Fail(errCode: Integer); {returns an error and exits the XCMD}
    BEGIN {Fail}
      CASE errCode OF {determine and assign the error type}
        paramErr: str := 'Wrong number of parameters';
        rangeErr: str := 'Level must be between 0-7';
      END; {Case}
      paramPtr^.returnValue := PasToZero(str); {load 'the result'}
      EXIT(Volume); {exit the XCMD}
    END; {Fail}
```

continued...

...from previous page

```
BEGIN {Main}
  IF paramPtr^.paramcount <> maxParams THEN Fail(paramErr);
  ZeroToPas(paramPtr^.params[1]^,str); {make the first parameter a Pascal string}
  sndLvl := StrToNum(str); {convert the string to a number}
  IF ((sndLvl < minSndLvl) or (sndLvl > maxSndLvl)) THEN Fail(rangeErr);
  SetSoundVol(sndLvl); {set the sound level to the volume passed}
END; {Main}
```

For the C Programmer

Following is the Volume XCMD (in LightspeedC™ format):

```
/*
    © 1988 by Gary Bond
    All Rights Reserved

    Translation to C by Sioux Lacy

    Volume --   a HyperCard XCMD that sets the speaker volume, ignoring
                parameter RAM

    Form:       Volume <number 0-7>

    Example:    Volume 5

    Note:       A volume of 0 will turn the sound off completely while a
                volume of 7 will make it as loud as possible.  Values outside
                the range 0-7 produce an error.

                In the HyperTalk script, "put the result" will display any
                returned error messages in the message box.
    _____

    Compile and link this file with the MacTraps and string libraries
*/
```

continued...

...from previous page

```
/*
   Includes
   Note that these header files are for LightspeedC development.
   Substitute the files that are appropriate for your compiler.
*/
#include    <MacTypes.h>
#include    "HyperXCmd.h"

/*
   LightspeedC Prototypes
*/
pascal   void main(XCmdBlockPtr);
Handle   CopyStrToHand(char *);
long     HandleToNum(XCmdBlockPtr, Handle);
char     *ToPstr(char *);


/*
   Defined Constants
*/
#define  requiredParamCount  (short) 1
#define  minSndLvl           (int) 0
#define  maxSndLvl           (int) 7


pascal   void main(paramPtr)
   XCmdBlockPtr  paramPtr;
{
   int      sndLvl;

   if (paramPtr->paramCount != requiredParamCount)
      {
         paramPtr->returnValue = (Handle) CopyStrToHand("Wrong number of params");
         return;
      }
   /*
      Convert the parameter to an unsigned number, and assign it to "sndLvl".
   */
   sndLvl = (int) HandleToNum(paramPtr, paramPtr->params[0]);

   if ((sndLvl > maxSndLvl) || (sndLvl < minSndLvl))
      {
         paramPtr->returnValue = (Handle) CopyStrToHand("Level must be 0-7");
         return;
      }
   SetSoundVol(sndLvl);      /* Set the sound level to param passed */
}
```

continued...

...from previous page

```
/*
   This utility function allocates heapspace and copies a string into it.
*/
Handle CopyStrToHand(str)
   char *str;
{
   Handle   newHndl;

   newHndl = (Handle) NewHandle((long) strlen(str) + 1);
   strcpy((char *)(*newHndl), str);
   return(newHndl);
}


/*
   This function makes a callback to HyperCard to convert a string to an
   unsigned long integer.  It takes a handle to a C string as an argument.
*/
long HandleToNum(paramPtr, hndl)
   XCmdBlockPtr   paramPtr;
   Handle         hndl;
{
   char  str[32];
   long  num;

   strcpy(str, *hndl);
   num = StrToLong(paramPtr, (Str31 *) ToPstr(str));
   return(num);
}


/*
   This utility function converts a C string to a Pascal string.
   Note that the C string is overwritten in the process.
*/
char *ToPstr(str)
   char *str;
{
   unsigned char length, i;

   for (i = 0, length = 0; str[i] != 0; ++i)      /* Find end of string */
      ++length;
   while (i--)                                    /* Shift string 1 byte to right */
      str[i+1] = str[i];
   str[0] = length;                               /* Put string length in 1st byte */
   return(str);
}
```

Defining Parameters to an XCMD

Think of a parameter as a kind of submessage that is carried along with the XCMD as it traverses the inheritance path. A parameter is an XCMD argument that contains a value you want to pass into that XCMD. For example, if you were to create an XCMD to eject a floppy disk, you might want to pass the disk drive number (1-3) as a parameter. Your XCMD could use that number to determine the disk it should eject. The EjectDisk XCMD, from HyperTalk, might resemble the following:

EjectDisk 2 -- where 2 is the parameter to EjectDisk

Parameters can be numbers, strings, containers, or almost anything. Following are some examples of items that can be passed in a parameter:

- numbers—including floating point numbers
- the number of cards
- a field name or the contents of a field
- a message
- a variable name or the contents of a variable
- string literals
- the contents of the selection
- any HyperTalk function
- numerical expressions like 5.14 * line 3 of field id 8
- string expressions like "My literal string" && myStringVar
- the contents of the message box

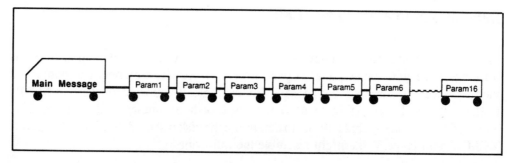

Figure 2.3

Parameters are submessages that get carried along with the main message that invoked the XCMD or XFCN.

Passing Parameters to an XCMD

Parameters are specified as a comma-separated list of items and are placed to the right of the XCMD's name, as shown below. While HyperTalk commands can be called with many parameters (up to 254 total characters including the command name), XCMD's are limited to only 16 parameters:

```
NameOfXCMD parameter1,parameter2,parameter3, ... paramter16
```

Following is an example of how you might pass several HyperTalk functions and values to an XCMD from within a HyperTalk handler:

```
on mouseUp
    myXCMD the time,myVar,"Lacy",line 3 of field 7,myVar/100
end mouseUp
```

> **Note:** There's a temptation (which you should resist) to extend the number of parameters an XCMD or XFCN can have by changing the params field of the XCmdBlock record. Doing so makes HyperCard crash. HyperCard expects the params array to be exactly 16 elements long. Due to a bug in HyperCard, if you provide more than 16 parameters, HyperCard will crash.

Specifying Content or Literal Value of a Parameter

When you specify a parameter, it's important to let HyperTalk know whether you want to pass the parameter as a *literal* value or whether you want to pass the *contents* of the parameter. For example, a literal value would be the name of a variable; the contents would be the value of the variable.

To pass the parameter as a literal value, place double quotes around it—even when they don't seem necessary (as in the case of a single word). The quotes eliminate any confusion HyperCard might encounter while interpreting the parameters.

Consider another example: *the selection* is a container that is two words long. If you want to pass the literal value "the selection", you would quote it as shown. If you want to pass the contents of *the selection*, you wouldn't need the quotes. Following are some more examples:

- Dialog "card field 1" -- sends the literal "card field 1"
- Dialog card field 1 -- sends the contents of card field 1
- Volume "7" -- sends the string value "7"
- Volume 7 -- sends the numeric value 7 as a string
- Sum "var" -- sends the literal "var"
- Sum var -- sends the contents of the variable var
- PrintField "the selection" -- sends the literal "the selection"
- PrintField the selection -- sends the contents of the selection

> **Note:** If HyperTalk can't find a variable or other container with the name you specify, it will send the name as a string literal. For example, Dialog myVar would send the literal value "myVar" if there was no variable with that name.

Using Parameter Data

When your XCMD is called from HyperTalk, a 16-element array of non-purgeable handles is allocated in a field of the XCmdBlock record of the external interface (see Chapter 3). Each element of the array contains a handle to a **zero-terminated string** that points to the information you passed in the corresponding parameter. If you don't supply all 16 parameters, the remaining handles are NIL.

To access the individual handles in the array, use the following syntax:

For the Pascal Programmer

```
paramPtr^.params[n] {handle to a parameter}
{where n is the number of the parameter 1-16}
```

For the C Programmer

```
paramPtr->params[n]   /* handle to a parameter */
/* where n is the number of the parameter 0-15 */
```

Dereferencing Parameter Handles

To access the parameter data pointed to by the handle, you must dereference the handle using the following syntax:

For the Pascal Programmer

```
paramPtr^.params[n]^ {allows access to the parameter data}
{Points to a zero-terminated string where n is the number of the parameter 1-16}
```

27

For the C Programmer

```
*(paramPtr->params[n] /* allows access to the parameter data */
/* Points to a zero-terminated string where n is the number of the parameter 0-15 */
/* Note:  zero is the first element of a C array */
```

Preventing a Pointer from Returning Random Garbage

Dereferencing a handle, as shown above, can get tricky because the parameter data is kept in a non-purgeable but **relocatable** block. If your XCMD makes any ROM calls that make the **memory manager** move things around on the **heap**, you could end up with a pointer to random garbage. The solution is to lock the handle before you access the data (see the next section). Locking the handle will lock the relocatable block, wherever it is on the heap.

For the Pascal Programmer

```
HLock(paramPtr^.params[3]); {Locks the parameter handle}
{You can now safely access the parameter data}
HUnlock(paramPtr^.params[3]); {Be sure to unlock the handle before your XCMD ends}
```

For the C Programmer

```
HLock(parasmPtr->params[3]); /* Locks the parameter handle */
/* You can now safely access the parameter data */
HUnlock(paramPtr->params[3]; /* Be sure to unlock the handle before your XCMD ends */
```

Heap Fragmentation

Because there's no way of knowing where the handle was allocated on the heap, locking the handle may cause heap fragmentation. This is generally not a problem for most XCMD's, but if it should become a problem, use the ROM routine MoveHHi to move the handle to the top of the heap. Following is a function that uses MoveHHi to perform this task.

For the Pascal Programmer

```
FUNCTION MoveParamHandle(VAR paramHandle: Handle): memError;
(*
This function will return one of three error codes:
```

Error	Means
noErr	There was no error.
nilHandleErr	There was a Nil master pointer in the handle you specified.
memLockedErr	The relocatable block specified was locked.

To move and lock a handle with this function, use the following syntax:

```
{Moves and locks the handle for parameter 1}
IF MoveParamHandle(paramPtr^.params[1]) = noError THEN Hlock(paramPtr^.params[1]);

*)
  BEGIN
    MoveHHi(paramHandle); {move the handle high on the heap}
    MoveParamHandle := MemError; {Return any errors}
  END;
```

For the C Programmer

```
/*
   To move and lock a handle with this function, use the following syntax:

   if (MoveParamHandle(paramPtr->params[0]) == noErr)
      HLock(paramPtr->params[0]);
*/

#include <MemoryMgr.h>

int MoveParamHandle(hndl)
   Handle hndl;
{
   MoveHHi(hndl);
   return(MemErr);
}
```

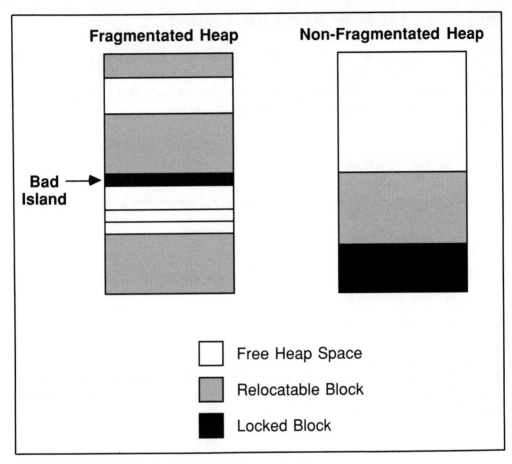

Figure 2.4

The heap can become fragmented when a handle gets locked in the middle of the heap.

Determining the Number of Parameters Passed

When an XCMD is called from HyperTalk, HyperCard automatically evaluates and stores the number of parameters that were passed with it and places that number in the paramCount field of the XCmdBlock record. The paramCount field is of type Integer, and you can access its contents with the following syntax:

For the Pascal Programmer

paramPtr^.paramCount {returns an integer number of parameters in the range 1-16}

For the C Programmer

```
paramPtr->paramCount /* returns an integer number of parameters in the range 1-16 */
```

Checking the Parameter Count

Because users sometimes make mistakes, it's a good idea to check for the correct number of parameters at the beginning of your XCMD (Samples 2.1 and 2.2 displayed next show a procedure you might use). To call the procedure in Sample 2.1, use the following syntax:

CheckParams(n) {where n represents the correct number of parameters to be passed}

If the user supplies the wrong number of parameters, CheckParams loads the result with "Wrong number of parameters" and exits the XCMD. If execution proceeds to the line of code following the CheckParams call, the number of parameters supplied is correct.

SAMPLE 2.1:   A Pascal procedure that can be used to check for the correct number of
               parameters passed to an XCMD.

```
PROCEDURE CheckParams(correctNumber: Integer);
   IF paramPtr^.paramcount <> correctNumber THEN
      BEGIN
         str := 'Wrong number of parameters';
         paramPtr^.returnValue := PasToZero(str); {load "the result" in HyperTalk}
         EXIT(myXCMD); {put the name of the XCMD in parenthesis}
      END;
```

SAMPLE 2.2:   A C function that can be used to check for the correct number of parameters
               passed to an XCMD.

```
void CheckParams(paramPtr, numParams)
   XCmdBlockPtr   paramPtr;
   short int      numParams;
{
   if (paramPtr->paramCount != numParams)
      {
         paramPtr->returnValue = (Handle) CopyStrToHand("Wrong number of params");
         return;
      }
}

Handle CopyStrToHand(str)
   char *str;
{
   Handle newHndl;

   newHndl = (Handle) NewHandle((long) strlen(str) + 1);
   strcpy((char *)(*newHndl), str);
   return(newHndl);
}
```

XCMD's, the Inheritance Path, and Pass

In Hypertalk, messages can be intercepted by message handlers. The message stops at the intercepting handler unless the handler chooses to *pass* the message. Passing the message makes it continue along the inheritance path, starting at the place it was intercepted.

XCMD's are unusual in that they act both as message handler and as command. XCMD's can pass messages they receive by setting a field of the XCmdBlock record called passFlag. The field passFlag is of type Boolean and must be set either TRUE or FALSE: TRUE to pass the message or FALSE to stop the message at the XCMD.

The following syntax shows how to manipulate the passFlag field:

For the Pascal Programmer

paramPtr^.passFlag := StrToBool('True'); {causes HyperTalk to pass the message}

paramPtr^.passFlag := StrToBool('False'); {causes HyperTalk to stop the message at the XCMD}

For the C Programmer

```
paramPtr->passFlag =  (short int) 1; /* causes HyperTalk to pass the message */

paramPtr->passFlag = (short int) 0;
   /* causes HyperTalk to stop the message at the XCMD */
```

> **Note:** When you pass the name of an XCMD, its parameters are automatically passed with it.

Using HyperTalk Commands in Your XCMD

While it is usually advantageous to have an XCMD operate independently from Hyper-Talk, it is possible for it to *call back* to HyperTalk by way of the call back interface. With the help of the glue routines (discussed in Chapter 3), an XCMD can send HyperTalk program statements back to HyperTalk. These statements are executed as if they had originated from within a message or function handler inside of a HyperTalk script.

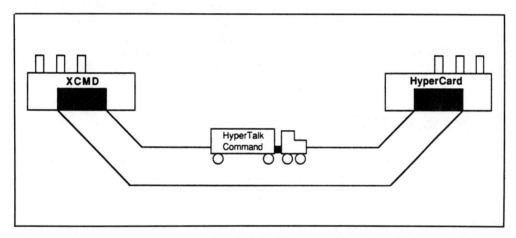

Figure 2.5

XCMD's and XFCN's can use HyperTalk commands and functions

Almost any command or function valid in HyperTalk is also valid from within an XCMD. There are three glue routines that support this capability: EvalExpr, SendCard-Message, and SendHCMessage (see Chapter 3 for more information).

For example, to get the name of a stack, you might use the EvalExpr call (this call evaluates and returns the result of a HyperTalk expression):

```
VAR    myStackName:          Str255;

myStackName := EvalExpr('short name of this stack'); {the name is placed in myStackName}
```

Following are some other examples of call backs you can make:

- SendHCMessage('go next card'); {moves from current card to next card in the stack}
- SendCardMessge('myMessageName'); {sends a user defined message to the current card}
- chunk := EvalExpr('word 4 of line 3 of field 1'); {gets a chunk from a field}
- numCardFields := EvalExpr('number of card fields'); {returns number of card fields}
- currTime := EvalExpr('the time'); {gets a string with the current time}
- SendHCMessage('answer "Are you sure?" with "Yes" or "No"'); {displays answer dialog}
- myMousePos := EvalExpr('the mouseloc'); {returns the mouse coordinates}
- SendCardMessage('set textfont of field 1 to "geneva"'); {sets field font}
- someValue := EvalExpr('cos(3.14)'); {can easily do floating point operations}
- SendCardMessage('choose brush tool'); {selects the brush tool}
- SendCardMessage('drag from 100,100 to 250,321'); {does a drag command}
- SendCardMessage('send mouseup to card button id 3'); {activate a card button}

Call Backs You Can't Make

Call backs to HyperCard are treated as if they had been entered from the message box. If a command, function, or expression works in the message box, it will work as a call back.

The following keywords do not work in the message box and, therefore, will not work with a call back:

do, else, end, exit, global, if, next, pass, repeat, return, send, then

Determining the Result of a Call Back

The result field of the XCmdBlock record indicates whether the call back succeeded or not. You should check the result field after every call back you make so you can take the appropriate action if it fails.

The result field is of type integer and can contain one of three values: 0, 1, or 2. The meaning of each value is explained as follows:

Result field = 0

A value of 0 indicates a successful call back.

Result field = 1

A value of 1 indicates that EvalExpr did not return a valid expression.

> **Note:** A result of 1 can also indicate that the glue routine StrToBool (discussed in Chapter 3) tried to convert a string that wasn't a Boolean value (TRUE or FALSE). In version of HyperCard greater than 1.1, the result field gets loaded after calling *any* glue routine.

Result field = 2

A value of 2 indicates that HyperCard didn't understand your call back message. This usually means that you misspelled something or made some kind of syntax error.

XCMD's Should Save and Restore the Environment

Because XCMD's work inside HyperCard, it's sometimes necessary to save **HyperCard's state** before the main body of the XCMD begins to execute. That way, HyperCard and HyperTalk don't become confused when your XCMD finally returns control to them.

For example, suppose you had created a window and changed the current port to that of the window. Suppose further that your XCMD finished executing and returned control to HyperCard. HyperCard would try to use the grafPort your XCMD created instead of the grafPort it should be using (because your XCMD changed the port). If you had deallocated the memory for your window before returning to HyperCard, HyperCard would try to draw into a space that no longer existed and would crash.

> **Note:** Don't forget to restore the state before your XCMD finishes.

Following is a list of common properties to save when working with ROM calls that affect them (see the individual managers in *Inside Macintosh* Volumes 1-5 for information on saving these properties):

• The current port (QuickDraw)
• The current pen information (QuickDraw)
• The current disk volume information (File Manager)
• The current print information (Print Manager)
• The condition of the serial port (Serial Drivers)
• The scrap (Scrap Manager)

Error Trapping Your XCMD's

Error trapping is a necessary, though time-consuming, part of creating any program. Unfortunately, many programmers do minimal or even no error trapping in their code. The temptation to ignore error trapping is especially strong with XCMD's because they are simple to create and are often created to solve specific problems, and it's only later that the XCMD or XFCN you created gets passed from person to person and errors start to occur.

> **Note:** When an error occurs in an XCMD, the Macintosh hardware can become confused and, in severe cases, can even crash HyperCard. Occasionally, the HyperCard stack you are using can become trashed when this happens. Once a stack is destroyed, there is no way to repair it.

HyperCard presents an environment that encourages experimentation. People *will* experiment with your XCMD's and XFCN's in ways that will rival your worst nightmares. They'll try many kinds of syntax, provide many kinds of input, scramble or omit parameters, and perform all sorts of other devilish deeds. Your best defense is to account for as many of these possibilities as you can by error trapping your XCMD's and XFCN's.

Common Errors to Check for

Following are some common areas in which error trapping might be useful:

• Correct number of parameters passed to your XCMD
• Correct type of information (i.e., integer, string) in the parameter list.
• NIL handles where appropriate.
• ROM call errors.
• File System Errors.
• Driver Errors.
• Insufficient memory for disk writes.

Detecting an Error

When an error occurs, your XCMD can (and should) detect the error and notify the calling script. It does this through a field in the external interface called returnValue. Sample 2.3 shows how returnValue might be used to return an error:

SAMPLE 2.3:   How to pass an error message from an XCMD back to a script.

```
(*
Put your error message into a string of type Str255 then use the routine PasToZero (discussed in
chapter 3) to convert the Pascal string to a zero-terminated string and pass it back to the script
through the returnValue field of the XCMDPtr record.  Storing a value in the returnValue field
automatically loads the HyperTalk function 'the result'.
*)

str := 'Your error message'; {load this string with your error message}
paramPtr^.returnValue := PasToZero(str); {the message appears in the result}
```

Note: If the returnValue field isn't used during the execution of an XCMD, *the result* will be set to empty.

Using a Central Error Handling Routine

To keep confusion and code size to a minimum, it's best to use a central error-handling routine. You should maintain an integer set of your own error codes that you pass to your central error-handling routine. That way, when an error occurs, your central routine will know what error message to return. Samples 2.4 and 2.5 show how you might construct such a routine in Pascal and C.

SAMPLE 2.4:   A typical error-handling routine in Pascal.

```
CONST RomError = 1; {Use appropriate names for your constants}
      O/S Error = 2;
      MyError = 3;

PROCEDURE Fail(errNumber: Integer); {call Fail with your own error code}
  BEGIN {Fail}
    CASE errNumber OF
      RomError: str := 'Error message 1'; {Use appropriate error messages}
      O/SError: str := 'Error message 2';
      MyError: str := 'Error message 3';
    OTHERWISE {If none found, return a generic error message}
      str := CONCAT('Unknown error: ', NumToStr(errNumber));
    END; {Case}
    paramPtr^.returnValue := PasToZero(str); {Load 'the result'}
    EXIT(myXCMD); {replace myXCMD with the name of your XCMD}
  END; {Fail}
```

SAMPLE 2.5: **A typical error-handling routine in C.**

```
#define RomError 1
#define OSError  2
#define MyError  3

void Fail(paramPtr, errorNumber)
   XCmdBlockPtr  paramPtr;
   int           errorNumber;
{
   switch (errorNumber)
     {
       case RomError:
          paramPtr->returnValue = (Handle) CopyStrToHand("Error message 1");
          break;
       case OSError:
          paramPtr->returnValue = (Handle) CopyStrToHand("Error message 2");
          break;
       case MyError:
          paramPtr->returnValue = (Handle) CopyStrToHand("Error message 3");
          break;
       default:
          paramPtr->returnValue = (Handle) ConcatErrorStr(paramPtr, "Unknown
             Error:", errorNumber);
          break;
     }
}

Handle ConcatErrorStr(paramPtr, errorString, errorNumber)
   XCmdBlockPtr  paramPtr;
   char          *errorString;
   int           errorNumber;
{
   Str31   str1, str2;

   strcpy(str1, errorString);
   LongToStr(paramPtr, (long) errorNumber, &str2);
   ToCstr((char *) str2);
   strcat(str1, str2);
   return((Handle) CopyStrToHand((char *) str1));
}

Handle CopyStrToHand(str)
   char *str;
{
   Handle  newHndl;

   newHndl = (Handle) NewHandle((long) strlen(str) + 1);
   strcpy((char *) (*newHndl), str);
   return(newHndl);
}
```

Some XCMD Absolutes

The one thing you must *never* do from within an XCMD or XFCN is INIT the GrafPort. This will cause HyperCard to crash and burn and might possibly destroy your stack. Following are some other things you should always pay attention to:

• Never INIT any of the other ROM-based managers.
• Never declare any global or static variables.
• Always save and restore HyperCard's state.
• Always do proper error trapping, retuning errors when necessary.
• Always deallocate the appropriate handles before exiting your XCMD or XFCN.

Note: XCMD's cannot share HyperCard's global data space, which makes it difficult to keep data around between each call to your XCMD. Two useful techniques for overcoming this restriction are detailed in Chapter 5.

For the Power Programmer

HyperCard relies heavily on the state of the A5 register. You must never do anything to change the value of that register. At first glance, it might seem like you could save the current contents, do what you need to do, and then restore the contents to its former state. This may work in isolated cases, but it's not generally a good idea. If one or more of the calls you make invoke HyperCard or HyperTalk, even in the most minor way, your XCMD could easily crash HyperCard.

PART TWO: XFCN'S

Much of the information found in the section about XCMD's also applies to the creation and use of XFCN's; therefore, you shoukd read the first part of this chapter before proceeding with the second part, which shows the unique ways in which XFCN's differ from XCMD's.

An XFCN is a Macintosh code segment that performs the work of a function. XFCN's—like XCMD's—have no header bytes and cannot be stand-alone applications. XFCN's are separately compiled resources that you can attach to the resource fork of your HyperCard application file or to any HyperCard stack. XFCN's attached to the Home stack or directly to HyperCard can be used by any HyperCard stack. XFCN's attached to any other stack can only be used by that stack.

SAMPLE 2.6:   **How to call an XFCN from HyperTalk.**

```
on sortMyField
    put sortField(field "myfield","ascending","text") into field 2
end sortMyField
```

Like the functions in HyperTalk, XFCN's usually return a value. For example, the function shown in Sample 2.6 returns the sorted contents of the field "myField".

Returning the Result of a Function

In other programming languages, when a function is called, the function itself is replaced by the result of the function call. This is also true of XFCN's (though it isn't necessary for them to return a result).

Unfortunately, XFCN's use the returnValue field of the XCmdBlock record to return their result—the same field XCMD's use to return an error message. This situation makes it difficult (but not impossible) for XFCN's to return error messages (see "Detecting an Error in an XFCN" later in this section).

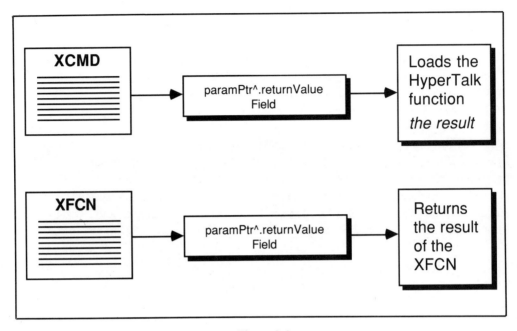

Figure 2.6

What the returnValue field of the XCmdBlock record returns for both XCMD's and XFCN's.

You can use the following syntax to return the result of an XFCN call:

For the Pascal Programmer

paramPtr^.returnValue := PasToZero(myFunctionResult);
(*
paramPtr^.returnValue must be assigned a handle. The glue routine PasToZero (discussed in chapter 3) creates one automatically. The variable myFunctionResult can be any variable of type Str255.
*)

For the C Programmer

```
paramPtr->returnValue = (Handle) CopyStrToHand("MacPlus");
```

A Typical XFCN

The name of the XFCN in this section is Machine, and it returns a string with the name of the machine (computer) you are currently running on. Machine takes no parameters.

Because a Macintosh II runs about four times faster than a Macintosh Plus, it would be useful to check the machine type before doing anything that might be timing-dependent (such as an animated sequence). The following example shows one way you can use the Machine XFCN to check the machine type and set a global flag:

```
on CheckMachine
    global speeedFlag --global for access by other handlers
    IF machine() is "MacII" THEN put "TRUE" into speeedFlag
    ELSE put "FALSE" into speeedFlag --slow case
end CheckMachine
```

Following is the source code for the Machine XFCN.

For the Pascal Programmer

```
{$R-} {MPW compiler directive}
(*
    © 1988 by Gary Bond
    All Rights Reserved

    Machine -- a HyperCard XFCN that returns the machine type (Mac plus, SE, Mac II)

    Form: Machine(takes no parameters)

    Example: Machine()

    Note:  Returns MacPlus, MacSE, MacII, or Type: # (for future machines)
    corresponding to the computer you are running on.
    _____

    To compile and link this file using MPW Pascal, select the following lines and press
    the ENTER key
    _____
```

continued...

...from previous page

```
pascal Machine.p
link -o "HD:HyperCard:Home" -rt XFCN=1 5 0 1 -sn Main=Machine Machine.p.o ∂
{MPW}Libraries:Interface.o -m ENTRYPOINT∂
{MPW}PLibraries:PasLib.o -m ENTRYPOINT
```

*)

{$S Machine } { Segment name must be the same as the command name. }

UNIT DummyUnit;

INTERFACE

USES MemTypes, QuickDraw, OSIntf, ToolIntf, HyperXCmd;

PROCEDURE ENTRYPOINT(paramPtr: XCmdPtr);

IMPLEMENTATION

TYPE Str31 = String[31]; {needed by many of the glue routines}

PROCEDURE Machine(paramPtr: XCmdPtr); FORWARD; {forward declaration}

PROCEDURE ENTRYPOINT(paramPtr: XCmdPtr); {main procedure}
  BEGIN
    Machine(paramPtr);
  END; {Entrypoint}

  PROCEDURE Machine(paramPtr: XCmdPtr); {begin XCDM Machine procedure}

    CONST macPlus = 1;
           macTwo = 2;
           macSE = 3;

    VAR str: Str255;
         romType: Integer;
         machineType: Integer;

{$I XCmdGlue.inc } {include the glue routines}

continued...

...from previous page

```
BEGIN {Main}
   Environs(romType,machineType); {get the info--ignore romType}
   CASE machineType OF {convert machineType to a string}
      macPlus: str := 'MacPlus';
      macTwo: str := 'MacII';
      macSE: str := 'MacSE';
   OTHERWISE {return type number if type unknown}
      str := CONCAT('Type:',NumToStr(machineType));
   END; {case}
   paramPtr^.returnValue := PasToZero(str); {set XFCN return value}
END; {Main}

END. {Machine}
```

For the C Programmer

Following is the Machine XFCN (in LightspeedC format):

```
/*
   © 1988 by Gary Bond
   All Rights Reserved

   Translation to C by Sioux Lacy

   Machine --    a HyperCard XFCN that returns the machine type
                 (Mac Plus, Mac SE, Mac II)

   Form:         Machine (takes no parameters)

   Example:      Machine()

   Note:         Returns MacPlus, MacSE, MacII, Unknown, or Type: #
                 (for future machines) of the computer you are running on.
   _____

   Compile and link this file with the MacTraps and string libraries
*/
```

continued...

...from previous page

```
/*
    Includes
    Note that these header files are for LightspeedC development.
    Substitute the files that are appropriate for your compiler.
*/
#include    <MacTypes.h>
#include    "HyperXCmd.h"

/*
    LightspeedC Prototypes
*/
pascal    void main(XCmdBlockPtr);
Handle    ConcatErrorStr(XCmdBlockPtr, char *, int);
Handle    CopyStrToHand(char *);
char      *ToCstr(char *);

/*
    Defined Constants
*/
#define  MACPLUS  1
#define  MACTWO   2
#define  MACSE    3


pascal void main(paramPtr)
    XCmdBlockPtr paramPtr;
{
    int     romType;
    int     machineType;

    Environs(&romType, &machineType);   /* Get the info. Ignore romType */
```

continued...

...from previous page

```
switch (machineType)
    {
        case MACPLUS:
            paramPtr->returnValue = (Handle) CopyStrToHand("MacPlus");
            break;
        case MACTWO:
            paramPtr->returnValue = (Handle) CopyStrToHand("MacTwo");
            break;
        case MACSE:
            paramPtr->returnValue = (Handle) CopyStrToHand("MacSE");
            break;
        default:
            paramPtr->returnValue = (Handle) ConcatErrorStr(paramPtr, "Type: ",
                machineType);
            break;
    }
}


/*
    This function concatenates an integer converted to a string onto a given
    error message. For consistency, it returns the handle and allows the caller
    to assign it to paramPtr->returnValue.
*/
Handle ConcatErrorStr(paramPtr, errorString, errorNumber)
    XCmdBlockPtr    paramPtr;
    char            *errorString;
    int             errorNumber;
{
    Str31    str1, str2;

    strcpy(str1, errorString);
    LongToStr(paramPtr, (long) errorNumber, &str2);
    ToCstr((char *) str2);
    strcat(str1, str2);
    return((Handle) CopyStrToHand((char *) str1));
}
```

continued...

...from previous page

```
/*
   This function allocates memory and copies the string, passed as a
   parameter, into it.  The handle to the string in memory is returned.
*/
Handle CopyStrToHand(str)
   char    *str;
{
   Handle  newHndl;

   newHndl = (Handle) NewHandle((long) strlen(str) + 1);
   strcpy((char *)(*newHndl), str);
   return(newHndl);
}


/*
   This function converts Pascal strings (a length byte, followed by that
   many characters) to zero-terminated (C) strings. Note that the conversion
   is in-place (the original string is overwritten).  A pointer to the
   string is returned.
*/
char *ToCstr(str)
   char  *str;
{
   unsigned char length, i;

   length = str[0];
   for (i = 0; i < length; ++i)        /* Shift string 1 byte to the left */
      str[i] = str[i+1];
   str[length] = 0;                    /* Put zero-terminator after string */
   return(str);
}
```

Detecting an Error in an XFCN

Error handling for XFCN's is slightly different from error handling for XCMD's. When an error occurs in an XCMD, you can load a field in the XCmdBlock record—called the returnValue—with an appropriate error message that is then automatically returned to the user in the HyperTalk function 'the result'. Unfortunately, XFCN's use the returnValue field to return the result of the XFCN call, which means that XFCN's can only return error messages as a result of the XFCN call.

Returning error messages in this way can become tricky at the script level because the HyperTalk routine expects a function result—not an error message. To get around this limitation, build a set of HyperTalk message handlers that check for an error message before returning the result of the function. Sample 2.7 shows one way to do this.

SAMPLE 2.7:   **How to trap for error messages returned from an XFCN call.**

```
on doMyFunction — the handler where your function gets called
    get myFunction(param1,param2)
    checkErrors it — call after every function
    —If no error, execution will continue with this line
    —Otherwise handleError handler returns the error message
end doMyFunction

on checkErrors errMsg — check for a known error
    —If errMsg matches a known error message, errMsg is sent
    —as a parameter to handleTheError
    if errMsg is "My error message 1" then handleTheError errMsg
    else if errMsg is "My error message 2" then handleTheError errMsg
    else if errMsg is "My error message 3" then handleTheError errMsg
    else if errMsg is "My error message 4" then handleTheError errMsg
end checkErrors — if execution gets here, there was no error

on handleTheError errMsg
    answer "Error in function:" && errMsg
    exit to HyperCard — stops execution
end handleTheError
```

HINTS AND TIPS

- In the same way that placing a HyperTalk handler in the home stack makes it available to other stacks, attaching an XCMD or XFCN to your home stack makes that command or function available to the scripts in your home stack as well as to all of your other stacks.

- Though HyperCard marks parameter handles as non-purgeable, it's a good idea to use the ROM routine HNoPurge on them anyway. While this approach is admittedly conservative, it never hurts to be sure.

- Number your XCMD's and XFCN's sequentially. Start with a number like 2000 and then each time you create another XCMD or XFCN, copy the last one you made, change the name, and increment the number by one. You will end up with a nice succession of numbers (2000,2001,2002....etc), making it easy to remember the next number in the sequence, which will prevent you from compiling over an existing XCMD or XFCN. Use the same strategy for XFCN's, but give them a number starting at, say, 3000.

- XCMD's and XFCN's, like any other resource, can be cut and pasted from one stack to another. Use a resource editor like Resedit to move or copy them.

- Using the call back interface, XCMD's and XFCN's can call other XCMD's and XFCN's.

- All HyperCard strings are zero-terminated. If you use Pascal to write your XCMD's and XFCN's, however, you'll find that it's easier to work with Pascal strings. The glue routine ZeroToPas (discussed in Chapter 3) converts a zero-terminated string to a Pascal string and stores it in a variable of type Str255. The one drawback to using Pascal strings is that they are limited to 255 characters. As a result, if you send more than 255 characters to the ZeroToPass routine, it will lose all characters from 256 on.

- XCMD's can be used to return a value other than an error message by loading the returnValue field with the desired value. This ability is particularly useful when debugging your XCMD.

SUMMARY

In this chapter, you learned that XCMD's and XFCN's are really code segments that are treated like regular HyperTalk commands and functions. You learned how to call them from HyperTalk and how to pass them parameters. You discovered that the manner in which they are called depends on their position in the inheritance path and what kind of parameters have been supplied. You learned that the parameter list for XFCN's must be put in parentheses and that, aside from the resource type, XFCN's and XCMD's are nearly identical. In addition, you learned how to call back to HyperTalk and discovered some of the do's and don'ts of XCMD's and XFCN's.

CHAPTER 3

ACCESSING HYPERCARD'S
INTERNAL STRUCTURES

The HyperCard application contains hundreds of unchangeable internal routines that contribute to the magic you experience when you launch HyperCard. Dan Winkler, the author of HyperTalk, created 29 *glue routines* to support what he considered to be the 29 most useful routines. The glue routines form a programmable interface through which you can access the corresponding internal routines. The glue routines contain code that specifically makes use of the inArgs, outArgs, request, and entryPoint fields of the XCmdBlock record.

Dan placed the XCmdBlock record into a file called *HyperXCmd* and the 29 glue routines into a file called *XCmdGlue*. He then named the entire structure the external interface. The external interface is the mechanism through which your XCMD's and XFCN's can communicate with HyperCard's internal structures. The external interface lets you, among other things, get and set the contents of a variable or field, convert between Pascal and zero-terminated strings, or even send HyperTalk commands and messages.

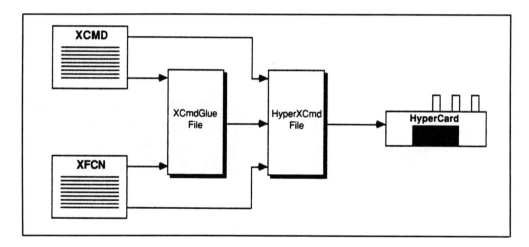

Figure 3.1

How XCMD's and XFCN's communicate with HyperCard through the XCmdGlue and HyperXCmd files.

This chapter discusses how to use the external interface, provides additional hints on accessing HyperCard's internal information, and even shows you how to build your own glue routines. Also, included at the end of the chapter are *starter files* you can use as templates for creating your own XCMD's and XFCN's from scratch.

THE EXTERNAL INTERFACE

The HyperXCmd file must be present at compile time for any communication between your finished XCMD or XFCN and HyperCard to occur. Without this file, you can't access HyperCard's internal information or perform any call backs.

The primary component of the file is the XCmdBlock record. The XCmdBlock record contains declarations for the nine fields through which the actual communication with HyperCard occurs. Unless you are a power programmer, you will only use five of those fields regularly (paramCount, params, returnValue, passFlag, and result). The XCmdBlock record and each of its fields are covered separately in later sections.

The XCmdBlock record resembles the following:

```
XCmdPtr = ^XCmdBlock;
XCmdBlock =
   RECORD
      paramCount:   Integer;
      params:       ARRAY[1..16] OF Handle;
      returnValue:  Handle;
      passFlag:     Boolean;

      entryPoint:   ProcPtr;
      request:      Integer;
      result:       Integer;
      inArgs:       ARRAY[1..8] OF LongInt;
      outArgs:      ARRAY[1..4] OF LongInt;
   END;
```

The HyperXCmd file is available as part of the *HyperCard Developers Workshop* (available through APDA). If you can't or don't want to send away for the *HyperCard Developers Workshop*, you can create the HyperXCmd file by typing it (exactly as shown below) into your compiler. Depending on the language you are using, the file should be saved using one of the following two names:

```
HyperXCmd.p {use this name if you are working in Pascal}
```

```
HyperXCmd.h /* use this name if you are working in C */
```

Declare the HyperXCmd.p file in the *uses* statement of your Pascal program, or declare the HyperXCmd.h file in the *include* statement of your C program.

The HyperXCmd File

Following is the HyperXCmd file shown first in MPW Pascal and then in LightSpeedC. The XCmdBlock record is shown at the bottom of the Pascal file and at the top of the C file:

For the Pascal Programmer

```
( *
 *       HyperXCmd.p-Interface to HyperTalk callback routines
 *       - Copyright Apple Computer, Inc. 1987,1988.
 *       - All Rights Reserved.
 *)

UNIT HyperXCmd;

INTERFACE

CONST

        { result codes }
        xresSucc          = 0;
        xresFail          = 1;
        xresNotImp        = 2;

        { request codes }
        xreqSendCardMessage = 1;
        xreqEvalExpr        = 2;
        xreqStringLength    = 3;
        xreqStringMatch     = 4;
        xreqSendHCMessage   = 5;
        xreqZeroBytes       = 6;
        xreqPasToZero       = 7;
        xreqZeroToPas       = 8;
        xreqStrToLong       = 9;
        xreqStrToNum        = 10;
        xreqStrToBool       = 11;
```

continued...

...from previous page

```
xreqStrToExt          = 12;
xreqLongToStr         = 13;
xreqNumToStr          = 14;
xreqNumToHex          = 15;
xreqBoolToStr         = 16;
xreqExtToStr          = 17;
xreqGetGlobal         = 18;
xreqSetGlobal         = 19;
xreqGetFieldByName    = 20;
xreqGetFieldByNum     = 21;
xreqGetFieldByID      = 22;
xreqSetFieldByName    = 23;
xreqSetFieldByNum     = 24;
xreqSetFieldByID      = 25;
xreqStringEqual       = 26;
xreqReturnToPas       = 27;
xreqScanToReturn      = 28;
xreqScanToZero        = 39;
```

TYPE

```
XCmdPtr = ^XCmdBlock;
XCmdBlock =
  RECORD
     paramCount:  INTEGER;
     params:      ARRAY[1..16] OF Handle;
     returnValue: Handle;
     passFlag:    BOOLEAN;

     entryPoint:  ProcPtr;
     request:     INTEGER;
     result:      INTEGER;
     inArgs:      ARRAY[1..8] OF LongInt;
     outArgs:     ARRAY[1..4] OF LongInt;
  END;
END;
```

For the C Programmer

The XCmdBlock record is handled differently in C and is shown at the top of the file beginning on this page. Also included in the C file are forward declarations for the glue routines:

```
/*
   © 1987 Apple Computer, Inc.
   All Rights Reserved
*/


typedef struct
   {
      short int     paramCount;        /* number of arguments    */
      Handle        params[16];        /* the arguments          */
      Handle        returnValue;       /* the result of this XCMD */
      Boolean       passFlag;          /* pass message on?  T/F  */

      void          (*entryPoint)();   /* call back to HyperCard  */
      short int     request;           /* what you want          */
      short int     result;            /* the answer it gives    */
      long          inArgs[8];         /* args for call back     */
      long          outArgs[4];        /* returned from call back */

   } XCmdBlock, *XCmdBlockPtr;


typedef unsigned char    Str31[32];
typedef double           extended;

/*
   Result codes
*/
#define xresSucc      0
#define xresFail      1
#define xresNotImp    2


/*
   Request codes
*/
#define xreqSendCardMessage    1
#define xreqEvalExpr           2
#define xreqStringLength       3
#define xreqStringMatch        4
#define xreqSendHCMessage      5
#define xreqZeroBytes          6
```

continued...

...from previous page

```
#define  xreqPasToZero            7
#define  xreqZeroToPas            8
#define  xreqStrToLong            9
#define  xreqStrToNum             10
#define  xreqStrToBool            11
#define  xreqStrToExt             12
#define  xreqLongToStr            13
#define  xreqNumToStr             14
#define  xreqNumToHex             15
#define  xreqBoolToStr            16
#define  xreqExtToStr             17
#define  xreqGetGlobal            18
#define  xreqSetGlobal            19
#define  xreqGetFieldByName       20
#define  xreqGetFieldByNum        21
#define  xreqGetFieldByID         22
#define  xreqSetFieldByName       23
#define  xreqSetFieldByNum        24
#define  xreqSetFieldByID         25
#define  xreqStringEqual          26
#define  xreqReturnToPas          27
#define  xreqScanToReturn         28
#define  xreqScanToZero           39


/*
** LightspeedC prototypes for the glue routines
*/
extern  pascal void     SendCardMessage (XCmdBlockPtr, StringPtr);
extern  pascal Handle   EvalExpr (XCmdBlockPtr, StringPtr);
extern  pascal long     StringLength (XCmdBlockPtr, StringPtr);
extern  pascal Ptr      StringMatch (XCmdBlockPtr, StringPtr, Ptr);
extern  pascal void     SendHCMessage (XCmdBlockPtr, StringPtr);
extern  pascal void     ZeroBytes (XCmdBlockPtr, Ptr, long);
extern  pascal Handle   PasToZero (XCmdBlockPtr, StringPtr);
extern  pascal void     ZeroToPas (XCmdBlockPtr, char *, StringPtr);
extern  pascal long     StrToLong (XCmdBlockPtr, Str31 *);
extern  pascal long     StrToNum (XCmdBlockPtr, Str31 *);
extern  pascal Boolean  StrToBool (XCmdBlockPtr, Str31 *);
extern  pascal void     StrToExt (XCmdBlockPtr, Str31 *, extended *);
extern  pascal void     LongToStr (XCmdBlockPtr, long, Str31 *);
extern  pascal void     NumToStr (XCmdBlockPtr, long, Str31 *);
```

continued...

...from previous page

```
extern    pascal void      NumToHex (XCmdBlockPtr, long, short, Str31 *);
extern    pascal void      BoolToStr (XCmdBlockPtr, Boolean, Str31 *);
extern    pascal void      ExtToStr (XCmdBlockPtr, extended *, Str31 *);
extern    pascal Handle    GetGlobal (XCmdBlockPtr, StringPtr);
extern    pascal void      SetGlobal (XCmdBlockPtr, StringPtr, Handle);
extern    pascal Handle    GetFieldByName (XCmdBlockPtr, Boolean, StringPtr);
extern    pascal Handle    GetFieldByNum (XCmdBlockPtr, Boolean, short);
extern    pascal Handle    GetFieldByID (XCmdBlockPtr, Boolean, short);
extern    pascal void      SetFieldByName (XCmdBlockPtr, Boolean, StringPtr, Handle);
extern    pascal void      SetFieldByNum (XCmdBlockPtr, Boolean, short, Handle);
extern    pascal void      SetFieldByID (XCmdBlockPtr, Boolean, short, Handle);
extern    pascal Boolean   StringEqual (XCmdBlockPtr, Str31 *, Str31 *);
extern    pascal void      ReturnToPas (XCmdBlockPtr, Ptr, StringPtr);
extern    pascal void      ScanToReturn  (XCmdBlockPtr, Ptr *);
extern    pascal void      ScanToZero (XCmdBlockPtr, Ptr *);
extern    pascal void      DoJsr (XCmdBlockPtr);
```

The XCmdBlock Record

The XCmdBlock record consists of a record definition that contains nine fields. Each field has its own data type and either passes information into HyperCard or receives information back from HyperCard.

The data type and size of each field is "hard-wired" so you can't change them. In Pascal, the XCmdBlock record looks like the following:

```
XCmdPtr = ^XCmdBlock;
XCmdBlock =
   RECORD
      paramCount:    Integer;
      params:        ARRAY[1..16] OF Handle;
      returnValue:   Handle;
      passFlag:      Boolean;

      entryPoint:    ProcPtr;
      request:       Integer;
      result:        Integer;
      inArgs:        ARRAY[1..8] OF LongInt;
      outArgs:       ARRAY[1..4] OF LongInt;
   END;
```

Writing to Read-Only Files

Each field can be read-only, write-only, or read-write (it varies with the field). You could write to a read-only field, but there wouldn't be any reason to. For example, the paramCount field is a read-only field that HyperCard automatically loads with the number of parameters present when your XCMD or XFCN was invoked. Writing to this field would produce unpredictable results and would serve no purpose.

Note: Reading the contents of a field doesn't affect the field in any way.

Referencing the Contents of the Individual Fields

You can reference the contents of the individual fields by placing paramPtr^ in front of the field's name if you are programming in Pascal. For example,

paramPtr^.paramCount

would access the contents of the paramCount field.

If you're programming in C, you would reference the contents of the individual elements of the structure by placing paramPtr-> in front of the field's name. For example,

```
paramPtr->paramCount
```

Following is a description of each field of the XCmdBlock record.

The paramCount Field

The paramcount field contains the total number of parameters (1-16) with which your XCMD or XFCN was called. This read-only field is set by HyperCard just before your XCMD or XFCN is invoked.

Data Type: Integer.

For the Pascal Programmer

paramPtr^.paramCount

Example:

IF paramPtr^.paramCount <> maxParams THEN doMyErrProcedure;

For the C Programmer

```
paramPtr->paramCount
```

Example:

```
if (paramPtr->paramCount != maxParams)
    {
        DoMyErrProcedure();
    }
```

The params Field

The params field contains a 16-element array of handles. Each handle points to the contents of the individual parameter passed. If nothing gets passed, the handle returns NIL. This read-only field is set by HyperCard just before your XCMD or XFCN is invoked.

Data Type: Array[1..16] OF Handle.

For the Pascal Programmer

paramPtr^.params[n] {where n is the number of the parameter (1-16)}

Example:

ZeroToPas(paramPtr^.params[1]^,str); {converts the contents of parameter one to a pascal string}

For the C Programmer

```
paramPtr->params[n] /* where n is the number of the parameter (1-16) */
```

Example:

```
Str255 pasStr;

strcpy (&str, *(paramPtr->params[0]));
```

The returnValue Field

The returnValue field passes values back to HyperCard. If your XCMD uses this field by passing a zero-terminated handle to it, HyperTalk's function *the result* will be set to the contents of the handle passed. If your XFCN uses this field by passing a handle to it, the *result of the XFCN* will be returned to HyperCard.

This write-only field should be loaded just before your XCMD or XFCN is finished. You must dispose of the handle you pass to the returnValue field unless you use the PasToZero glue routine. (If you use PasToZero, HyperCard will dispose of the handle for you.) The returnValue field passes EMPTY back to HyperCard if no value is supplied.

Data Type: Handle.

For the Pascal Programmer

```
paramPtr^.returnValue := myHandle;
```

Example:

```
str := NumToStr(myResult); {return a numeric result}
paramPtr^.returnValue := PasToZero(str); {don't need to dispose of this handle - HyperCard
does it}
```

For the C Programmer

```
paramPtr->returnValue
```

Example:

```
void AssignReturnValue(paramPtr, str)
   XCmdBlockPtr   paramPtr;
   char           *str;
{
   paramPtr->returnValue = (Handle) NewHandle((long) strlen(str) + 1);
   strcpy((char *) *(paramPtr->returnValue), str);
   return;
}
```

The passFlag Field

The passFlag field instructs HyperCard as to whether or not you want to pass the XCMD or XFCN message that invoked your code along the inheritance path. This is a write-only field that you can set anytime before exiting your XCMD or XFCN. The passFlag field defaults to 'don't pass' if no value is supplied.

Data Type: Boolean.

For the Pascal Programmer

paramPtr^.passFlag

Example:

paramPtr^.passFlag:= StrToBool('TRUE'); {pass the message}

For the C Programmer

```
paramPtr->passFlag
```

Example:

```
paramPtr->passFlag = 1; /* pass the message */
```

The entryPoint Field

The read-write entryPoint field contains a jump address (put there by HyperCard) used to pass temporary control from your XCMD or XFCN back to HyperCard while your XCMD or XFCN is running. If you put your own address into this field, it can be used to pass control to the code at that address.

Note: The entryPoint field is commonly used by the glue routines to jump to an **INLINE** HyperCard procedure. HyperCard loads the jump address into the entryPoint field as it is reading in the XCmdBlock record just after your XCMD or XFCN is invoked. The entryPoint field should only be manipulated by the power programmer.

Data Type: ProcPtr.

For the Pascal Programmer

paramPtr^.entryPoint

Example:

DoJsr(entryPoint); (DoJsr is a glue routine which does an INLINE procedure call to $205F,$4E90}

For the C Programmer

```
paramPtr->entryPoint
```

Example:

```
(*paramPtr->entryPoint)();
```

The request Field

The request field contains an integer representation of the procedure to be called when jumping to the address in the entryPoint field. The jump codes for HyperCard's internal procedures are listed in the HyperXCmd file shown in "The External Interface" section of this chapter.

Because the data type of this field is integer, it will restrict the maximum number of INLINE procedures you can write to 255.

While you can manipulate this field to call HyperCard's internal routines, HyperCard isn't set up to accept numbers outside of the range 1–28 and 39 (see the HyperXCmd file shown in "The External Interface" section in this chapter). The request field is used extensively by the glue routines.

Data Type: Integer.

For the Pascal Programmer

paramPtr^.request

Example:

paramPtr^.request := 5; {modifies the contents of the request field}

For the C Programmer

```
paramPtr->request
```

Example:

```
paramPtr->request = 5; /* modifies the contents of the request field */
```

The result Field

The read-only result field contains an integer (0, 1, or 2) representing the success of the EvalExpr glue routine:

Result field = 0

A value of 0 indicates a successful call back.

Result field = 1

A value of 1 indicates that EvalExpr did not return a valid expression.

Note: A result of 1 can also indicate that the glue routine StrToBool (discussed later in this chapter) tried to convert a string that wasn't a Boolean value.

Result field = 2

A value of 2 indicates that HyperCard didn't understand your call back message. This usually means that you misspelled something or made some kind of syntax error.

Data Type: Integer.

For the Pascal Programmer

paramPtr^.result

Example:

```
myHandle := EvalExpr('number of card buttons');
IF paramPtr^.result <> 0 THEN doMyCallFailed;
```

For the C Programmer

```
paramPtr->result /* to access the contents of the field */
```

Example:

```
Str255 str;
Strcpy(str,"number of card buttons");
ToPstr (str);
myhandle = EvalExpr(paramPtr,str);
if (paramPtr->result != 0)
    {
       DoMyCallFailed;
    }
```

The inArgs Field

The inArgs field is used with the entryPoint and request fields to send the arguments of the various glue routines to HyperCard (this field can also be used to send information to your own INLINE procedures).

This is a write-only field that should only be manipulated by experienced programmers (see the "Managing Your Own Calls to HyperCard" section later in this chapter).

Data Type: Array[1..8] OF LongInt.

For the Pascal Programmer

paramPtr^.inArgs[n] {where n is the number of the argument(0-7)}

Example:

paramPtr^.inArgs[1] := ORD(@myVar); {send the pointer address of a variable}

For the C Programmer

```
paramPtr->inArgs[n] /* where n is the number of the argument (0-7) */
```

Example:

```
paramPtr->inArgs[0] = (long) myVar;
```

The outArgs Field

The outArgs field is used to return a value from HyperCard to the routine that managed the jump to the address in the entryPoint field. (This field can also be used to return values to your own INLINE procedure.)

This is a read-only field that should only be manipulated by experienced programmers (see the "Managing Your Own Calls to HyperCard" section later in this chapter).

Data Type: Array[1..4] OF LongInt.

For the Pascal Programmer

paramPtr^.outArgs[n] {where n is the number of the element of the array(1-4)}

Example:

myHandle := Handle(outArgs[1]); {HyperCard has passed a handle back to the caller}

For the C Programmer

```
paramPtr->outArgs[n] /* where n is the number of the element of the array(0-3) */
```

Example:

```
myHandle = (handle) paramPtr->outArgs[0];
```

Managing Your Own Calls to HyperCard

The internal code that performs the work for each glue routine is hard-wired into HyperCard and cannot be changed. The way in which the code is called, however, can be changed. To manage your own calls, you must perform the following steps in the order given:

1. Redefine the XCmdBlock record inside of your XCMD or XFCN.
2. Load the request field with the appropriate request code (see the constants in the HyperXCmd file).
3. Load the inArgs field with the appropriate input information.
4. Execute a jump instruction to the address in the entryPoint field.

To execute a jump instruction to the address in the entryPoint field, you can use the built-in glue routine DoJsr:

```
PROCEDURE DoJsr(addr: ProcPtr); INLINE $205F,$4E90;
{pops the address in register A0 and does a JSR(A0)}
```

HyperCard places the result of the call into the outArgs field. If you want to know what specific values are returned in the outArgs field, see the glue routine that corresponds to the request code you are using.

Doing the Work Yourself

It is possible to build your own routines to handle calls to the external interface. To do so, you need to construct a block of code that somehow makes use of HyperCard's internal structures. While the file formats contain part of the information you would need, the rest is locked within the source code for HyperCard. Unfortunately, Apple has no plans for releasing either the file formats or the source code, which makes it difficult to extend access to HyperCard's internal structures.

> **Note:** If you decide to **reverse engineer** the file formats, you do so at your own peril. Apple considers HyperCard's file formats to be proprietary.

THE GLUE ROUTINES

The 29 glue routines presented in this section are a collection of procedures and functions that provide access to some of the routines and data inside HyperCard. The glue routines are the only method by which you can set and get the contents of a HyperCard field, set and get the contents of a HyperTalk global variable, evaluate a HyperTalk expression, or send a HyperCard message.

While a few of the glue routines provide access to HyperCard's internal information, the majority are utilitarian in nature. For example, there are routines to convert zero-terminated strings to Pascal strings, to convert numbers to strings and strings to numbers, and to make various string comparisons and measurements.

The glue routines must be placed in a file called XCmdGlue. The XCmdGlue file and each of the glue routines will be explained in a separate section.

> **Note:** You cannot access any part of HyperCard's file formats using the glue routines.

The XCmdGlue File

The XCmdGlue file contains all 29 glue routines and is part of the *HyperCard Developers Workshop* (available from APDA). To create your own file, type the contents of Appendix C for Pascal programmers or the contents of Appendix D for C programmers into your compiler and save the file using the appropriate file name shown below:

```
XCmdGlue.inc {for pascal programmers}
```

```
XCmdGlue.c {for C programmers}
```

In C, the XCmdGlue file is declared in an *include* statement. In Pascal, the XCmdGlue file is declared in a special *$I include compiler directive* (see the Pascal starter file later in this chapter).

Note: To call the glue routines from C, you must pass the XCmdBlock pointer as an argument.

SendCardMessage

SendCardMessage sends a card message (HyperCard command) to the current card. From there, the message traverses the inheritance path in the normal way. Any command can be sent as a message (including user-defined commands), with the exception of HyperTalk keywords; the use of keywords produces an error dialog.

Parameters

The SendCardMessage procedure takes a string of type Str255, representing the card message as its only argument:

```
PROCEDURE SendCardMessage(msg: Str255);
```

Example

```
SendCardMessage('doMenu "New Card"');
SendCardMessage('go next card');
SendCardMessage('go stack "address"');
SendCardMessage('choose brush tool');
SendCardMessage('myMessage param1,param2');
SendCardMessage('put 5 into field 1');
SendCardMessage('add var1 to var2');
```

Additional Information

Most of the time, the current card will be the card that was visible when the XCMD or XFCN was called. If the XCMD or XFCN causes movement to another card, the card moved to becomes the current card and receives the card message generated by SendCardMessage.

Note: You can use SendCardMessage to call other XCMD's and XFCN's, but they must be attached to stacks that will inherit the card message.

WARNING: If an error occurs during the SendCardMessage call back, an internal abort flag is set in HyperCard that causes all future SendCardMessage calls to automatically fail. At present, there is no way to detect such an error in versions of HyperCard through 1.1. In versions greater than 1.1, you can check the result field for an error (see "The XCmdBlock record" earlier in this chapter.

For the Pascal Programmer

```
PROCEDURE SendCardMessage(msg: Str255);

BEGIN
    WITH paramPtr^ DO
        BEGIN
            inArgs[1] := ORD(@msg);
            request := xreqSendCardMessage;
            DoJsr(entryPoint);
        END;
END;
```

For the C Programmer

```
pascal void SendCardMessage (paramPtr, msg)
    XCmdBlockPtr   paramPtr;
    StringPtr      msg;
{
    paramPtr->inArgs[0] = (long) msg;
    paramPtr->request = xreqSendCardMessage;
    DoJsr (paramPtr);
}

/* Note: msg is a pointer to a Pascal format string.  */
```

SendHCMessage

SendHCMessage sends a HyperCard message directly to HyperCard, bypassing the normal chain of inheritance. Any command—with the exception of HyperTalk keywords—can be sent as a message, including user-defined commands. (Keywords cause an error dialog to appear.)

Parameters

The SendHCMessage procedure takes a Pascal string of type Str255, representing the message to be sent as its only argument:

PROCEDURE SendHCMessage(msg: Str255);

Example

SendHCMessage('play "harpsichord" tempo 200 c d e f g');
SendHCMessage('click at the loc of card button id 18');
SendHCMessage('delete line 4 to 7 of field "data"');
SendHCMessage('push card');
SendHCMessage('visual effect dissolve');
SendHCMessage('set name of button id 3 to "Floor Wax"');
SendHCMessage('set lockScreen to true');

Additional Information

You can use SendHCMessage to call other XCMD's and XFCN's (as long as they are attached directly to HyperCard).

For the Pascal Programmer

PROCEDURE SendHCMessage(msg: Str255);

```
BEGIN
    WITH paramPtr^ DO
      BEGIN
        inArgs[1] := ORD(@msg);
        request := xreqSendHCMessage;
        DoJsr(entryPoint);
      END;
END;
```

For the C Programmer

```
pascal void SendHCMessage (paramPtr, msg)
   XCmdBlockPtr  paramPtr;
   StringPtr     msg;
{
   paramPtr->inArgs[0] = (long) msg;
   paramPtr->request = xreqSendHCMessage;
   DoJsr (paramPtr);
}

/* Note: msg is a pointer to a Pascal format string */
```

EvalExpr

EvalExpr evaluates a HyperTalk expression. EvalExpr returns a handle to a zero-terminated string that points to the result of the evaluation. Your XCMD or XFCN is responsible for disposing of the handle when you've finished with the data.

Parameters

The EvalExpr function takes a Pascal string of type Str255, representing the expression to be evaluated, and returns a handle:

FUNCTION EvalExpr(expr: Str255): Handle;

Example

```
ZeroToPas(EvalExpr('short name of this stack',stackName)^,str);
ZeroToPas(EvalExpr('the long date',dateInfo)^,str);
ZeroToPas(EvalExpr('the mouseLoc',mouseLocation)^,str);
ZeroToPas(EvalExpr('word 3 of line 5 of card 7',getWord)^,str);
ZeroToPas(EvalExpr('the optionKey',optionKey)^,str);
ZeroToPas(EvalExpr('the userLevel,currentUserLevel);
ZeroTopas(EvalExpr('the target',messageTarget);
ZeroTopas(EvalExpr('number of items in var',numberListItems);
```

   continued...

...from previous page

```
ZeroToPas(EvalExpr('the number of cards')^,str));
numberOfCards := StrToNum(str);

ZeroToPas(EvalExpr('field 3 is EMPTY')^,str));
fieldEmpty := StrToBool(str);

ZeroToPas(EvalExpr('textSize of card field "Lacy"')^,str));
fieldTextSize := StrToNum(str);

ZeroToPas(EvalExpr('"mystring" is in card field 6')^,str));
stringInField := StrToBool(str);
```

Additional Information

To convert the evaluated expression to a Pascal string, use the ZeroToPas glue routine (discussed later in this chapter). To convert the evaluated expression to a number or Boolean, first convert it to a Pascal string and then use any of the following glue routines to complete the conversion as necessary: StrToLong, StrToNum, StrToBool, or StrToExt. (These routines are also discussed later in this chapter.)

For the Pascal Programmer

```
FUNCTION EvalExpr(expr: Str255): Handle;

BEGIN
    WITH paramPtr^ DO
        BEGIN
            inArgs[1] := ORD(@expr);
            request := xreqEvalExpr;
            DoJsr(entryPoint);
            EvalExpr := Handle(outArgs[1]);
        END;
END;
```

For the C Programmer

```
pascal void ZeroToPas (paramPtr, zeroStr, passtr)
   XCmdBlockPtr   paramPtr;
   char           *zeroStr;
   StringPtr      passtr;
{
   paramPtr->inArgs[0] = (long) zeroStr;
   paramPtr->inArgs[1] = (long) passtr;
   paramPtr->request = xreqZeroToPas;
   DoJsr (paramPtr);
}
```

StringLength

StringLength returns the total number of characters (not counting the zero) contained in the zero-terminated string passed as its argument. Pascal strings cannot be used with this call.

Parameters

The StringLength function takes a pointer to a zero-terminated string and returns a long integer that represents the number of ASCII characters in the string (up to but not including the zero):

FUNCTION StringLength(strPtr: Ptr): LongInt;

Example

stringSize := StringLength(myPtr);
fieldSize := StringLength(paramPtr^.params[1]^); {measure size of a parameter}

Additional Information

To measure the length of a Pascal string, use either the Pascal language command LENGTH, or convert the Pascal string to a zero-terminated string, using the glue routine PasToZero (discussed later in this chapter).

For the Pascal Programmer

```
FUNCTION StringLength(strPtr: Ptr): LongInt;

BEGIN
   WITH paramPtr^ DO
      BEGIN
        inArgs[1] := ORD(strPtr);
        request := xreqStringLength;
        DoJsr(entryPoint);
        StringLength := outArgs[1];
      END;
END;
```

For the C Programmer

```
pascal long StringLength (paramPtr, strPtr)
   XCmdBlockPtr    paramPtr;
   StringPtr       strPtr;
{
   paramPtr->inArgs[0] = (long) strPtr;
   paramPtr->request = xreqStringLength;
   DoJsr (paramPtr);
   return (long) paramPtr->outArgs[0];
}
```

StringMatch

StringMatch performs a case-insensitive search to locate a Pascal string within a zero-terminated string. StringMatch cannot be used to compare two Pascal strings. If the source characters are found within the zero-terminated string, StringMatch returns a pointer to the first character of the match; otherwise, it returns NIL.

Parameters

The StringMatch function takes two arguments. The first argument is a Pascal string that contains the characters you are trying to match. The second argument is a pointer to a zero-terminated string.

```
FUNCTION StringMatch(pattern: Str255; target: Ptr): Ptr;
```

Example

```
myPtr := StringMatch('look for this string',destPtr);

{Search for one zero-terminated string within another}
ZeroToPas(sourceZeroPtr,searchString);
myPtr := StringMatch(searchString, destPtr);

{Find the string and then convert its pointer to a handle}
myStringPtr := StringMatch(myPascalString, ptrToDestString);

IF myStringPtr <> Nil THEN
   BEGIN
      osErr := PtrToHand(myStringPtr , myHandle, StringLength(myStringPtr ));
      IF osErr <> noErr THEN HandleError;
   END;
```

Additional Information

To search for one zero-terminated string within another, convert the second zero-terminated string to a Pascal string, using the ZeroToPas glue routine discussed later in this chapter.

For the Pascal Programmer

```
FUNCTION StringMatch(pattern: Str255; target: Ptr): Ptr;

BEGIN
   WITH paramPtr^ DO
      BEGIN
         inArgs[1] := ORD(@pattern);
         inArgs[2] := ORD(target);
         request := xreqStringMatch;
         DoJsr(entryPoint);
         StringMatch := Ptr(outArgs[1]);
      END;
END;
```

For the C Programmer

```
pascal Ptr StringMatch (paramPtr, pattern, target)
    XCmdBlockPtr  paramPtr;
    StringPtr     pattern;
    Ptr           target;
{
    paramPtr->inArgs[0] = (long) pattern;
    paramPtr->inArgs[1] = (long) target;
    paramPtr->request = xreqStringMatch;
    DoJsr (paramPtr);
    return (Ptr)paramPtr->outArgs[0];
}

/* Note: pattern is a Pascal string */
```

PasToZero

PasToZero converts the contents of a Pascal string to a zero-terminated string, returning a handle to the converted string. You must dispose of the handle when you are finished with it (use the DisposHandle ROM routine; see "Additional Information" below).

Parameters

The PasToZero function takes a Pascal string representing the string to be converted as its only argument:

FUNCTION PasToZero(str: Str255): Handle;

Example

```
{ PasToZero is particularly useful in setting the returnValue field}
{ Note that in this case, you don't need to dispose of the handle}
{ HyperTalk does it for you}

str := 'store my error message in this string';
paramPtr^.returnValue := PasToZero(str);

anyPascalString := 'contents of the pascal string';
myHandle := PasToZero(anyPascalString);
{...supply your own code dealing with the new handle}
DisposHandle(myHandle);
```

Additional Information

When you use PasToZero to assign a handle to the returnValue field of the XCmdBlock record, HyperTalk disposes of the handle for you. It would be impossible for HyperTalk to read the contents of the handle if you dispose of it when your XCMD ends.

For the Pascal Programmer

```
FUNCTION PasToZero(str: Str255): Handle;

BEGIN
    WITH paramPtr^ DO
        BEGIN
            inArgs[1] := ORD(@str);
            request := xreqPasToZero;
            DoJsr(entryPoint);
            PasToZero := Handle(outArgs[1]);
        END;
END;
```

For the C Programmer

```
pascal Handle PasToZero (paramPtr, pasStr)
    XCmdBlockPtr    paramPtr;
    StringPtr       pasStr;
{
    paramPtr->inArgs[0] = (long) pasStr;
    paramPtr->request = xreqPasToZero;
    DoJsr (paramPtr);
    return (Handle) paramPtr->outArgs[0];
}
```

ZeroToPas

ZeroToPas is particularly useful for converting an XCMD's or XFCN's incoming parameters to Pascal strings.

Parameters

The ZeroToPas procedure takes two parameters. The first is a pointer to a zero-terminated string, and the second is a string variable of type Str255 into which the converted string will be placed:

PROCEDURE ZeroToPas(zeroStr: Ptr; VAR pasStr: Str255);

Example

ZeroToPas(paramPtr^.params[2]^,str); {converts the second parameter and stores it in str);

myHandle := EvalExpr('line 1 of card field 5'); {get line 1 of card field 5}
ZeroToPas(myHandle^,myString); {convert it to a pascal string storing it in myString}

Additional Information

ZeroToPas is particularly useful for converting an XCMD's or XFCN's incoming parameters.

For the Pascal Programmer

PROCEDURE ZeroToPas(zeroStr: Ptr; VAR pasStr: Str255);

```
BEGIN
   WITH paramPtr^ DO
     BEGIN
        inArgs[1] := ORD(zeroStr);
        inArgs[2] := ORD(@pasStr);
        request := xreqZeroToPas;
        DoJsr(entryPoint);
     END;
END;
```

For the C Programmer

```
pascal void ZeroToPas (paramPtr, zeroStr, pasStr)
   XCmdBlockPtr   paramPtr;
   char           *zeroStr;
   StringPtr      pasStr;
{
   paramPtr->inArgs[0] = (long) zeroStr;
   paramPtr->inArgs[1] = (long) pasStr;
   paramPtr->request = xreqZeroToPas;
   DoJsr (paramPtr);
}

/* Note: You allocate space for the Pascal string and pass a pointer to it
   as a parameter */
```

ZeroBytes

ZeroBytes writes a longInt number of zeros into memory, starting at the address passed in dst Ptr pointer.

Parameters

The ZeroBytes procedure takes two parameters. The first is a pointer to a memory address into which the zeros will be written. The second is the number of zeros to write:

PROCEDURE ZeroBytes(dstPtr: Ptr; longCount: LongInt);

Example

ZeroBytes(myPtr,1); {zeros 1 byte}
ZeroBytes(myHandle^,10); {zeros 10 bytes}

myNewHandle := NewHandle(50); {allocate a handle}
ZeroBytes(myNewHandle^,50); {zero a block of memory}

Additional Information

You can use the ZeroBytes procedure to add a zero to a string that you've built in memory, making it a zero-terminated string.

For the Pascal Programmer

```
PROCEDURE ZeroBytes(dstPtr: Ptr; longCount: LongInt);

BEGIN
   WITH paramPtr^ DO
      BEGIN
         inArgs[1]  :=  ORD(dstPtr);
         inArgs[2]  :=  longCount;
         request  :=  xreqZeroBytes;
         DoJsr(entryPoint);
      END;
END;
```

For the C Programmer

```
pascal void ZeroBytes (paramPtr, dstPtr, longCount)
   XCmdBlockPtr   paramPtr;
   Ptr            dstPtr;
   long           longCount;
{
   paramPtr->inArgs[0] = (long) dstPtr;
   paramPtr->inArgs[1] = longCount;
   paramPtr->request = xreqZeroBytes;
   DoJsr (paramPtr);
}
```

StrToLong

StrToLong converts a Pascal string of type Str31 to an unsigned long integer.

Parameters

The StrToLong function takes a single parameter of type Str31 that contains the value to be converted. It returns an unsigned long integer:

FUNCTION StrToLong(str: Str31): LongInt;

Example

```
myLongInt := StrToLong(myString);
myLongInt := StrToLong('5783');

{converts unsigned parameter into a long integer}

TYPE    Str31:              String[31];

VAR     convertedNumber:    LongInt;
        str:                Str255;

ZeroToPas(paramPtr^.params[1]^,str);
convertedNumber := StrToLong(str); {slip from Str255 to Str31 is allowed}
```

Additional Information

The Pascal string can have no more than 31 characters and must contain ASCII decimal digits. StrToLong is useful for converting incoming parameters to numbers that Pascal or C can understand.

For the Pascal Programmer

```
FUNCTION StrToLong(str: Str31): LongInt;

BEGIN
    WITH paramPtr^ DO
        BEGIN
            inArgs[1] := ORD(@str);
            request := xreqStrToLong;
            DoJsr(entryPoint);
            StrToLong := outArgs[1];
        END;
END;
```

For the C Programmer

```
pascal long StrToLong (paramPtr, strPtr)
    XCmdBlockPtr   paramPtr;
    Str31          *strPtr;
{
    paramPtr->inArgs[0] = (long) strPtr;
    paramPtr->request = xreqStrToLong;
    DoJsr (paramPtr);
    return (long) paramPtr->outArgs[0];
}
```

StrToNum

StrToNum converts a Pascal string of type Str31 to a signed long integer.

Parameters

The StrToNum function takes a single parameter of type Str31 and returns a signed long integer:

FUNCTION StrToNum(str: Str31): LongInt;

Example

myLongInt := StrToNum(myString);
myLongInt := StrToNum('-800001');

{converts signed parameter into a long integer}

TYPE   Str31:   String[31];

VAR   convertedNumber: LongInt;
        myStr: Str255;

ZeroToPas(paramPtr^.params[4]^,myStr);
convertedNumber := StrToNum(myStr); {slip from Str255 to Str31 is allowed}

Additional Information

The Pascal string can include no more than 31 characters and must contain ASCII decimal digits. A negative sign is allowed.

For the Pascal Programmer

FUNCTION StrToNum(str: Str31): LongInt;

```
BEGIN
   WITH paramPtr^ DO
      BEGIN
        inArgs[1] := ORD(@str);
        request := xreqStrToNum;
        DoJsr(entryPoint);
        StrToNum := outArgs[1];
      END;
END;
```

For the C Programmer

```
pascal long StrToNum (paramPtr, str)
   XCmdBlockPtr   paramPtr;
   Str31          *str;
{
   paramPtr->inArgs[0] = (long) str;
   paramPtr->request = xreqStrToNum;
   DoJsr (paramPtr);
   return (long) paramPtr->outArgs[0];
}
```

StrToBool

StrToBool converts a Pascal string of type Str31 to a Pascal Boolean. The Pascal string should include no more than 31 characters and must contain either the string 'TRUE' or the string 'FALSE'.

Parameters

The StrToBool function takes a single parameter of type Str31 and returns a Pascal Boolean value of either TRUE or FALSE:

FUNCTION StrToBool(str: Str31): BOOLEAN;

Example

myFlag := StrToBool(myString);

IF StrToBool(myString) THEN DoTrueRoutine
ELSE DoFalseRoutine;

{converts a TRUE/FALSE parameter into a true pascal boolean}

TYPE   Str31: String[31];

VAR   param3:   Boolean;
       myStr: Str255;

ZeroToPas(paramPtr^.params[3]^,myStr);
param3 := StrToBool(myStr);

Additional Information

StrToBool is not case-sensitive.

For the Pascal Programmer

```
FUNCTION StrToBool(str: Str31): BOOLEAN;

BEGIN
   WITH paramPtr^ DO
      BEGIN
         inArgs[1] := ORD(@str);
         request := xreqStrToBool;
         DoJsr(entryPoint);
         StrToBool := BOOLEAN(outArgs[1]);
      END;
END;
```

For the C Programmer

```
pascal Boolean StrToBool (paramPtr, str)
   XCmdBlockPtr   paramPtr;
   Str31          *str;
{
   paramPtr->inArgs[0] = (long) str;
   paramPtr->request = xreqStrToBool;
   DoJsr (paramPtr);
   return (Boolean) paramPtr->outArgs[0];
}

/* Note: Converts the Pascal strings 'true' and 'false' to booleans */
```

StrToExt

StrToExt converts a Pascal string of type Str31 to a Pascal floating-point value of type Extended. The Pascal string should include no more than 31 characters and can contain a decimal point.

Parameters

The StrToExt function takes a single parameter of type Str31, representing the number to be converted, and returns a floating-point value:

```
FUNCTION StrToExt(str: Str31): Extended;
```

Example

```
VAR     radius:         Extended;

radius:=  StrToExt(myString);

{converts and places a floating point parameter into a pascal variable of type Extended}

TYPE  Str31:          String[31];

VAR     myReal:        Extended;
        myStr:         Str255;

ZeroToPas(paramPtr^.params[1]^,myStr);
myReal := StrToExt(myStr);
```

Additional Information

You can use StrToExt to pass floating-point values between HyperTalk and your XCMD or XFCN.

For the Pascal Programmer

FUNCTION StrToExt(str: Str31): Extended;

VAR x: Extended;

```
BEGIN
    WITH paramPtr^ DO
      BEGIN
        inArgs[1] := ORD(@str);
        inArgs[2] := ORD(@x);
        request := xreqStrToExt;
        DoJsr(entryPoint);
        StrToExt := x;
      END;
END;
```

For the C Programmer

```
pascal void StrToExt (paramPtr, str, myext)
   XCmdBlockPtr   paramPtr;
   Str31          *str;
   extended       *myext;
{
   paramPtr->inArgs[0] = (long) str;
   paramPtr->inArgs[1] = (long) myext;
   paramPtr->request = xreqStrToExt;
   DoJsr (paramPtr);
}

/* Note: StrToExt expects you to create myext and pass it in to be loaded */
```

LongToStr

LongToStr converts an unsigned long integer into a Pascal string of type Str31. This function is the inverse of the StrToLong function discussed earlier.

Parameters

The LongToStr function takes a longInt representing the number to be converted as its only argument and returns a string of type Str31:

```
FUNCTION LongToStr(posNum: LongInt): Str31;
```

Example

```
myString := LongToStr(4089);
myString := LongToStr(myLongInt);

myString := LongToStr(myCalcTotal);
paramPtr^.returnValue := PasToZero(myString);  {returns a value to HyperTalk}

{The SetGlobal call sets the contents of the specified HyperTalk global variable}
{SetGlobal is discussed later in this chapter}
myString := LongToStr(myCalcTotal);
SetGlobal('globalVarName',PasToZero(myString));
```

Additional Information

LongToStr is useful for returning the value of a computation to HyperTalk. Converted values can be stored directly in fields or global variables or can be returned via the returnValue field.

For the Pascal Programmer

```
FUNCTION LongToStr(posNum: LongInt): Str31;

VAR  str:        Str31;

BEGIN
   WITH paramPtr^ DO
      BEGIN
         inArgs[1] := posNum;
         inArgs[2] := ORD(@str);
         request := xreqLongToStr;
         DoJsr(entryPoint);
         LongToStr := str;
      END;
END;
```

For the C Programmer

```
pascal void LongToStr (paramPtr, posNum, mystr)
   XCmdBlockPtr   paramPtr;
   long           posNum;
   Str31          *mystr;
{
   paramPtr->inArgs[0] = (long) posNum;
   paramPtr->inArgs[1] = (long) mystr;
   paramPtr->request = xreqLongToStr;
   DoJsr (paramPtr);
}

/* Note: LongToStr expects you to create a variable mystr and pass it in
         to be loaded */
```

NumToStr

NumToStr converts a signed long integer into a Pascal string of type Str31. This function is the inverse of the StrToNum function discussed earlier.

Parameters

The NumToStr function takes a longInt representing the number to be converted as its only argument and returns a string of type Str31:

```
FUNCTION NumToStr(num: LongInt): Str31;
```

Example

```
myString := NumToStr(-650987);
myString := NumToStr(mySignedLongInt);

myString := NumToStr(myCalcTotal);
paramPtr^.returnValue := PasToZero(myString); {returns a value to HyperTalk}

{The SetFieldByNum routine sets the contents of the numbered HyperTalk field}
{SetFieldByNum is discussed later in this chapter}
myString := NumToStr(myCalcTotal);
SetFieldByNum(StrToBool('TRUE'),1,PasToZero(myString));
```

Additional Information

NumToStr is useful for returning the signed value of a computation to HyperTalk. Values can be stored directly in fields or global variables or can be returned via the returnValue field.

For the Pascal Programmer

```
FUNCTION NumToStr(num: LongInt): Str31;

VAR  str:       Str31;

BEGIN
   WITH paramPtr^ DO
     BEGIN
       inArgs[1]  :=  num;
       inArgs[2]  :=  ORD(@str);
       request  :=  xreqNumToStr;
       DoJsr(entryPoint);
       NumToStr  :=  str;
     END;
END;
```

For the C Programmer

```
pascal void NumToStr (paramPtr, num, mystr)
   XCmdBlockPtr  paramPtr;
   long          num;
   Str31         *mystr;
{
   paramPtr->inArgs[0] = num;
   paramPtr->inArgs[1] = (long) mystr;
   paramPtr->request = xreqNumToStr;
   DoJsr (paramPtr);
}

/* Note: NumToStr expects you to create a variable mystr and pass it in
         to be loaded */
```

BoolToStr

BoolToStr converts the Boolean values TRUE and FALSE to Pascal strings of type Str31. This function is the inverse of the StrToBool function explained earlier.

Parameters

The BoolToStr function takes a Boolean representing the value to be converted as its only argument and returns a string of type Str31:

```
FUNCTION BoolToStr(bool: BOOLEAN): Str31;
```

Example

```
IF condition THEN flag := TRUE; {metaphorically shown}
paramPtr^.returnValue := PasToZero(BoolToStr(flag));
```

Additional Information

Use BoolToStr when it is necessary to send a Pascal Boolean value back to HyperTalk.

For the Pascal Programmer

```
FUNCTION BoolToStr(bool: BOOLEAN): Str31;

VAR  str:        Str31;

BEGIN
   WITH paramPtr^ DO
      BEGIN
         inArgs[1]  :=  LongInt(bool);
         inArgs[2]  :=  ORD(@str);
         request  :=  xreqBoolToStr;
         DoJsr(entryPoint);
         BoolToStr  :=  str;
      END;
END;
```

For the C Programmer

```
pascal void BoolToStr (paramPtr, bool, mystr)
   XCmdBlockPtr   paramPtr;
   Boolean        bool;
   Str31          *mystr;
{
   paramPtr->inArgs[0] = (long) bool;
   paramPtr->inArgs[1] = (long) mystr;
   paramPtr->request = xreqBoolToStr;
   DoJsr (paramPtr);
}

/* Note: BoolToStr expects you to create a variable mystr and pass it in
         to be loaded */
```

ExtToStr

ExtToStr converts a Pascal floating-point number of type extended to a Pascal string of type Str31. The string contains ASCII decimal digits and, possibly, a decimal point after the conversion.

Parameters

The ExtToStr function takes a floating-point number of type extended as its only argument and returns a string of type Str31:

FUNCTION ExtToStr(num: Extended): Str31;

Example

```
myString := ExtToStr(36.4591);
myString := ExtToStr(myFloatingPointVar);
```

Additional Information

It is much faster to manipulate floating-point numbers from Pascal or C than it is from HyperTalk.

For the Pascal Programmer

```
FUNCTION ExtToStr(num: Extended): Str31;

VAR  str:       Str31;

BEGIN
   WITH paramPtr^ DO
      BEGIN
         inArgs[1] := ORD(@num);
         inArgs[2] := ORD(@str);
         request := xreqExtToStr;
         DoJsr(entryPoint);
         ExtToStr := str;
      END;
END;
```

For the C Programmer

```c
pascal void ExtToStr (paramPtr, myext, mystr)
   XCmdBlockPtr   paramPtr;
   extended       *myext;
   Str31          *mystr;
{
   paramPtr->inArgs[0] = (long) myext;
   paramPtr->inArgs[1] = (long) mystr;
   paramPtr->request = xreqExtToStr;
   DoJsr (paramPtr);
}

 /* Note: ExtToStr expects you to create a variable mystr and pass it in
          to be loaded */
```

NumToHex

NumToHex converts a long integer to its hexadecimal equivalent and places it into a Pascal string of type Str31.

Parameters

The NumToHex function takes two parameters. The first is a long integer to be converted to hexadecimal. The second is an integer representing the number of hexadecimal digits desired in the final output:

```
FUNCTION NumToHex(num: LongInt; nDigits: INTEGER): Str31;
```

Example

```
myString := NumToHex(32,2); {Outputs a string of: 20}
myString := NumToHex(40000,4); {Outputs a string of: 9C40}
myString := NumToHex(myLongIntVar,2);
```

Additional Information

If you supply more digits than the conversion requires, the converted value is padded with zeros. For example, converting the decimal number 16 to hex would yield $10 if you had specified two digits for the conversion. If you had specified four digits, however, the decimal number 16 would yield $0010.

For the Pascal Programmer

```
FUNCTION NumToHex(num: LongInt; nDigits: INTEGER): Str31;

VAR str:        Str31;

BEGIN
   WITH paramPtr^ DO
      BEGIN
         inArgs[1]  :=  num;
         inArgs[2]  :=  nDigits;
         inArgs[3]  :=  ORD(@str);
         request := xreqNumToHex;
         DoJsr(entryPoint);
         NumToHex := str;
      END;
END;
```

For the C Programmer

```
pascal void NumToHex (paramPtr, num, nDigits, mystr)
   XCmdBlockPtr   paramPtr;
   long           num;
   short int      nDigits;
   Str31          *mystr;
{
   paramPtr->inArgs[0] = num;
   paramPtr->inArgs[1] = nDigits;
   paramPtr->inArgs[2] = (long) mystr;
   paramPtr->request = xreqNumToHex;
   DoJsr (paramPtr);
}

 /* Note: NumToHex expects you to create a variable mystr and pass it in
          to be loaded */
```

GetGlobal

GetGlobal returns a handle to the contents of a HyperTalk global variable. The global variable must have been declared in a HyperTalk handler prior to calling the XCMD or XFCN and must be passed by name.

Parameters

The GetGlobal function takes a string of type Str255 (representing the name of the global variable) as its only argument and returns a handle that points to the zero-terminated contents of that variable:

```
FUNCTION GetGlobal(globName: Str255): Handle;
```

Example

```
{This example assumes a HyperTalk global was first declared with the name fieldTotal}

VAR     myHandle:       Handle;
        str:            Str255;
        inTotal:        LongInt;

myHandle := GetGlobal('fieldTotal');
ZeroToPas(myHandle^,str);
inTotal := StrToNum(str); {Now in number form}

{This example assumes a HyperTalk global was first declared with the name myList}

VAR     myHandle:       Handle;
        inList:         Str255;

myHandle := GetGlobal('myList');
ZeroToPas(myHandle^,inList); {Stores the string in the Pascal string variable inList}
```

Additional Information

If GetGlobal cannot find a variable with the name you supply, HyperTalk will beep once to signal the error. Unfortunately, there is no way to determine whether the global variable exists, and—in versions of HyperCard through 1.1—it is difficult to create it from within your XCMD or XFCN (see Chapter 5). Subsequent versions of HyperCard, however, create a global variable when the set global call fails (see "SetGlobal" for more information).

For the Pascal Programmer

```
FUNCTION GetGlobal(globName: Str255): Handle;

BEGIN
   WITH paramPtr^ DO
      BEGIN
         inArgs[1] := ORD(@globName);
         request := xreqGetGlobal;
         DoJsr(entryPoint);
         GetGlobal := Handle(outArgs[1]);
      END;
END;
```

For the C Programmer

```
pascal Handle GetGlobal (paramPtr,globName)
   XCmdBlockPtr   paramPtr;
   StringPtr      globName;
{
   paramPtr->inArgs[0] = (long) globName;
   paramPtr->request = xreqGetGlobal;
   DoJsr (paramPtr);
   return (Handle) paramPtr->outArgs[0];
}
```

SetGlobal

SetGlobal sets the contents of the specified HyperTalk global variable to the contents of a zero-terminated string.

Parameters

The SetGlobal procedure takes two parameters. The first parameter is a string of type Str255 that contains the name of the global to be set, and the second parameter is a handle to a zero-terminated string:

```
PROCEDURE SetGlobal(globName: Str255; globValue: Handle);
```

Example

```
{This example assumes a HyperTalk global was first declared with the name fieldTotal}

VAR    myHandle:      Handle;

SetGlobal('fieldTotal',myHandle); {set global 'fieldTotal' to contents of myHandle}
DisposHandle(myHandle); {must dispose of the handle after setting the global}
```

Additional Information

The contents of the zero-terminated string will replace the contents of the specified global variable. If there is no global variable with the name you supply, HyperTalk will beep once, indicating an error. (In HyperCard versions greater than 1.1, SetGlobal will create the global variable and then assign the contents of the zero-terminated string to the newly created variable.) HyperTalk copies the contents of the handle, so you must dispose of it before exiting the XCMD or XFCN.

For the Pascal Programmer

```
PROCEDURE SetGlobal(globName: Str255; globValue: Handle);

BEGIN
   WITH paramPtr^ DO
      BEGIN
         inArgs[1] := ORD(@globName);
         inArgs[2] := ORD(globValue);
         request := xreqSetGlobal;
         DoJsr(entryPoint);
      END;
END;
```

For the C Programmer

```
pascal void SetGlobal (paramPtr, globName, globValue)
   XCmdBlockPtr  paramPtr;
   StringPtr     globName;
   Handle        globValue;
{
   paramPtr->inArgs[0] = (long)globName;
   paramPtr->inArgs[1] = (long)globValue;
   paramPtr->request = xreqSetGlobal;
   DoJsr (paramPtr);
}
```

GetFieldByName

GetFieldByName returns a handle to a zero-terminated string that points to the contents of a card or background field. The field is specified by its name.

Parameters

The GetFieldByName function takes two parameters. The first parameter is of type Boolean and determines what kind of field—card or background—will be accessed; use TRUE for a card field or FALSE for a background field. The second parameter is of type Str255 and contains the name of the field whose contents you want to get:

```
FUNCTION GetFieldByName(cardFieldFlag: BOOLEAN; fieldName: Str255): Handle;
```

Example

```
{This example assumes a HyperTalk global was first declared with the name fieldTotal}

VAR     myHandle:      Handle;
        myCardField:   Boolean;
        fieldName:     Str255;
        pasStr:        Str255;

fieldName := 'Kamins';
myCardField := StrToBool('TRUE'); {make it a card field}
{get contents of card field "Kamins"}
myHandle := GetFieldByName(myCardField,fieldName);
ZeroToPas(myHandle^,pasStr);
{optionally convert field contents to a pascal string}
DisposHandle(myHandle); {must dispose of the handle before exiting}
```

Additional Information

Use the glue routine ZeroToPas to convert the contents of the handle to a Pascal string. HyperTalk copies the contents of the handle you define, so you must dispose of the handle before your XCMD or XFCN ends. The handle is a copy of the field data. Changing the contents of the handle will not automatically change the field.

For the Pascal Programmer

```
FUNCTION GetFieldByName(cardFieldFlag: BOOLEAN; fieldName: Str255): Handle;

BEGIN
   WITH paramPtr^ DO
      BEGIN
         inArgs[1] := ORD(cardFieldFlag);
         inArgs[2] := ORD(@fieldName);
         request := xreqGetFieldByName;
         DoJsr(entryPoint);
         GetFieldByName := Handle(outArgs[1]);
      END;
END;
```

For the C Programmer

```
pascal Handle GetFieldByName (paramPtr, cardFieldFlag, fieldName)
   XCmdBlockPtr   paramPtr;
   Boolean        cardFieldFlag;
   StringPtr      fieldName;
{
   paramPtr->inArgs[0] = (long) cardFieldFlag;
   paramPtr->inArgs[1] = (long) fieldName;
   paramPtr->request = xreqGetFieldByName;
   DoJsr (paramPtr);
   return (Handle) paramPtr->outArgs[0];
}
```

GetFieldByNum

GetFieldByNum returns a handle to a zero-terminated string that points to the contents of a card or background field. The field is specified by its object number.

Parameters

The GetFieldByNum function takes two parameters. The first parameter contains a Boolean value that determines what kind of field—card or background—will be accessed; use TRUE for a card field or FALSE for a background field. The second parameter contains an integer that represents the object number (not ID number) of the field whose contents you want to get:

```
FUNCTION GetFieldByNum(cardFieldFlag: BOOLEAN; fieldNum: INTEGER): Handle;
```

Example

{This example assumes a HyperTalk global was first declared with the name fieldTotal}

```
CONST  fieldNum = 3;

VAR    myHandle:     Handle;
       myCardField:  Boolean;
       fieldNum:     Integer;
       pasStr:       Str255;

myCardField := StrToBool('FALSE'); {make it a backgroundfield}
myHandle := GetFieldByNum(myCardField,fieldNum); {get contents of bkgnd field 3}
ZeroToPas(myHandle^,pasStr); {optionally convert field contents to a pascal string}
DisposHandle(myHandle); {must dispose of the handle before exiting}
```

Additional Information

Use the glue routine ZeroToPas to convert the contents of the handle to a Pascal string. HyperTalk copies the contents of the handle, so you must dispose of it before exiting your XCMD or XFCN. The handle is a copy of the field data, so changing the contents of the handle will not automatically change the field.

For the Pascal Programmer

```
FUNCTION GetFieldByNum(cardFieldFlag: BOOLEAN; fieldNum: INTEGER): Handle;

BEGIN
   WITH paramPtr^ DO
      BEGIN
         inArgs[1] := ORD(cardFieldFlag);
         inArgs[2] := fieldNum;
         request := xreqGetFieldByNum;
         DoJsr(entryPoint);
         GetFieldByNum := Handle(outArgs[1]);
      END;
END;
```

For the C Programmer

```
pascal Handle GetFieldByNum (paramPtr, cardFieldFlag, fieldNum)
   XCmdBlockPtr   paramPtr;
   Boolean        cardFieldFlag;
   short int      fieldNum;
{
   paramPtr->inArgs[0] = (long) cardFieldFlag;
   paramPtr->inArgs[1] = fieldNum;
   paramPtr->request = xreqGetFieldByNum;
   DoJsr (paramPtr);
   return (Handle) paramPtr->outArgs[0];
}
```

GetFieldByID

GetFieldByID returns a handle to a zero-terminated string representing the contents of the specified card or background field. The field is specified using its ID number.

Parameters

GetFieldByID takes two parameters. The first parameter contains a Boolean value that determines what kind of field—card or background—will be accessed; use TRUE for a card field or FALSE for a background field. The second parameter is of type integer and contains the ID number (not object number) of the field whose contents you want to get:

```
FUNCTION GetFieldByID(cardFieldFlag: BOOLEAN; fieldID: INTEGER): Handle;
```

Example

```
CONST  fieldID = 29847;

VAR    myHandle:     Handle;
       myCardField:  Boolean;
       pasStr:       Str255;

myCardField := StrToBool('FALSE'); {make it a background field}
myHandle := GetFieldByID(myCardField,fieldID); {get contents of bkgnd field ID 29847}
ZeroToPas(myHandle^,pasStr); {optionally convert field contents to a pascal string}
DisposHandle(myHandle); {must dispose of the handle before exiting}
```

Additional Information

Use the glue routine ZeroToPas to convert the contents of the handle to a Pascal string. HyperTalk copies the contents of the handle, so you must dispose of it before exiting the XCMD or XFCN. The handle is a copy of the field data, so changing the contents of the handle will not automatically change the field.

For the Pascal Programmer

```
FUNCTION GetFieldByID(cardFieldFlag: BOOLEAN; fieldID: INTEGER): Handle;

BEGIN
   WITH paramPtr^ DO
      BEGIN
         inArgs[1]  :=  ORD(cardFieldFlag);
         inArgs[2]  :=  fieldID;
         request  :=  xreqGetFieldByID;
         DoJsr(entryPoint);
         GetFieldByID  :=  Handle(outArgs[1]);
      END;
END;
```

For the C Programmer

```
pascal Handle GetFieldByID (paramPtr, cardFieldFlag, fieldID)
   XCmdBlockPtr   paramPtr;
   Boolean        cardFieldFlag;
   short int      fieldID;
{
   paramPtr->inArgs[0] = (long) cardFieldFlag;
   paramPtr->inArgs[1] = fieldID;
   paramPtr->request = xreqGetFieldByID;
   DoJsr (paramPtr);
   return (Handle) paramPtr->outArgs[0];
}
```

SetFieldByName

SetFieldByName sets the contents of a card or background field to a zero-terminated string. The field is specified by name.

Parameters

The SetFieldByName procedure takes three parameters. The first parameter contains a Boolean value that determines what kind of field—card or background—will be set; use TRUE for a card field or FALSE for a background field. The second parameter is of type Str255 and contains the name of the field to set. The third parameter contains a handle that points to a zero-terminated string:

```
PROCEDURE SetFieldByName(cardFieldFlag: BOOLEAN; fieldName: Str255; fieldVal: Handle);
```

Example

```
VAR    myHandle:      Handle;
       myCardField:   Boolean;
       fieldName:     Str255;

fieldName := 'Lacy'; {set the field name}
myCardField := StrToBool('TRUE'); {make it a card field}
SetFieldByName(myCardField,fieldName,myHandle); {set contents of card field "Lacy"}
DisposHandle(myHandle); {must dispose of the handle before exiting}
```

Additional Information

HyperTalk copies the handle you provide, so you must dispose of it before exiting your XCMD or XFCN. The contents of the zero-terminated string appear immediately in the named field, replacing the previous contents.

For the Pascal Programmer

PROCEDURE SetFieldByName(cardFieldFlag: BOOLEAN; fieldName: Str255; fieldVal: Handle);

```
BEGIN
   WITH paramPtr^ DO
      BEGIN
         inArgs[1] := ORD(cardFieldFlag);
         inArgs[2] := ORD(@fieldName);
         inArgs[3] := ORD(fieldVal);
         request := xreqSetFieldByName;
         DoJsr(entryPoint);
      END;
END;
```

For the C Programmer

```
pascal void SetFieldByName (paramPtr, cardFieldFlag, fieldName, fieldVal)
   XCmdBlockPtr   paramPtr;
   Boolean        cardFieldFlag;
   StringPtr      fieldName;
   Handle         fieldVal;
{
   paramPtr->inArgs[0] = (long) cardFieldFlag;
   paramPtr->inArgs[1] = (long) fieldName;
   paramPtr->inArgs[2] = (long) fieldVal;
   paramPtr->request = xreqSetFieldByName;
   DoJsr (paramPtr);
}
```

SetFieldByNum

SetFieldByNum sets the contents of a card or background field to a zero-terminated string. The field is specified by its object number.

Parameters

The SetFieldByNum procedure takes three parameters. The first parameter contains a Boolean value that determines what kind of field—card or background—will be set; use TRUE for a card field or FALSE for a background field. The second parameter is of type Integer and contains the object number (not the ID number) of the field to set. The third parameter contains a handle that points to a zero-terminated string:

```
PROCEDURE SetFieldByNum(cardFieldFlag: BOOLEAN; fieldNum: INTEGER; fieldVal: Handle);
```

Example

```
CONST  fieldNum = 12;

VAR    myHandle:    Handle;
       myCardField: Boolean;

myCardField := StrToBool('FALSE'); {make it a background field}
SetFieldByNum(myCardField,fieldNum,myHandle); {set bkgnd field 12 to myHandle}
DisposHandle(myHandle); {must dispose of the handle before exiting}
```

Additional Information

HyperTalk copies the handle you provide; therefore, you must dispose of it before exiting your XCMD or XFCN. The contents of the zero-terminated string appears immediately in the numbered field, replacing the previous contents.

For the Pascal Programmer

```
PROCEDURE SetFieldByNum(cardFieldFlag: BOOLEAN; fieldNum: INTEGER; fieldVal: Handle);

BEGIN
   WITH paramPtr^ DO
      BEGIN
         inArgs[1] := ORD(cardFieldFlag);
         inArgs[2] := fieldNum;
         inArgs[3] := ORD(fieldVal);
         request := xreqSetFieldByNum;
         DoJsr(entryPoint);
      END;
END;
```

For the C Programmer

```
pascal void SetFieldByNum (paramPtr, cardFieldFlag, fieldNum, fieldVal)
   XCmdBlockPtr   paramPtr;
   Boolean        cardFieldFlag;
   short int      fieldNum;
   Handle         fieldVal;
{
   paramPtr->inArgs[0] = (long) cardFieldFlag;
   paramPtr->inArgs[1] = fieldNum;
   paramPtr->inArgs[2] = (long) fieldVal;
   paramPtr->request = xreqSetFieldByNum;
   DoJsr (paramPtr);
}
```

SetFieldByID

SetFieldByID sets the contents of a card or background field to a zero-terminated string. The field is specified by its ID number.

Parameters

The SetFieldByID procedure takes three parameters. The first parameter contains a Boolean value that determines what kind of field—card or background—will be set; use TRUE for a card field or FALSE for a background field. The second parameter is of type Integer and contains the ID number of the field to set. The third parameter contains a handle to a zero-terminated string:

PROCEDURE SetFieldByID(cardFieldFlag: BOOLEAN; fieldID: INTEGER; fieldVal: Handle);

Example

```
CONST  fieldID = 1291;

VAR    myHandle:     Handle;
       myCardField:  Boolean;

myCardField := StrToBool('FALSE'); {make it a background field}
SetFieldByID(myCardField,fieldID,myHandle); {set bkgnd field ID 1291 to myHandle}
DisposHandle(myHandle); {must dispose of the handle before exiting}
```

Additional Information

HyperTalk copies the handle you provide; therefore, you must dispose of it before exiting the XCMD or XFCN. The contents of the zero-terminated string appear immediately in the field, replacing the previous contents.

For the Pascal Programmer

PROCEDURE SetFieldByID(cardFieldFlag: BOOLEAN; fieldID: INTEGER; fieldVal: Handle);

```
BEGIN
   WITH paramPtr^ DO
      BEGIN
        inArgs[1] := ORD(cardFieldFlag);
        inArgs[2] := fieldID;
        inArgs[3] := ORD(fieldVal);
        request := xreqSetFieldByID;
        DoJsr(entryPoint);
      END;
END;
```

For the C Programmer

```
pascal void SetFieldByID (paramPtr, cardFieldFlag, fieldID, fieldVal)
   XCmdBlockPtr  paramPtr;
   Boolean       cardFieldFlag;
   short int     fieldID;
   Handle        fieldVal;
{
   paramPtr->inArgs[0] = (long) cardFieldFlag;
   paramPtr->inArgs[1] = fieldID;
   paramPtr->inArgs[2] = (long) fieldVal;
   paramPtr->request = xreqSetFieldByID;
   DoJsr (paramPtr);
}
```

StringEqual

StringEqual compares two strings of type Str255. It returns the Boolean value TRUE if the strings contain the same characters or FALSE if they don't.

Parameters

StringEqual takes two paramters. Both parameters are of type Str255, and each parameter contains one of the two strings to be compared:

```
FUNCTION StringEqual(str1,str2: Str255): BOOLEAN;
```

Example

```
VAR    inString:      Str255;
       outString:     Str255;
       diffSame:      Boolean;

inString := 'ABCDE';
outString := 'abcde'; {assign values to the two strings used for the comparison}
diffSame := StringEqual(inString,outString); {these two strings are the same}

{This example shows you how to check an incoming parameter for the correct value. It
assumes that the word "ascending" was passed as paramter 2}


ZeroToPas(paramPtr^.params[2]^,paramStr); {convert the parameter to a pascal string}
IF NOT StringEqual('ascending',paramStr) THEN {exit if they aren't equal and load the result}
    BEGIN
        paramStr := 'Error in the second parameter';
        paramPtr^.returnValue := PasToZero(paramStr);
        EXIT{myXCMD}; {load the result and abort execution}
    END;
{If execution makes it here, the param checks out ok}
```

Additional Information

StringEqual is not case-sensitive or diacritical-sensitive.

For the Pascal Programmer

```
FUNCTION StringEqual(str1,str2: Str255): BOOLEAN;

BEGIN
   WITH paramPtr^ DO
      BEGIN
         inArgs[1] := ORD(@str1);
         inArgs[2] := ORD(@str2);
         request := xreqStringEqual;
         DoJsr(entryPoint);
         StringEqual := BOOLEAN(outArgs[1]);
      END;
END;
```

For the C Programmer

```
pascal Boolean StringEqual (paramPtr, str1, str2)
   XCmdBlockPtr   paramPtr;
   Str31          *str1, *str2;
{
   paramPtr->inArgs[0] = (long) str1;
   paramPtr->inArgs[1] = (long) str2;
   paramPtr->request = xreqStringEqual;
   DoJsr (paramPtr);
   return (Boolean) paramPtr->outArgs[0];
}
```

ReturnToPas

ReturnToPas collects the characters from the pointer to the first zero character marking the end of the zero-terminated string (or the first return character) and places them in the specified Pascal string.

Parameters

The ReturnToPas function takes two parameters. The first parameter is a pointer to a zero-terminated string. The second parameter is of type Str255 and contains the characters collected (the return or zero character is not included):

```
PROCEDURE ReturnToPas(zeroStr: Ptr; VAR pasStr: Str255);
```

Example

```
{gets the first line of a field}

VAR    myField:      Str255;
       chunkStr:     Str255;
       cardField:    Booelan;
       myHandle:     Handle;

cardField := StrToBool('TRUE'); {make it a card field}
myField := 'Winkler';
myHandle := GetFieldByName(cardField,myField); {contents of card field "Winkler"}
ReturnToPas(myHandle^,chunkStr); {chunkStr now contains line 1 of the field}
```

Additional Information

If a return character isn't found, ReturnToPas collects only the first 255 characters from the zero-terminated string. If the end of the string (a zero character) is encountered before that, ReturnToPas collects the characters up to—but not including—the zero character.

For the Pascal Programmer

```
PROCEDURE ReturnToPas(zeroStr: Ptr; VAR pasStr: Str255);

BEGIN
   WITH paramPtr^ DO
      BEGIN
         inArgs[1] := ORD(zeroStr);
         inArgs[2] := ORD(@pasStr);
         request := xreqReturnToPas;
         DoJsr(entryPoint);
      END;
END;
```

For the C Programmer

```
pascal void ReturnToPas (paramPtr, zeroStr, pasStr)
   XCmdBlockPtr  paramPtr;
   Ptr           zeroStr;
   StringPtr     pasStr;
{
   paramPtr->inArgs[0] = (long)zeroStr;
   paramPtr->inArgs[1] = (long)pasStr;
   paramPtr->request = xreqReturnToPas;
   DoJsr (paramPtr);
}
```

ScanToReturn

ScanToReturn moves a pointer along a zero-terminated string until it points to the first zero character marking the end of the zero-terminated string (or the first return character).

Parameters

The ScanToReturn procedure takes a single VAR parameter of type Ptr that contains the string to be scanned:

PROCEDURE ScanToReturn(VAR scanPtr: Ptr);

Example

{gets the nth line of a field}

```
VAR     myField:        Str255;
        chunkStr:       Str255;
        cardField:      Booelan;
        myHandle:       Handle;
        getLine:        Integer;

cardField := StrToBool('TRUE'); {make it a card field}
myField := 'Atkinson';
getLine := 4;
myHandle := GetFieldByName(cardField,myField); {gets contents of card field "Leffler"}
FOR i := 1 to getLine DO ScanToReturn(myHandle^); {scan to the fourth line}
myHandle^ := Pointer(ORD(myPtr)+1); {move the pointer to the right of the return character}
ReturnToPas(myHandle^,chunkStr); {chunkStr now contains line 4 of field "Leffler"}
```

Additional Information

If a return character isn't found, ScanToReturn ends up pointing to the zero character marking the end of the zero-terminated string.

For the Pascal Programmer

```
PROCEDURE ScanToReturn(VAR scanPtr: Ptr);

BEGIN
   WITH paramPtr^ DO
      BEGIN
        inArgs[1] := ORD(@scanPtr);
        request := xreqScanToReturn;
        DoJsr(entryPoint);
      END;
END;
```

For the C Programmer

```
pascal void ScanToReturn (paramPtr, scanHndl)
   XCmdBlockPtr  paramPtr;
   Ptr           *scanHndl;
{
   paramPtr->inArgs[0] = (long) scanHndl;
   paramPtr->request = xreqScanToReturn;
   DoJsr (paramPtr);
}
```

ScanToZero

ScanToZero moves a pointer along a zero-terminated string until it points at a zero character.

Parameters

The ScanToZero procedure takes a single VAR parameter of type Ptr that contains the string to be scanned:

PROCEDURE ScanToZero(VAR scanPtr: Ptr);

Example

ScanToZero(myPtr); {move the pointer to the end of the zero-terminated string}

Additional Information

You can use ScanToZero to scan through memory for the first zero character.

For the Pascal Programmer

PROCEDURE ScanToZero(VAR scanPtr: Ptr);

```
BEGIN
    WITH paramPtr^ DO
        BEGIN
            inArgs[1] := ORD(@scanPtr);
            request := xreqScanToZero;
            DoJsr(entryPoint);
        END;
END;
```

For the C Programmer

```
pascal void ScanToZero (paramPtr, scanHndl)
    XCmdBlockPtr   paramPtr;
    Ptr            *scanHndl;
{
    paramPtr->inArgs[0] = (long) scanHndl;
    paramPtr->request = xreqScanToZero;
    DoJsr (paramPtr);
}
```

A QUICK REFERENCE GUIDE TO THE GLUE ROUTINES

The 29 glue routines and their parameters are summarized in alphabetical order as follows:

BoolToStr

FUNCTION BoolToStr(bool: Boolean): Str31;

EvalExpr

FUNCTION EvalExpr(expr: Str255): Handle;

ExtToStr

FUNCTION ExtToStr(num: Extended): Str31;

GetFieldByID

FUNCTION GetFieldByID(cardFieldFlag: Boolean; fieldID: Integer): Handle;

GetFieldByName

FUNCTION GetFieldByName(cardFieldFlag: Boolean; fieldName: Str255): Handle;

GetFieldByNum

FUNCTION GetFieldByNum(cardFieldFlag: Boolean; fieldNum: Integer): Handle;

GetGlobal

FUNCTION GetGlobal(globName: Str255): Handle;

LongToStr

FUNCTION LongToStr(posNum: LongInt): Str31;

NumToHex

FUNCTION NumToHex(num: LongInt): Str31;

continued...

...from previous page

NumToStr

FUNCTION NumToStr(num: LongInt): Str31;

PasToZero

FUNCTION PasToZero(str: Str255): Handle;

ReturnToPas

PROCEDURE ReturnToPas(zeroStr: Ptr;   VAR pasStr: Str255);

ScanToReturn

PROCEDURE ScanToReturn(VAR scanPtr: Ptr);

ScanToZero

PROCEDURE ScanToZero(VAR scaPtr: Ptr);

SendCardMessage

PROCEDURE SendCardMessage(msg: Str255);

SendHCMessage

PROCEDURE SendHCMessage(msg: Str255);

SetFieldByID

PROCEDURE SetFieldByID(cardFieldFlag: Boolean; fieldID: Integer: fieldVal: Handle);

SetFieldByName

PROCEDURE SetFieldByName(cardFieldFlag: Boolean; fieldName: Str255: fieldVal: Handle);

SetFieldByNum

PROCEDURE SetFieldByNum(cardFieldFlag: Boolean; fieldNum: Integer: fieldVal: Handle);

continued...

...from previous page

SetGlobal

PROCEDURE SetGlobal(globName: Str255; globValue: Handle);

StringEqual

FUNCTION StringEqual(str1,str2: Str255): Boolean;

StringLength

FUNCTION StringLength(strPtr: Ptr): LongInt;

StringMatch

FUNCTION StringMatch(pattern: Str255;   target: Ptr): Ptr;

StrToBool

FUNCTION StrToBool(str: Str31): Boolean;

StrToExt

FUNCTION StrToExt(str: Str31): Extended;

StrToLong

FUNCTION StrToLong(str: Str31): LongInt;

StrToNum

FUNCTION StrToNum(str: Str31): LongInt;

ZeroToPas

PROCEDURE ZeroToPas(zeroStr: Ptr; VAR pasStr: Str255);

ZeroBytes

PROCEDURE ZeroBytes(dstPtr: Ptr; longCount: longInt);

WRITING YOUR OWN TOOLS

Every good programmer keeps a set of procedures and functions that help make life a little easier. As you get farther into XCMD's and XFCN's, you will discover things you tend to do all the time—such as incrementing a pointer or collecting all the characters between a pointer and the nearest comma. Routines that handle repetitive tasks can make great additions to your own tool library.

To create your own tools, write them in Pascal or C as you normally would; then, add them to the XCmdGlue file discussed earlier in this chapter. Use the same procedure to include routines you have already created. Tools added to the XCmdGlue file are called like any other glue routine.

Following are some routines you might find useful.

IncrementPointer

Increments a pointer by the number of bytes specified by the variable count. ScanPtr^ returns the contents of the byte pointed to.

For the Pascal Programmer

```
PROCEDURE IncrementPointer(VAR scanPtr: Ptr; count: LongInt);

    BEGIN
      scanPtr := Pointer(ORD(scanPtr)+count);
    END;
```

Example:

```
IncrementPointer(myPointer,incNum);
```

For the C Programmer

Because you would use pointer arithmetic in C to handle this task easily, an equivalent routine is not presented here.

ScanToSpace

Moves the VAR pointer along a zero-terminated string until it points to the first zero character marking the end of the zero-terminated string or the first space character (ASCII 32).

For the Pascal Programmer

```
PROCEDURE ScanToSpace(VAR scanPtr: Ptr);

   VAR  exitloop: BOOLEAN;

   BEGIN
      exitloop := FALSE;
      REPEAT
         IF ((scanPtr^ = $20) OR (scanPtr^ = 0)) THEN exitloop := TRUE
         ELSE scanPtr := Pointer(ORD(scanPtr)+1);
      UNTIL exitloop = TRUE;
   END;
```

Example:

```
myPointer := paramPtr^.params[1]^;
ScanToSpace(myPointer);
```

For the C Programmer

```
char *ScanToSpace(str)
   char *str;
{
   while ((*str != ' ') && (*str != 0))
      ++str;
   return(str);
}

/*
   Example:

   myPointer = *(paramPtr->params[0]);
   myPointer = ScanToSpace(myPointer);
*/
```

ScanToComma

Moves the VAR pointer along a zero-terminated string until it points to the first zero character marking the end of the zero-terminated string or the first comma character (ASCII 44).

For the Pascal Programmer

```
PROCEDURE ScanToComma(VAR scanPtr: Ptr);

   VAR  exitloop: BOOLEAN;

   BEGIN
      exitloop := FALSE;
      REPEAT
         IF ((scanPtr^ = $2C) OR (scanPtr^ = 0)) THEN exitloop := TRUE
         ELSE scanPtr := Pointer(ORD(scanPtr)+1);
      UNTIL exitloop = TRUE;
   END;
```

Example:

```
myPointer := paramPtr^.params[5]^;
ScanToComma(myPointer);
```

For the C Programmer

```
char *ScanToComma(str)
   char *str;
{
   while ((*str != ',') && (*str != 0))
      ++str;
   return(str);
}

/*
   Example:

   myPointer = *(paramPtr->params[0]);
   myPointer = ScanToComma(myPointer);
*/
```

ScanToSpec

Moves the VAR pointer along a zero-terminated string until it points to the first zero character marking the end of the zero-terminated string or the character specified by the ASCII value in myChar.

For the Pascal Programmer

```
PROCEDURE ScanToSpec(VAR scanPtr: Ptr; myChar: Integer);

   VAR  exitloop: BOOLEAN;

   BEGIN
      exitloop := FALSE;
      REPEAT
         IF ((scanPtr^ = myChar) OR (scanPtr^ = 0)) THEN exitloop := TRUE
         ELSE scanPtr := Pointer(ORD(scanPtr)+1);
      UNTIL exitloop = TRUE;
   END;
```

Example:

```
myPointer := paramPtr^.params[15]^;
scanCharacter := 59;
ScanToSpec(myPointer,scanCharacter); {scan until semi-colon}
```

For the C Programmer

```
char *ScanToSpec(str, myChar)
   char *str;
   char myChar;
{
   while ((*str != myChar) && (*str != 0))
      ++str;
   return(str);
}

/*
   Example (scan until $):

   myPointer = *(paramPtr->params[0]);
   myPointer = ScanToSpec(myPointer, '$');
*/
```

CollectToComma

Moves the VAR pointer along a zero-terminated string, collecting characters until it points to the first zero character marking the end of the zero-terminated string or to the first comma character (ASCII 44). CollectToComma returns up to 255 characters and leaves the pointer pointing to the comma character.

For the Pascal Programmer

```
FUNCTION CollectToComma(VAR scanPtr: Ptr): Str255;

   TYPE Str1  =  String[1];

   VAR  exitloop:  BOOLEAN;
        tempStr: Str1;
        collectStr: Str255;

BEGIN
   exitloop := FALSE;
   tempStr[0]  :=  chr(1);
   collectStr  :=  ''; {initialize it}
   REPEAT
      IF ((scanPtr^ = $2C) OR (scanPtr^ = 0)) THEN exitloop := TRUE
      ELSE
         BEGIN
            tempStr[1]  :=  chr(scanPtr^);
            collectStr  :=  Concat(collectStr,tempStr);
            scanPtr  :=  Pointer(ORD(scanPtr)+1);
         END;
   UNTIL exitloop = TRUE;
   CollectToComma := collectStr;
END;
```

Example:

```
myPointer  :=  paramPtr^.params[3]^;
collectedChars  :=  CollectToComma(myPointer); {collectedChars is of type Str255}
```

For the C Programmer

```
char *CollectToComma(targetStr, subStr)
   char  *targetStr;
   char  *subStr;
{
   while ((*targetStr != ',') && (*targetStr != 0))
      *subStr++ = *targetStr++;

   return(targetStr);
}

/*
   Example: (Note that the subString does not get 0 terminated)

   Str255 mySubstring;

   myPointer = *(paramPtr->params[0]);
   myPointer = CollectToComma(myPointer, (char *) mySubstring);
*/
```

CollectToSpace

Moves the VAR pointer along a zero-terminated string, collecting characters until it points to the first zero character marking the end of the zero-terminated string or to the first space character (ASCII 32). CollectToSpace returns up to 255 characters and leaves the pointer pointing at the space character.

For the Pascal Programmer

```
FUNCTION CollectToSpace(VAR scanPtr: Ptr): Str255;

TYPE Str1  =  String[1];

VAR  exitloop:   BOOLEAN;
     tempStr: Str1 ;
     collectStr: Str255;

  BEGIN
     exitloop := FALSE;
     tempStr[0]  :=  chr(1);
     collectStr  :=  ''; {initialize it}
     REPEAT
       IF ((scanPtr^ = $20) OR (scanPtr^ = 0)) THEN exitloop := TRUE
       ELSE
          BEGIN
             tempStr[1]  :=  chr(scanPtr^);
             collectStr  :=  Concat(collectStr,tempStr);
             scanPtr  :=  Pointer(ORD(scanPtr)+1);
          END;
     UNTIL exitloop = TRUE;
     CollectToSpace := collectStr;
  END;
```

Example:

```
myPointer  :=  paramPtr^.params[10]^;
collectedChars  :=  CollectToSpace(myPointer); {collectedChars is of type Str255}
```

For the C Programmer

```
char *CollectToSpace(targetStr, subStr)
   char *targetStr;
   char *subStr;
{
   while ((*targetStr != ' ') && (*targetStr != 0))
      *subStr++ = *targetStr++;

   return(targetStr);
}

/*
   Example: (Note that the subString does not get 0 terminated)

   Str255   mySubstring;

   myPointer = *(paramPtr->params[0]);
   myPointer = CollectToSpace(myPointer, (char *) mySubstring);
*/
```

CollectToSpec

Moves the VAR pointer along a zero-terminated string, collecting characters until it points to the first zero character marking the end of the zero-terminated string or the character specified by the ASCII value in myChar. CollectToSpec returns up to 255 characters and leaves the pointer pointing at the character specified by the ASCII value in myChar.

For the Pascal Programmer

```
FUNCTION CollectToSpec(VAR scanPtr: Ptr; myChar: Integer): Str255;

TYPE Str1  =  String[1];

VAR  exitloop:  BOOLEAN;
     tempStr: Str1;
     collectStr: Str255;

   BEGIN
     exitloop := FALSE;
     tempStr[0]  :=  chr(1);
     collectStr := ''; {initialize it}
     REPEAT
       IF ((scanPtr^ = myChar) OR (scanPtr^ = 0)) THEN exitloop := TRUE
       ELSE
          BEGIN
             tempStr[1]  :=  chr(scanPtr^);
             collectStr  :=  Concat(collectStr,tempStr);
             scanPtr  :=  Pointer(ORD(scanPtr)+1);
          END;
     UNTIL exitloop = TRUE;
     CollectToSpec := collectStr;
   END;
```

Example:

```
myPointer  :=  paramPtr^.params[14]^;
scanChar := 65; {collect characters up to a capital 'A'}
collectedChars  :=  CollectToComma(myPointer,scanChar); {collectedChars is of type Str255}
```

For the C Programmer

```
char *CollectToSpec(targetStr, subStr, myChar)
   char *targetStr;
   char *subStr;
   char myChar;
{
   while ((*targetStr != myChar) && (*targetStr != 0))
      *subStr++ = *targetStr++;

   return(targetStr);
}

/*
   Example: (Note that the subString does not get 0 terminated)

   Str255  mySubstring;

   myPointer = *(paramPtr->params[0]);
   myPointer = CollectToSpace(myPointer, (char *) mySubstring, '$');
*/
```

XCMD AND XFCN STARTER FILES

XCMD and XFCN starter files are files that contain the minimum code necessary to create an XCMD or XFCN, using either MPW Pascal or LightSpeedC. You should enter the code for the appropriate file into your compiler and save it as a template for future use. Later, when you need to create an XCMD or XFCN, copy the file and customize it with your own procedures and functions.

Customizing the Starter File

Following are the steps necessary to customize the starter file.

For the Pascal Programmer

1. Duplicate the template using CMD-D in the Finder.
2. Rename the copy, giving it the exact name of your XCMD or XFCN.
3. Double-click the copy to launch it.
4. Replace all occurrences of the string "myXCMDName" with the name of your XCMD or XFCN.

5. If you are creating an XFCN, change all occurrences of the string "XCMD" to XFCN.
6. Modify the resource number.
7. Modify the pathname, "yourVolume:yourFilename," to match your situation.
8. As you work, add the appropriate libraries and link files.

For the C Programmer

To customize the C starter file, eliminate steps 6 and 7 above.

Pascal Starter File

The following file is for use with the MPW Pascal compiler. You may need to modify it for your particular compiler.

Directives that are specific to the MPW compiler are preceded by the dollar sign character ($R-) or the hyphen character (-rt); you may need to remove or change these characters when using other compilers.

(*

© Add your appropriate copyright information
All Rights Reserved

myXCMDName— Describe what your XCMD or XFCN does

Form: Describe the parameters your XCMD or XFCN takes

Example: Give an exact example of your XCMD or XFCN in use

Note: Put any notes about your XCMD or XFCN here

To compile and link this file using MPW Pascal, select the following lines and press ENTER

---

continued...

...from previous page

```
pascal myXCMDName.p
link -o "HD:HyperCard:Home" -rt XCMD=1614 -sn Main=myXCMDName myXCMDName.p.o ∂
{MPW}Libraries:Interface.o -m ENTRYPOINT ∂
{MPW}PLibraries:PasLib.o -m ENTRYPOINT
```

Note: Include other link files as necessary. Use option-D in MPW to continue the line.

```
* )

{$R-} {Dollar sign R and S are MPW compiler directives}

{$S myXCMDName}
{The name of the segment must be the same as the name of your XCMD or  XFCN}

UNIT DummyUnit;
{DummyUnit is what HyperTalk jumps to as it begins to run your XCMD or  XFCN}

INTERFACE

USES MemTypes, QuickDraw, OSIntf, ToolIntf, PasLibIntf, HyperXCmd;
{HyperXCmd is the  interface  file}

PROCEDURE EntryPoint(paramPtr: XCmdPtr);

IMPLEMENTATION

TYPE Str31 = String[31];

{Put other type definitions here}

PROCEDURE myXCMDName(paramPtr: XCmdPtr); FORWARD;

   PROCEDURE EntryPoint(paramPtr: XCmdPtr);

   BEGIN
      myXCMDName(paramPtr);
   END;

   PROCEDURE myXCMDName(paramPtr: XCmdPtr);

   CONST {Constant declarations for your main procedure - eliminate if not necessary}
```
continued...

...from previous page

VAR {Variable declarations for your main procedure - eliminate if not necessary}

{Put any sub-procedures or sub-functions that are called by your main procedure here}

{$I XCmdGlue.inc } {This is an MPW directive which includes the glue routines}

BEGIN {main}

    {Your main procedure goes here}

END; {main}

END. {myXCMDName}

C Starter File

Use the following file with the LightSpeedC compiler. You may need to modify it for your particular compiler.

Following is the starter file in LightSpeedC:

```
/*
    © Add appropriate copyright information
    All Rights Reserved

    myXCMDName --    Describe what your XCMD or XFCN does

    Form:            Describe the parameters your XCMD or XFCN takes

    Example:         Give an exact example of your XCMD or XFCN in use

    Note:            Put any notes about your XCMD or XFCN here
    _____

    Compile and link this file with the MacTraps and string libraries
*/
```

continued...

...from previous page

```
/*
   Includes:
   Substitute the header files that are appropriate for your compiler.
*/
#include    <MacTypes.h>
#include    "HyperXCmd.h" /* This header file appears earlier in this chapter */

pascal void main(XCmdBlockPtr);

/* Define your constants here */

/* Include type definitions here */


pascal void main(paramPtr)
   XCmdBlockPtr paramPtr;
{
   /* Insert the main body of your XCMD here */
}


/* Put your subroutines here */
```

FOR THE POWER PROGRAMMER

For brave souls who program entirely in assembly language, following is the Flash
XCMD done entirely in 68000 code:

```
*
*        Flash.a - A sample HyperCard XCMD in 68000 Assembly
*        - Copyright Apple Computer, Inc.  1988.
*        - All Rights Reserved.
*
*        Build Instructions for MPW:
*
*        Asm  Flash.a -o Flash.a.o
*        Link Flash.a.o -sg AFlash -rt XCMD=7 -o StackName
*
*
```

continued...

...from previous page

```
          INCLUDE 'QuickEqu.a'
          INCLUDE 'Traps.a'

          SEG 'AFlash'              ; Segname must be same as command name

AFlash  PROC                       ; uses a0,a1,d1
          link     a6,#-4
          move.l   d4,-(sp)         ; save
          move.l   8(a6),a0         ; get paramPtr in a temp reg
          move.l   2(a0),a1         ; get handle to flashCount (as c string)
          move.l   (a1),a1          ; deref
          move.w   #3,d4            ; StrToNum default result

@1        move.b   (a1)+,d1         ; get a char
          cmp.b    #'0',d1          ; test for a number
          blt.s    @2               ; less than valid
          cmp.b    #'9',d1
          bgt.s    @2               ; greater than valid

          and.w    #$000F,d1        ; mask to value of legal char
          move.w   d1,d4            ; stick value into result

@2        pea      -4(a6)           ; var result of GetPort
          _GetPort
          bra.s    @4               ; get into DBRA loop

@3        move.l   -4(a6),a0        ; get port
          pea      portRect(a0)     ; address of portRect
          _InverRect
          move.l   -4(a6),a0        ; get port
          pea      portRect(a0)     ; address of portRect
          _InverRect
```

continued...

...from previous page

```
@4      dbra    d4,@3

        move.l  (sp)+,d4        ;  restore
        unlk    a6

        move.l  (sp)+,a0        ; rts Pascal style
        add.l   #4,a7
        jmp     (a0)

        END
```

HINTS AND TIPS

• If you are using MPW to compile and link your XCMD's and XFCN's, a make file is not necessary. To compile and link each XCMD or XFCN using MPW, you need only highlight the set of lines indicated in the source code listings found in this book (see the Introduction for details).

• Use the glue routines wherever possible; many are optimized for speed.

• You should not modify or add anything to the stack file formats; they are likely to change in future versions of HyperCard.

SUMMARY

In this chapter, you explored the various fields of the external interface file called "HyperXCmd." You learned what each of the glue routines does and how to write your own routines. Also, you learned how to enter and customize the starter files for building your own XCMD's and XFCN's from scratch.

CHAPTER 4

CREATING YOUR FIRST XCMD

In this chapter, you will apply what you have learned about the design and coding of XCMD's and XFCN's by following the creation of an XCMD from beginning to end. You will take a serious look at the design process and an in-depth look at the code necessary to implement the design. Feel free to make changes to the design or the code shown in this chapter.

If you are new to XCMD's and XFCN's, the following section—"What Kind of XCMD Should You Create"—provides information on how to get started and teaches you how to develop ideas for your own XCMD's and XFCN's. You can skip this section if you want to move on to the design phase for the sample XCMD used in this chapter.

WHAT KIND OF XCMD SHOULD YOU CREATE?

When you think about creating an XCMD or XFCN, you may feel overwhelmed by the many possibilities. You may find yourself asking questions such as "What kind of XCMD or XFCN should I create? What should it do? How should it do it?"

One way to start is by making a list of tasks you wish HyperCard could perform. Such a list will help you to begin thinking about extending HyperCard's abilities. Following are some examples:

• Print the contents of a field or variable
• Sort the contents of a field or variable
• Display larger and more useful dialogs
• Display custom menus
• Control the sound volume
• Speak the contents of a field or variable
• Determine the model of computer your XCMD is running on

When you have finished compiling your "wish" list, start a second list of HyperCard's qualities that *annoy* you, such as the inability to print the contents of a field or variable or not being able to change more than one global variable at a time.

As you examine your lists, you might find that a few items appear on both lists; these are the items on which you should concentrate. By creating XCMD's and XFCN's to handle your most common wishes and complaints, you will not only be providing a solution for them, you will learn a tremendous amount about XCMD's, HyperCard, and the Macintosh.

And, as you begin to use your own XCMD's and XFCN's, you will find ideas for new ones around every corner.

The remaining sections in this chapter cover the design and coding of an XCMD named Dialog.

DESIGNING THE DIALOG BOX

The XCMD you will be learning about in this chapter was chosen for both its "wish" value (many people want it) and technical simplicity. It is named Dialog, and it lets you create a modal dialog that displays up to 255 characters (many times more than HyperTalk's answer dialog can display).

When creating any XCMD, you'll want to keep the design as friendly and intuitive as possible; the user will suffer if you don't. As you follow the creation of the Dialog XCMD in this chapter, frequently ask yourself "is this the best thing for the user?"

Following are some possible uses for the Dialog XCMD:

- Display long explanations or instructions
- Display warnings
- Attract the user's attention to a fact or condition
- Help debug HyperTalk scripts
- Display the contents of hidden fields
- Display the script of an object
- Replace the message box (where appropriate)
- Replace HyperTalk's answer dialog

Building the Dialog XCMD provides a thorough integration of what you learned in the first three chapters. As you create the Dialog XCMD, you will use the external interface, some of the glue routines, the call back interface, and some ROM and system routines.

To produce the dialog window for the Dialog XCMD, you will use an already created **DLOG** (number 107) resource from HyperCard's resource fork. The DLOG 107 resource contains a typical modal style dialog window that looks like the following:

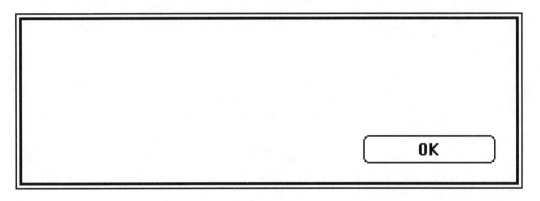

Figure 4.1

The dialog window of HyperCard's DLOG 107 resource. Note that it is larger than HyperTalk's answer dialog but doesn't include the default outline around the OK button (you will draw one later).

By using an existing resource, you will save coding time and space. You can access the DLOG resource, including the single button control (OK button), with the ROM routine GetNewDialog.

> **Note:** The possible drawback to the strategy of using an existing resource is that resources are not guaranteed to be around from one version of HyperCard to another. (The one you use for the Dialog XCMD, however, is likely to be around a while because it is used to return errors in HyperCard.)

Making Some Decisions

Before you start building the Dialog XCMD, there are some design issues you must consider. Your decisions about these issues should be based on what you know of Apple's user interface guidelines, what you know of the way HyperTalk handles similar situations, and your own experience as a user and designer.

Following are some of the questions you must answer before completing the design of the Dialog XCMD; each is covered in detail in its own section:

• What should the parameters to the Dialog XCMD be?
• What order should the parameters be in?
• Can the user leave out some parameters without doing damage?
• Should the dialog window be displayed at a user-specified location?
• What should the dialog window look like?
• Should the text inside the dialog be displayed in a user-specified font?
• Should the Dialog XCMD return a result of any kind?

What Should Dialog XCMD Parameters Be?

You should give this question the most thought because the XCMD's parameters will reflect both its feature set and interface. It is one of the most important questions you can ask of any XCMD or XFCN.

Start a list of the features you think would be appropriate for your XCMD. Don't worry about having too many features; you can narrow the list after you get it on paper. Following are some possibilities for the Dialog XCMD:

• Display the contents of any field or variable.
• Specify the font to be used when displaying the information.
• Specify the location of the dialog window.
• Have default values if the user doesn't specify a font or window location.
• Be flexible about the number and type of parameters it accepts.
• Return the correct parameters if a mistake is made.
• Look and behave like a standard Macintosh modal dialog.

HyperTalk's standard answer dialog allows you to display the contents of any field or variable in a dialog window that always appears in the same place, regardless of the position of the card window itself.

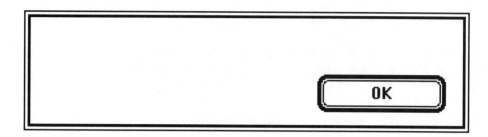

Figure 4.2

HyperTalk's standard answer dialog. Compare it to the larger dialog shown in Figure 4.1

The finished Dialog XCMD should display the contents of any string or container (field, variable, the selection) in a window approximately centered within the card window's boundaries. (This feature would be especially useful when the card window is on a large-screen monitor or on a screen other than the main one.)

It would be advantageous, however, to let the user modify the location of the dialog window by providing a top left point at which the user wants the dialog window to be placed. A good solution to both problems would be to show the dialog window at the user-specified location when the user provides one or to center the dialog window when the user does not.

The next-most desirable feature would be to let the user specify the font in which to display the text. For simplicity, you should probably have the user specify the font by name rather than by number.

At this point, you have covered the main feature set for the dialog XCMD. You could allow more features, such as a user-defined dialog type or extra buttons in the dialog window, but the following four features will provide you with a good learning example while maintaining a minimum technical complexity. These features also provide the parameters your XCMD will need to be passed.

Following are the four parameters (features):

• A container or string with the information to be displayed (field, variable, the selection)
• A font name to use when displaying the information
• A *left* screen coordinate at which to display the dialog window
• A *top* screen coordinate at which to display the dialog window

What Order Should the Parameters Be In?

Now that you know what parameters you'll need, you must decide whether or not you want them to be passed in a fixed order.

It would be convenient to be able to pass the parameters in any order, but it would complicate your XCMD. On the other hand, if the parameters are fixed, the user must supply every parameter with every call in exactly the right order.

One solution to this problem is to provide *partial* freedom by allowing the user to omit some parameters while still requiring that the parameters be supplied in a fixed order. Allowing this freedom creates the illusion that your parameters can be supplied in almost any order. For example, any of the following combinations would break the strict rule of supplying all of the parameters while maintaining the basic order your XCMD will need (container refers to a string, field, variable, or the selection):

• Dialog container
• Dialog container,font
• Dialog container,top,left

It seems natural to position the information to be displayed in the first parameter. You should pay particular attention to parameters that have such an implied or natural order.

The top-left order is another example of natural ordering. Because the combined top and left coordinates specify a single point in space, you do not want to break them up. The coordinates should always be listed in the following order: top,left.

One decision remains: should the window location come before the font name, or should the font name come before the window location? At first glance, it might seem like the two are interchangeable, but it can be tricky.

Because two of the parameters are numbers (the location) and two are strings (the information and the font name), you would have no way of knowing whether the parameters have been supplied in the correct order; therefore, you must make certain assumptions.

You can safely assume that if there is only one parameter, it describes the information to be displayed. You can also assume that if there are four parameters, you have been passed *all* of the necessary information. Likewise, if there are two parameters, it is valid to assume that those parameters are the information to be displayed and the font name because the location would require a minimum of three parameters (container,top,left).

From this analysis, you should see that the font name works equally well in parameter 2 and parameter 4, and the location works equally well in parameter 2 or parameter 3. For the greatest flexibility, however, the font name should probably follow the location.

The complete parameter specification now looks like the following:

Dialog container,top,left,font name

The first parameter is the container that provides the information to be displayed; the second and third parameters are the screen (global) coordinates at which to show the dialog window; and the fourth parameter is the font to use when displaying the contents of the container.

> **Note:** If the font name is two words or is separated by a hyphen, the entire name must appear within double quotes (as in "Narrow Helvetica").

Can the User Leave Out Some Parameters?

The only parameter the user must supply is parameter 1—the container. The location and font name should be optional. If you make them optional, any of the following combinations would be valid:

- Dialog container,top,left,font
- Dialog container,top,left
- Dialog container,font
- Dialog container

If you code the XCMD properly, bad combinations will not cause a problem for either you or the user. One method for accomplishing this task is to establish default values.

Should the Dialog Window Be Displayed at a User-Specified Location?

The dialog window *should* be displayed at a user-defined location, but if the user forgets to specify a location, your XCMD should center the dialog window within the boundaries of the current card window. This includes centering the dialog window on a Mac II monitor or other large-screen monitor where the card window can move around.

What Should the Dialog Window Look Like?

The dialog window in the DLOG 107 resource measures 376 pixels (horizontally) by 116 pixels (vertically) and resembles a typical modal dialog box. A single OK button appears in the lower right corner of the window (see Figure 4.1).

The button doesn't include the 3-pixel line surrounding it that the interface guidelines require to denote a default button. To conform to the interface guidelines, you must draw a round rectangle around the button.

Should the Text Inside the Dialog Be Specified in a User-Specified Font?

Text inside the dialog box *should* be displayed in a user-specified font, but you should consider cases in which the user omits the font name, spells it incorrectly, or specifies a font name that doesn't exist. In such cases, you have two options: you can abort the XCMD returning an "incorrect font" error, or you can choose a font you know will always be there. The second solution is better; it lets the user display the contents of the field or variable—regardless of errors—while providing visual feedback about the error.

Should the Dialog XCMD Return a Result?

Your XCMD's or XFCN's should always return appropriate errors or information via the returnValue field of the XCmdBlock. In the case of the Dialog XCMD, you need only return a result when a fatal error occurs. Fatal errors for the Dialog XCMD include:

- Missing parameters
- More than four parameters passed
- A call-back failure
- A fatal error in a ROM routine
- A fatal error in a System routine

Note: If the error is in the parameter count, it would be convenient to provide the user with an error message containing the correct form. There are several ways in which you can perform this task, but the method that should cause the least interference with the existing environment is to load the result with a string containing the correct form before exiting back to HyperTalk. For example:

```
paramPtr^.returnValue := PasToZero('Form: Dialog,container,top,left,"font name"')
```

WRITING THE CODE

After you complete the preliminary design for your XCMD or XFCN, the next step is to write the code for it. In this step, you must implement the decisions you made while designing the XCMD. Sometimes, implementing these decisions is not as easy as it sounds. Difficulties in coding can cause design changes that make life easier for the programmer but aren't good for the user (such as requiring that the user supply a font number rather than a font name). Avoid making those kinds of changes; they only lessen the quality of your XCMD or XFCN.

The best way to start coding an XCMD or XFCN is to duplicate the starter file (see the end of Chapter 3) in the Finder and rename it using the new name of your XCMD. For the Dialog XCMD, you should name the file Dialog.p if you are working in Pascal or Dialog.c if you are working in C.

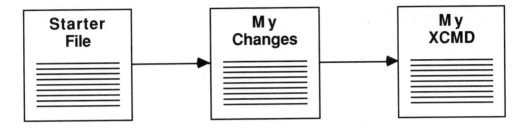

Figure 4.3

The transformation from starter file to finished XCMD.

Next, you must modify the starter file as discussed in Chapter 3. The following Dialog XCMD starter file (in Pascal) is shown with the appropriate modifications:

```
{$R-}
( *
    Dialog: a HyperCard XCMD that displays a modal dialog.  The caller can provide the
    text, font and display location. Dialog uses dialog box number 107 from HyperCard's
    resource fork, automatically centering the dialog window within the card window.  Up
    to 255 characters can be displayed.

    Form: Dialog "String to display",Top,Left,Font Name

    Example: Dialog "Display this text",100,80,geneva

    Note: Top and Left are integers that specify the top-left point at which to display the
    dialog. If these values aren't supplied, the dialog automatically centers itself within
    the boundaries of the card window.  The font to display the text in is passed by name;
    its size cannot be changed.

    _____

    To compile and link this file using MPW Pascal, select the following lines and press
    the ENTER key
    _____

pascal Dialog.p
link -o "HD:Home" -rt  XCMD=1502 -sn Main=Dialog Dialog.p.o ∂
{MPW}Libraries:Interface.o -m ENTRYPOINT
```

continued...

...from previous page

```
* )

{$S Dialog }    { Segment name must be the same as the command name. }

UNIT DummyUnit;

INTERFACE

USES MemTypes, QuickDraw, OSIntf, ToolIntf, HyperXCmd;

PROCEDURE ENTRYPOINT(paramPtr: XCmdPtr);

IMPLEMENTATION

TYPE  Str31  =  String[31];

PROCEDURE Dialog(paramPtr: XCmdPtr);                 FORWARD;

PROCEDURE ENTRYPOINT(paramPtr: XCmdPtr);

    BEGIN
        Dialog(paramPtr);
    END;

PROCEDURE Dialog(paramPtr: XCmdPtr);

{$I XCmdGlue.inc } {This is an MPW directive which includes the glue routines}

    BEGIN {main}

        {Your main procedure goes here}

    END; {main}

END. {Dialog}
```

You will be adding to the starter file as you progress, but only the main procedure of that file will be shown from this point on (the entire Dialog XCMD is shown at the end of the chapter). Following is the main procedure without additional code:

```
PROCEDURE Dialog(paramPtr: XCmdPtr);

{$I XCmdGlue.inc } {This is an MPW directive which includes the glue routines}

      BEGIN {main}

      {Your main procedure goes here}

      END; {main}

END. {Dialog}
```

Defining Your Subprocedures

The next step is to define subprocedures that you know you will need to call from the main procedure. For the Dialog XCMD, you will need procedures to check the correct parameter count (a good addition to your own tools library), to set default values, to get the location of the card window, and to abort the XCMD if necesssary. Each of these procedures is discussed in a separate section.

CheckParamCount Procedure

The CheckParamCount procedure checks the current parameter count against prede-fined minimum and maximum values. If the number of parameters passed to the Dialog XCMD does not fall within the specified range, CheckParamCount aborts the Dialog XCMD, returning a string (that represents the correct form to use when calling the Dialog XCMD) in *the result*.

CheckParamCount takes no parameters and looks like the following:

```
PROCEDURE CheckParamCount; {checks for the correct parameter count}
   BEGIN
      numParams := paramPtr^.paramCount; {store the number of parameters passed}
      IF (numParams < minParamCount) OR (numParams > maxParamCount) THEN
         BEGIN {Exit loading the result with the correct form}
            errStr := 'Form: Dialog "Display string",Top,Left,"Font Name"';
            paramPtr^.returnValue := PasToZero(errStr); {load the result}
            EXIT(Dialog); {leave the XCMD}
         END;
   END; {CheckParamCount}
```

CheckParamCount takes the value from the paramCount field and stores it in a variable called numParams. NumParams is then compared to two constants—minParamCount and maxParamCount—to see whether or not it falls within the legal range.

If the comparison succeeds, execution will proceed to the line of the main procedure that follows the CheckParamCount procedure call. If the comparison does not succeed, errStr is loaded with the correct form, and the returnValue field is used to pass that form back to HyperTalk's result function. The XCMD is then aborted, and control is returned to HyperTalk.

SetDefaults Procedure

The SetDefaults procedure sets the default values your XCMD can fall back on if the user chooses to omit any parameters. The four defaults and their values are as follows:

- The font number is set to zero (the system font —font name— is converted to a number later).
- The top coordinate of the dialog window is set to zero for centering.
- The left coordinate of the dialog window is set to zero for centering.
- The dialog resource ID is set to 107 to use the built-in DLOG resource.

The SetDefaults procedure takes no parameters and resembles the following:

```
PROCEDURE SetDefaults; {set default values for friendly params}
   BEGIN
      myFontNum := 0; {default to the system font}
      dialogID := 107; {use an existing dialog resource}
      userLeft := 0; {center dialog within card window}
      userTop := 0; {center dialog within card window}
   END; {SetDefaults}
```

GetLocOfCardWindow Procedure

The GetLocOfCardWindow procedure uses the EvalExpr glue routine and the call back interface to retrieve the current top-left coordinates of the card window. These values are stored in the variables named windTop and windLeft, respectively.

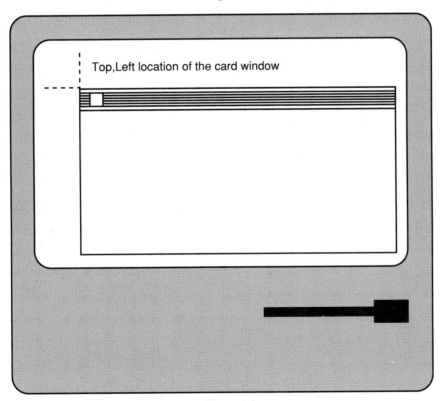

Figure 4.4

The top-left global coordinate of the card window as it appears on the screen.

The GetLocOfCardWindow procedure takes no parameters and looks like the following:

```
PROCEDURE GetLocOfCardWindow; {gets the left and top edges of the card window}
    BEGIN {use call backs to get current window loc}
        tempHandle := EvalExpr('Item 1 of rect of card window'); {left edge}
        IF (paramPtr^.result <> noErr) THEN Fail('Unable to find the card window');
        ZeroToPas(tempHandle^,tempStr); {convert to a string and then an integer}
        windLeft := StrToNum(tempStr); {now have left edge of card window}
        disposHandle(tempHandle); {don't need this any longer}
        tempHandle := EvalExpr('Item 2 of rect of card window'); {top edge}
        IF (paramPtr^.result <> noErr) THEN Fail('Unable to find the card window');
        ZeroToPas(tempHandle^,tempStr); {convert to a string and then an integer}
        windTop := StrToNum(tempStr); {now have top edge of card window}
        disposHandle(tempHandle); {don't need this any longer}
    END; {GetLocOfCardWindow}
```

HyperCard always knows the location of its card window, so you can use the EvalExpr glue routine to determine the location of the card window. To perform this task, you must make two separate calls back to HyperTalk: one that retrieves item 1 of the rect of the card window (the left coordinate) and one that retrievs item 2 (the top coordinate). Each item is returned as a zero-terminated string that you must convert to an integer number. You can then store the integers in the windLeft and windTop variables for later use.

While it is unlikely that HyperCard will ever fail to evaluate the expressions passed to it by the EvalExpr glue routine, it is possible; thus, you should check for errors after each use of the EvalExpr routine. Because this type of error is likely to be fatal, you should call the Fail procedure shown in the next section to let the user know that you are having trouble getting the location of the card window.

Note: Make sure you dispose of the handles needed by the EvalExpr glue routine when you are finished with them.

Fail Procedure

The Fail procedure loads *the result* function of HyperTalk with the string passed and aborts execution of the XCMD. Because Fail can be called at any time during execution of the XCMD, it can leave things dangling or in a modified state. As a result, your Fail routine must dispose of any dangling handles and restore any values saved or changed along the way. (For example, if you have used SetDAFont to change the font for your dialog, you must restore the system font with a value of zero, or all future HyperCard dialogs will be displayed in the new font.)

The Fail procedure takes a single parameter of type Str255 that represents the string to be returned in HyperTalk's result function. The Fail procedure resembles the following:

```
PROCEDURE Fail(errMsg: Str255); {Abort execution of the XCMD}
   BEGIN
      SetDaFont(0); {reset to system font or all future dialogs will retain the new font}
      SetPort(savePort); {restore the port}
      SetPenState(savePen); {restore the penstate}
      paramPtr^.returnValue := PasToZero(errMsg); {load the result}
      EXIT(Dialog); {leave the XCMD}
   END;
```

> **Note:** Because the port and pen state are saved early in the main program, you must restore them within the Fail procedure before exiting back to HyperCard.

Taking a Peek

While you have not yet written any code for the main procedure, the subprocedures include many constants and variables that must be declared at the beginning of your main procedure. At this point, the Dialog XCMD looks like the following:

```
PROCEDURE Dialog(paramPtr: XCmdPtr);

    CONST   minParamCount = 1;
            maxParamCount = 4;

    VAR     errStr:         Str255;
            tempStr:        Str255;
            dialogID:       Integer;
            myFontNum:      Integer;
            windLeft:       Integer;
            windTop:        Integer;
            numParams:      Integer;
            tempHandle:     Handle;
            savePort:       GrafPtr;
            savePen:        PenState;

{$I XCmdGlue.inc } {includes the glue routines}

    PROCEDURE Fail(errMsg: Str255); {Abort execution of the XCMD}
        BEGIN
            SetDaFont(0); {reset to system font or all future dialogs will retain new font}
            SetPort(savePort); {restore the port}
            SetPenState(savePen); {restore the penstate}
            paramPtr^.returnValue := PasToZero(errMsg); {load the result}
            EXIT(Dialog); {leave the XCMD}
        END;
```

continued...

...from previous page

```
PROCEDURE CheckParamCount; {checks for the correct parameter count}
    BEGIN
        numParams := paramPtr^.paramCount; {store number of params passed}
        IF (numParams < minParamCount) OR (numParams > maxParamCount) THEN
            BEGIN {Exit loading the result with the correct form}
                errStr := 'Form: Dialog "Display string",Left,Top,"Font Name"';
                paramPtr^.returnValue := PasToZero(errStr); {load the result}
                EXIT(Dialog); {leave the XCMD}
            END;
    END; {CheckParamCount}

PROCEDURE SetDefaults; {set default values for friendly params}
    BEGIN
        myFontNum := 0; {default to the system font}
        dialogID := 107; {use an existing dialog resource}
        userLeft := 0; {center dialog within card window}
        userTop := 0; {center dialog within card window}
    END; {SetDefaults}

PROCEDURE GetLocOfCardWindow; {gets the left and top edges of the card window}
    BEGIN {use call backs to get current window loc}
        tempHandle := EvalExpr('Item 1 of rect of card window'); {left edge}
        IF (paramPtr^.result <> noErr) THEN Fail('Unable to find the card window');
        ZeroToPas(tempHandle^,tempStr); {convert to a string and then an integer}
        windLeft := StrToNum(tempStr); {now have left edge of card window}
        disposHandle(tempHandle); {don't need this any longer}
        tempHandle := EvalExpr('Item 2 of rect of card window'); {top edge}
        IF (paramPtr^.result <> noErr) THEN Fail('Unable to find the card window');
        ZeroToPas(tempHandle^,tempStr); {convert to a string and then an integer}
        windTop := StrToNum(tempStr); {now have top edge of card window}
        disposHandle(tempHandle); {don't need this any longer}
    END; {GetLocOfCardWindow}

BEGIN {main}

    {Your main procedure goes here}

END; {main}

END. {Dialog}
```

CODING YOUR XCMD'S MAIN PROCEDURE

The first task the main procedure should accomplish is checking the parameter count. By immediately checking the parameter count, you can exit with a minimum of effort if there is a problem. Because you have already built a procedure to check the parameter count, all you must do is call it. The code looks like the following:

```
BEGIN {Main}
   CheckParamCount; {check for min and max paramcount}
END; {Main}
```

You will be changing the port to that of the dialog window and drawing a 3-pixel line around the OK button in that window, so you will want to save both the current state of the port and the current state of the pen (to restore them later). You can perform this task by using the ROM routines GetPort and GetPenState. GetPort stores the current port in a variable of type GrafPtr that you supply. GetPenState saves the current pen information in a variable of type PenState. You can choose any name for these variables as long as you declare them ahead of time. Try to choose variable names that reflect the contents or the action of the variable. For example, the variables used to save the port and pen information in the Dialog XCMD are called savePort and savePen.

Next, you will want to call the ROM routine InitCursor to ensure that the pointer resembles an arrow before the dialog window is displayed. (This stops people from clicking the OK button in the dialog window with an I-beam or hand pointer, which would be a violation of the user interface guidelines and might be confusing.)

To complete the setup sequence, you must retrieve the current location of the card window and establish the default values for the font and location. You can accomplish both these tasks by using the procedures you created earlier: use the SetDefaults procedure to initialize the default values, and use the GetLocOfCardWindow procedure to put the left and top window coordinates into the variables windLeft and windTop.

At this point, the main procedure looks like the following:

```
BEGIN {main}
    CheckParamCount; {check for min and max paramcount}
    GetPort(savePort); {save the current port}
    GetPenState(savePen); {save the current pen stuff}
    InitCursor; {set the arrow cursor so no I-beam or hand when we go modal}
    SetDefaults; {set default values for friendly params}
    GetLocOfCardWindow; {get the card windows current position}
END {main}
```

Dealing with the Parameters

Once you have completed the setup, you should think about the parameters. You will want to treat the contents of the parameters differently, depending on the number of parameters that get passed.

Dialog XCMD's Parameters

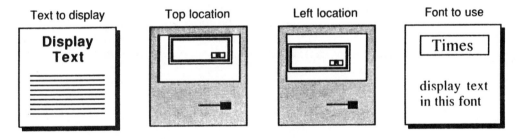

Text to display   Top location   Left location   Font to use

Figure 4.5

The parameters for the Dialog XCMD.

Because of the assumptions made earlier in this chapter, you know that the first parameter will always contain the information to be displayed (see Figure 4.5). Thus, the next step is to convert the first parameter into a Pascal string that can later be passed to the ParamText ROM routine. You will use the ParamText ROM routine because the DLOG 107 resource only accepts the special strings ^0 through ^3. (The ParamText ROM routine is used to change those special strings.)

Use the following syntax to convert the first parameter to a Pascal string and to store it in the string variable displayStr:

```
ZeroToPas(paramPtr^.params[1]^,displayStr); {the string to display}
```

There are three possible combinations for the remaining parameters, as follows:

- Dialog container,font (two total parameters)
- Dialog container,left,top (three total parameters)
- Dialog container,left,top,font name (four total parameters)

You can use a CASE statement to handle each possible combination:

```
CASE numParams OF {make assumptions based on the param count}

    2: {string,font} {set font and use default values for left and top}
       BEGIN {GetFNum returns system font if it can't find requested font}
           ZeroToPas(paramPtr^.params[2]^,tempStr); {convert to a font number}
           GetFNum(tempStr,myFontNum);
       END; {case 2}

    3: {string,top,left} {set top, left and use default value for font}
       BEGIN {use default value for font}
           ZeroToPas (paramPtr^.params[2]^,tempStr); {param2 is top coord}
           userTop := StrToNum(tempStr); {now have desired top coord}
           ZeroToPas (paramPtr^.params[3]^,tempStr); {param3 is left coord}
           userLeft := StrToNum(tempStr); {now have desired left coord}
       END; {case 3}

    4: {string,top,left,font} {set left, top and font}
       BEGIN
           ZeroToPas (paramPtr^.params[2]^,tempStr); {param2 is top coord}
           userTop := StrToNum(tempStr); {now have desired top coord}
           ZeroToPas (paramPtr^.params[3]^,tempStr); {param3 is left coord}
           userLeft := StrToNum(tempStr); {now have desired left coord}
           ZeroToPas(paramPtr^.params[4]^,tempStr); {param4 is font number}
           GetFNum(tempStr,myFontNum); {convert param4 to a font number}
       END; {case 4}

END; {case} {done parsing the parameters}
```

Following is an explanation of each case combination.

The Case of Two Parameters

If your XCMD is passed only two parameters, you should assume that the first parameter contains the information to be displayed and the second parameter contains the font name. Because the SetDAFont ROM routine requires the number of the font rather than the name, you must convert the font name to a number.

The GetFNum ROM routine does the conversion for you. You needn't perform any error checking on the font name because GetFNum returns a zero (number of the system font) if it cannot find a font with the name you pass to it.

You have already converted the first parameter to a Pascal string, so all you must do is convert the second parameter to a Pascal string and pass it to the GetFNum routine shown previously in case 2. GetFNum will return the number of the font in the variable myFontNum.

The Case of Three Parameters

In the design discussion, you learned that if the user supplies three parameters, they are as follows: container, top, and left. You have already converted the first parameter to a Pascal string, so all you must do is convert the second and third parameters as shown in case 3 of the previous case statement. You can store the resulting integer values in the userTop and userLeft variables for later use.

The Case of Four Parameters

When your XCMD is passed all four parameters, you must convert and store the top coordinate, the left coordinate, and the font name. Case 4 of the previous case statement shows you how to do this. (Case 4 is nothing more than a combination of cases 2 and 3.)

With all of the parameters converted to values that can be used by the rest of your program, you can proceed to build and show the dialog window itself.

Putting the Pieces Together

Up to this point, you have been saving bits and pieces of items for later use. You will now combine them as you build, show, and manipulate the dialog window. Before continuing, review the sizeable portion of the XCMD you have already completed:

```
PROCEDURE    Dialog(paramPtr: XCmdPtr);

      CONST  minParamCount = 1;
             maxParamCount = 4;

      VAR    errStr:         Str255;
             tempStr:        Str255;
             dialogID:       Integer;
             myFontNum:      Integer;
             windLeft:       Integer;
             windTop:        Integer;
             userLeft:       Integer;
             userTop:        Integer;
             numParams:      Integer;
             tempHandle:     Handle;
             savePort:       GrafPtr;
             savePen:        PenState;

{$I XCmdGlue.inc } {includes the glue routines}

   PROCEDURE Fail(errMsg: Str255); {Abort execution of the XCMD}
      BEGIN
         SetDaFont(0); {reset to system font or future dialogs will retain new font}
         SetPort(savePort); {restore the port}
         SetPenState(savePen); {restore the penstate}
         paramPtr^.returnValue := PasToZero(errMsg); {load the result}
         EXIT(Dialog); {leave the XCMD}
      END;
```

continued...

...from previous page

```
PROCEDURE CheckParamCount; {checks for the correct parameter count}
   BEGIN
      numParams := paramPtr^.paramCount; {store number of params passed}
      IF (numParams < minParamCount) OR (numParams > maxParamCount) THEN
         BEGIN {Exit loading the result with the correct form}
            errStr := 'Form: Dialog "Display string",Left,Top,"Font Name"';
            paramPtr^.returnValue := PasToZero(errStr); {load the result}
            EXIT(Dialog); {leave the XCMD}
         END;
   END; {CheckParamCount}


PROCEDURE SetDefaults; {set default values for friendly params}
   BEGIN
      myFontNum := 0; {default to the system font}
      dialogID := 107; {use an existing dialog resource}
      userLeft := 0; {center dialog within card window}
      userTop := 0; {center dialog within card window}
   END; {SetDefaults}


PROCEDURE GetLocOfCardWindow; {gets the left and top edges of the card window}
   BEGIN {use call backs to get current window loc}
      tempHandle := EvalExpr('Item 1 of rect of card window'); {left edge}
      IF (paramPtr^.result <> noErr) THEN Fail('Unable to find the card window');
      ZeroToPas(tempHandle^,tempStr); {convert to a string and then an integer}
      windLeft := StrToNum(tempStr); {now have left edge of card window}
      disposHandle(tempHandle); {don't need this any longer}
      tempHandle := EvalExpr('Item 2 of rect of card window'); {top edge}
      IF (paramPtr^.result <> noErr) THEN Fail('Unable to find the card window');
      ZeroToPas(tempHandle^,tempStr); {convert to a string and then an integer}
      windTop := StrToNum(tempStr); {now have top edge of card window}
      disposHandle(tempHandle); {don't need this any longer}
   END; {GetLocOfCardWindow}

BEGIN {Main}
   CheckParamCount; {check for min and max paramcount}
   GetPort(savePort); {save the current port}
   GetPenState(savePen); {save the current pen stuff}
   InitCursor; {set the arrow cursor so no I-beam or hand when we go modal}
   SetDefaults; {set default values for friendly params}
   GetLocOfCardWindow; {get the card windows current position}
```

continued...

...from previous page

```
ZeroToPas(paramPtr^.params[1]^,displayStr); {first param = string to display}

CASE numParams OF {make assumptions based on the param count}

    2: {string,font} {set font and use default values for left and top}
       BEGIN {GetFNum returns system font if it can't find requested font}
           ZeroToPas(paramPtr^.params[2]^,tempStr); {convert param2 to a number}
           GetFNum(tempStr,myFontNum);
       END; {case 2}

    3: {string,top,left} {set left and top and use default value for font}
       BEGIN {use default value for font}
           ZeroToPas (paramPtr^.params[2]^,tempStr); {param2 is top coord}
           userTop := StrToNum(tempStr); {now have desired top coord}
           ZeroToPas (paramPtr^.params[3]^,tempStr); {param3 is left coord}
           userLeft := StrToNum(tempStr); {now have desired left coord}
       END; {case 3}

    4: {string,top,left,font} {set left, top and font}
       BEGIN
           ZeroToPas (paramPtr^.params[2]^,tempStr); {param2 is top coord}
           userTop := StrToNum(tempStr); {now have desired top coord}
           ZeroToPas (paramPtr^.params[3]^,tempStr); {param3 is left coord}
           userLeft := StrToNum(tempStr); {now have desired left coord}
           ZeroToPas(paramPtr^.params[4]^,tempStr); {param4 is font number}
           GetFNum(tempStr,myFontNum); {convert param4 to a font number}
       END; {case 4}

END; {case} {done parsing the parameters - let's work on the dialog}

END; {main}

END. {Dialog}
```

The next step is to make the dialog manager aware of the text you want to display. You can use the ParamText ROM routine to perform this task:

```
ParamText(displayStr,'',''); {DLOG 107 already set up for this call}
```

> **Note:** You must pass an empty string for each parameter of the ParamText ROM routine you don't use.

The ParamText ROM call will copy the contents of the variable displayStr into special string ^0 in preparation for making the dialog visible. At the same time, you will want to specify the font in which the text is to be displayed with the SetDAFont ROM routine:

```
SetDAFont(myFontNum); {sets the font to display the text with}
```

After you perform these tasks, move to the resource fork and retrieve a pointer to the dialog record for DLOG resource 107 with the GetNewDialog ROM routine.

GetNewDialog takes three parameters. The first parameter is the ID number of the dialog resource (number 107 in this case). The second parameter determines where the dialog record will be allocated space. (If you pass a NIL for this parameter, you are instructing the memory manager to allocate space for the dialog record *any place* it can on the heap.) The third parameter specifies the window behind which your dialog window will be placed. If you want your dialog window to be the front-most window, you must pass a value of -1. (Because this parameter takes a windowPtr, you can pass the -1 as follows: POINTER(-1).)

The GetNewDialog ROM call with the appropriate additional information looks like the following:

```
myDialogPtr := GetNewDialog(dialogID,NIL,POINTER(-1)); {get ptr to dialog 107}
```

This is a good time to make changes to the dialog window's position. The dialog window is still invisible, so moving it won't disorient the user.

Adjusting the Position of the Dialog Window

Use a conditional to center the dialog window within the boundaries of the card window; If the user hasn't passed you a location, center the dialog window; otherwise, show it at the specifed location as follows:

```
IF ((userLeft = 0) AND (userTop=0)) {then center it}
    THEN MoveWindow(myDialogPtr,offsetLeft+windLeft,offsetTop+windTop,TRUE)
    ELSE MoveWindow(myDialogPtr,userLeft+windLeft,userTop+windTop,TRUE);
```

Because you set the default values for userTop and userLeft to 0, you know that unless the user has changed them, they will still be 0; therefore, if the equality test reveals that no values have been supplied, you can add the constants offsetLeft and offsetTop to the variables windLeft and windTop to center the dialog window (see Figure 4.6).

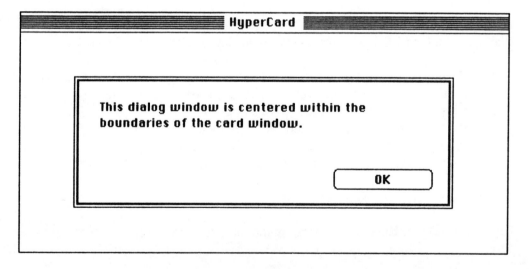

Figure 4.6

The dialog window centered within the boundaries of the card window.

You should use two constants (offsetLeft and offsetTop) when centering the dialog. You can determine the value for the offsetLeft constant by calculating the difference between the width of the dialog window and the overall card width and dividing the value by 2 (512 - 376/2). Use the same approach for the offsetTop coordinate, but subtract the height of the dialog window from the card height (342 - 116/2).

If coordinate values have been passed into your XCMD, you should add them to the left and top edges of the card window. Negative or large positive values can be used to show the dialog outside the card window or anywhere in the GrafPort.

Finally, the MoveWindow ROM routine is what actually does the moving. MoveWindow takes the following parameters: a pointer to the window to move, the left window coordinate to move to, the top window coordinate to move to, and a Boolean flag that, when set to TRUE, makes the window become the active window.

Making the Dialog Window Visible

The only tasks that remain are making the dialog visible, making the dialog modal, and drawing the line around the OK button.

You show the dialog window the same way you would show any other window: with the ShowWindow ROM routine. The ShowWindow ROM routine takes only one argument—a pointer to the window to be shown:

```
ShowWindow(myDialogPtr); {Make the dialog visible}
```

Drawing the Outline Around the OK Button

You must make the dialog window the current drawing port before you draw the default outline around the OK button. If you don't, you won't be able to draw within the window. Use the SetPort ROM routine to make the dialog window the current port:

```
SetPort(myDialogPtr); {make the dialog window the current port for drawing}
```

Next, you will want to set the drawing pen size to 3,3 to draw a 3-pixel-wide line. Use the PenSize ROM routine to change the pen height and width (you will use the FrameRoundRect call to do the actual drawing):

```
PenSize(3,3); {set the pensize for a 3 pixel line width}
```

Once you have set the port and pen size, you must get the rect of the OK button; this task can be performed with the GetDItem ROM routine. GetDItem returns the rect of the specified control plus the item type and a handle to the item. You will not need these extra bits of information, but you must declare variables for them.

The only items you must supply to the GetDItem routine are a pointer to the dialog record in parameter 1 and the item number of the item for which you are trying to get some information in parameter 2. (The item number of the OK button is 1 because it is the first control in the control list.)

There is a global constant called OK, which contains a value of 1. By using the constant instead of the number 1, you will make the GetDItem ROM call a little clearer:

```
GetDItem(myDialogPtr,OK,itemType,tempHandle,ctlRect); {get rect of OK button}
```

Next, you must widen the rectangle by four pixels (to conform to the user interface guidelines) and draw the rounded rectangle around the OK button. You can use the QuickDraw ROM routine InsetRect to widen the rectangle. (In this example, a constant is used in place of gap values to allow flexibility in changing the values and to make the InsetRect call more readable.)

```
InsetRect(ctlRect,gap,gap); {expand the rectangle by 4 pixels}
```

You must supply the FrameRoundRect ROM routine with the rectangle to use when drawing as well as the amount of curve the corners of the rectangle should have. A value of 16 is perfect for most round-rect button controls:

```
FrameRoundRect(ctlRect,edgeCurve,edgeCurve); {draw the expanded rectangle}
```

Taking a Peek

The following is what you have added so far:

```
ParamText(displayStr,"","",""); {dialog 107 already set up for this call}
SetDaFont(myFontNum);
myDialogPtr := GetNewDialog(dialogID,NIL,POINTER(-1)); {get ptr to dialog 107}
IF ((userLeft = 0) AND (userTop=0)) {then center it}
    THEN  MoveWindow(myDialogPtr,offsetLeft+windLeft,offsetTop+windTop,TRUE)
    ELSE  MoveWindow(myDialogPtr,userLeft+windLeft,userTop+windTop,TRUE);

ShowWindow(myDialogPtr); {Make the dialog visible}

SetPort(myDialogPtr); {make the dialog window the current port for drawing}

PenSize(3,3); {set the pensize for a 3 pixel line width}

GetDItem(myDialogPtr,OK,itemType,tempHandle,ctlRect); {get rect of OK button}
InsetRect(ctlRect,gap,gap); {expand the rectangle by 4 pixels}
FrameRoundRect(ctlRect,edgeCurve,edgeCurve); {draw the expanded rectangle}
```

Going Modal

The dialog window is now visible and in the correct position with a 3-pixel line drawn around the OK button. Before you make the call to ModalDialog, however, you should call the FlushEvents ROM routine to empty the event queue of pending events, which will guarantee that the dialog will not disappear as soon as it is shown. The only remaining task is to make the dialog modal. Following are the two calls that complete the manipulation of the dialog window:

```
FlushEvents(everyEvent,0); {flush all events to be safe}

REPEAT
   ModalDialog(NIL,itemHit); {stay modal until the user clicks OK}
UNTIL itemHit = OK;
```

> **Note:** You should put the modal dialog routine into a repeat loop that waits for a mouse
> click on the OK button (itemHit equal to 1). You can leave the repeat structure out, but
> if you do, a mouse click anywhere inside the dialog window will cause the window to
> disappear.

Cleaning Up

When the OK button is clicked, it is time to clean up and return to HyperTalk. You must
dispose of the dialog, set the font back to the system font, and restore the port and pen.
The last four lines of the main procedure perform these functions:

```
DisposDialog(myDialogPtr); {Get rid of the dialog and dialog handle}
SetDaFont(0); {reset to system font or all future dialogs will retain the new font}
SetPort(savePort); {restore the port}
SetPenState(savePen); {restore the penstate}
```

The only items still missing are the comment blocks, which will help you decipher your
code six months from now. These blocks are added to the finished XCMD shown in the
next section.

LOOKING AT THE FINISHED XCMD

The finished XCMD appears in the following section. You can type the code directly into your MPW Pascal compiler, change the pathname, and compile it. (The C version immediately follows the Pascal version.)

For the Pascal Programmer

Following is the Dialog XCMD, complete with comments:

```
{$R-}
( *
    Dialog: a HyperCard XCMD that displays a modal dialog. The caller can provide the
    text, font and display location. Dialog uses dialog box number 107 from HyperCard's
    resource fork, automatically centering the dialog window within the card window. Up
    to 255 character can be displayed.

    Form: Dialog "String to display",Top,Left,Font Name

    Example: Dialog "Display this text",100,80,geneva

    Note: Top and Left are integers that specify the top-left point at which to display the
    dialog. If these values aren't supplied, the dialog automatically centers itself within
    the boundaries of the card window. The font to display the text in is passed by name;
    its size cannot be changed.

    ───────────────────────────────────────────────────────────────────

    To compile and link this file using MPW Pascal, select the following lines and press
    the ENTER key

    ───────────────────────────────────────────────────────────────────

    pascal Dialog.p
    link -o "M2HD:Home" -rt  XCMD=1502-sn Main=Dialog Dialog.p.o ∂
    {MPW}Libraries:Interface.o -m ENTRYPOINT
```

continued...

...from previous page

*)

{$S Dialog }   { Segment name must be the same as the command name. }

UNIT DummyUnit;

INTERFACE

USES MemTypes, QuickDraw, OSIntf, ToolIntf, HyperXCmd;

PROCEDURE ENTRYPOINT(paramPtr: XCmdPtr);

IMPLEMENTATION

TYPE Str31 = String[31];

PROCEDURE Dialog(paramPtr: XCmdPtr);   FORWARD;

PROCEDURE ENTRYPOINT(paramPtr: XCmdPtr);

```
  BEGIN
    Dialog(paramPtr);
  END;
```

PROCEDURE Dialog(paramPtr: XCmdPtr);

```
  CONST  minParamCount = 1; {minimum number of parameters allowed}
         maxParamCount = 4; {maximum number of parameters allowed}
         edgeCurve = 16; {curve of the corner of the round rect rectangle}
         gap = -4; {distance to enlarge the rectangle}
         offsetLeft = 68; {left offset for centering within the card window}
         offsetTop =113; {top offset for centering within the card window}

  VAR    tempStr:      Str255;
         errStr:       Str255;
         displayStr:   Str255;
         itemHit:      Integer;
         dialogID:     Integer;
```

continued...

...from previous page

userLeft:	Integer;
userTop:	Integer;
myFontNum:	Integer;
windLeft:	Integer;
windTop:	Integer;
numParams:	Integer;
itemType:	Integer;
myDialogPtr:	DialogPtr;
tempHandle:	Handle;
ctlRect:	Rect;
savePort:	GrafPtr;
savePen:	PenState;

```
{$I XCmdGlue.inc } {includes the glue routines}

   PROCEDURE Fail(errMsg: Str255); {Abort execution of the XCMD}
      BEGIN
         SetDaFont(0); {reset to system font or future dialogs will retain new font}
         SetPort(savePort); {restore the port}
         SetPenState(savePen); {restore the penstate}
         paramPtr^.returnValue := PasToZero(errMsg); {load the result}
         EXIT(Dialog); {leave the XCMD}
      END;

   PROCEDURE CheckParamCount; {checks for the correct parameter count}
      BEGIN
         numParams := paramPtr^.paramCount; {store number of params passed}
         IF (numParams < minParamCount) OR (numParams > maxParamCount) THEN
            BEGIN {Exit loading the result with the correct form}
               errStr := 'Form: Dialog "Display string",Left,Top,"Font Name"';
               paramPtr^.returnValue := PasToZero(errStr); {load the result}
               EXIT(Dialog); {leave the XCMD}
            END;
      END; {CheckParamCount}

   PROCEDURE SetDefaults; {set default values for friendly params}
      BEGIN
         myFontNum := 0; {default to the system font}
         dialogID := 107; {use an existing dialog resource}
         userLeft := 0; {center dialog within card window}
         userTop := 0; {center dialog within card window}
      END; {SetDefaults}
```

continued...

...from previous page

```
PROCEDURE GetLocOfCardWindow; {gets the left and top edges of the card window}
    BEGIN {use call backs to get current window loc}
        tempHandle := EvalExpr('Item 1 of rect of card window'); {left edge}
        IF (paramPtr^.result <> noErr) THEN Fail('Cannot get rect of card window');
        ZeroToPas(tempHandle^,tempStr); {convert to a string and then an integer}
        windLeft := StrToNum(tempStr); {now have left edge of card window}
        disposHandle(tempHandle); {don't need this any longer}
        tempHandle := EvalExpr('Item 2 of rect of card window'); {top edge}
        IF (paramPtr^.result <> noErr) THEN Fail('Cannot get rect of card window');
        ZeroToPas(tempHandle^,tempStr); {convert to a string and then an integer}
        windTop := StrToNum(tempStr); {now have top edge of card window}
            disposHandle(tempHandle); {don't need this any longer}
        END; {GetLocOfCardWindow}

BEGIN {Main}
    ( *
    _____

    Do the set up stuff.
    _____

    * )

    CheckParamCount; {check for minimum and maximum parameter count}
    GetPort(savePort); {save the current port}
    GetPenState(savePen); {save the current pen stuff}
    InitCursor; {set the arrow cursor so no I-beam or hand when we go modal}
    SetDefaults; {set default values for friendly params}
    GetLocOfCardWindow; {get the card windows current position}

    ( *
    _____

    Convert the first parameter. CheckParamCount ensures at least 1 parameter
    so make the first parameter the display string.
    _____

    * )

    ZeroToPas(paramPtr^.params[1]^,displayStr); {first params the string to display}
```

continued...

...from previous page

(*

Parse the rest of the parameters. Fall back on the default values when params aren't supplied.

---

*)

CASE numParams OF {make assumptions based on the param count}

```
    2: {string,font} {set font and use default values for left and top}
       BEGIN {GetFNum returns system font if it can't find requested font}
          ZeroToPas(paramPtr^.params[2]^,tempStr); {convert param2 to a number}
          GetFNum(tempStr,myFontNum);
       END; {case 2}

    3: {string,top,left} {set left and top and use default value for font}
       BEGIN {use default value for font}
          ZeroToPas (paramPtr^.params[2]^,tempStr); {param2 is top coord}
          userTop := StrToNum(tempStr); {now have desired top coord}
          ZeroToPas (paramPtr^.params[3]^,tempStr); {param3 is left coord}
          userLeft := StrToNum(tempStr); {now have desired left coord}
       END; {case 3}

    4: {string,top,left,font} {set left, top and font}
       BEGIN
          ZeroToPas (paramPtr^.params[2]^,tempStr); {param2 is top coord}
          userTop := StrToNum(tempStr); {now have desired top coord}
          ZeroToPas (paramPtr^.params[3]^,tempStr); {param3 is left coord}
          userLeft := StrToNum(tempStr); {now have desired left coord}
          ZeroToPas(paramPtr^.params[4]^,tempStr); {param4 is font number}
          GetFNum(tempStr,myFontNum); {convert param4 to a font number}
       END; {case 4}

END; {case} {done parsing the parameters}
```

continued...

...from previous page

(*
_____

Use the paramText to make the dialog manager display the text.
_____

*)

ParamText(displayStr,",",""); {dialog 107 already set up for this call}

(*
_____

Use the SetDaFont call to set the font for the dialog box.
_____

*)

SetDaFont(myFontNum);

(*
_____

Look in the resource fork for dialog 107 and return a handle if found and
make it the upper most window. The dialog is still invisible at this point.
_____

*)

myDialogPtr := GetNewDialog(dialogID,NIL,POINTER(-1)); {get ptr to dialog 107}

(*
_____

Move the dialog window to its correct screen position before showing it. If the
user hasn't supplied a location, center the dialog within the card window.
Otherwise use the supplied location. Then make the dialog window the active
window and make it visible.
_____

*)

IF ((userLeft = 0) AND (userTop=0)) {then center it}
    THEN MoveWindow(myDialogPtr,offsetLeft+windLeft,offsetTop+windTop,TRUE)
    ELSE MoveWindow(myDialogPtr,userLeft+windLeft,userTop+windTop,TRUE);

ShowWindow(myDialogPtr); {Make the dialog visible}

continued...

...from previous page

(*

Make the dialog window the current port and make the OK button the
default by drawing a 3 pixel line around it. Use the constant 'OK' for the item
number when getting the rect.

---

*)

SetPort(myDialogPtr); {make the dialog window the current port for drawing}

PenSize(3,3); {set the pensize for a 3 pixel line width}

GetDItem(myDialogPtr,OK,itemType,tempHandle,ctlRect); {get rect of OK button}
InsetRect(ctlRect,gap,gap); {expand the rectangle by 4 pixels}
FrameRoundRect(ctlRect,edgeCurve,edgeCurve); {draw the expanded rectangle}

(*

Before we make the dialog modal, flush events so pending key and mouse
events won't put the dialog away too early. Once modal, hit test for a click
of the OK button.

---

*)

FlushEvents(everyEvent,0); {flush all events to be safe}

REPEAT
    ModalDialog(NIL,itemHit); {display dialog until the user clicks OK}
UNTIL itemHit = OK;

(*

When the user clicks the OK button, it's time to clean up and restore the state.

---

*)

continued...

...from previous page

```
    DisposDialog(myDialogPtr); {Get rid of the dialog and dialog handle}
    SetDaFont(0); {reset to system font or all future dialogs will retain the new font}
    SetPort(savePort); {restore  the  port}
    SetPenState(savePen); {restore  the  penstate}

END; {Main}

END. {Dialog}
```

For the C Programmer

Here's the complete Dialog XCMD shown in C:

```
/*
  © 1988 by Gary Bond
  All Rights Reserved

  Translation to C by Sioux Lacy

  Dialog:    a Hypercard XCMD that displays a modal dialog.
             The caller can provide the text, font and display location.
             Dialog uses dialog box number 107 from HyperCard's resource
             fork, automatically centering the dialog window within the
             card window.  Up to 255 characters can be displayed.

  Form:      Dialog "String to display", Top, Left, Font, Name

  Example:   Dialog "Display this text", 100, 80, Geneva

  Note:      Top and Left are integers that specify the upper left point
             at which to display the dialog.  If you don't supply values
             for these, the dialog automatically centers itself within the
             card window.  The font to display the text in is passed by
             name; its size cannot be changed.
  _____

  Compile and link this file with the MacTraps and string libraries
*/
```

continued...

...from previous page

```
/*
   Includes
   Note that these header files are for LightspeedC development.
   Substitute the files that are appropriate for your compiler.
*/
#include <MacTypes.h>
#include <DialogMgr.h>
#include <EventMgr.h>
#include <QuickDraw.h>
#include "HyperXCmd.h"

/*
   LightspeedC Prototypes
*/
pascal   void main(XCmdBlockPtr);
int      GetLocOfCardWindow(XCmdBlockPtr, Point *);
short    GetParamCount(XCmdBlockPtr, char *);
Handle   CopyStrToHand(char *);
long     HandleToNum(XCmdBlockPtr, Handle);
void     HandleToPstr(Str255, Handle);
char     *ToCstr(char *);
char     *ToPstr(char *);


/*
   Defined Constants
*/
#define minParamCount    (short)   1
#define maxParamCount    (short)   4
#define errorFlag        (short)  -1
#define edgeCurve        (int)    16
#define gapBetween       (int)    -4
#define lineSize         (int)     3


pascal void   main(paramPtr)
   XCmdBlockPtr paramPtr;
{
   short      numParams;
   Str255     displayStr;
   Str255     fontName;
   int        itemHit;
   int        dialogID;
   int        offsetLeft;
   int        offsetTop;
   int        myFontNum;
   int        itemType;
```

continued...

...from previous page

```
DialogPtr    myDialogPtr;
Handle       tempHandle;
Point        cardWindowLoc;
Rect         ctlRect;
GrafPtr      savePort;
PenState     savePen;


if ((numParams = GetParamCount(paramPtr, "Form: Dialog \"string\",top,left,font")
       == errorFlag)
    return;
GetPort(&savePort);
GetPenState(&savePen);
InitCursor();

/*
   Set default values for friendly params
*/
myFontNum =    (int) 0;
dialogID =     (int) 107;
offsetLeft =   (int) 68;
offsetTop =    (int) 113;

if ((GetLocOfCardWindow(paramPtr, &cardWindowLoc)) == errorFlag)
    return;

/*
   Get the 1st param: the display string
   CheckParamCount ensures at least 1 param.
*/
HandleToPstr(displayStr, paramPtr->params[0]);

switch (numParams)  /* Make assumptions based on paramCount */
    {
        case 2:        /* Params = string, font. Use default top, left */
            HandleToPstr(fontName, paramPtr->params[1]);
            GetFNum(fontName, &myFontNum);
            break;

        case 3:        /* Params = string, top, and left. Use default font. */
            offsetTop = (int) HandleToNum(paramPtr, paramPtr->params[1]);
            offsetLeft = (int) HandleToNum(paramPtr, paramPtr->params[2]);
            break;
```

continued...

...from previous page

```
     case 4:        /* Params = string, top, left, font */
        offsetTop = (int) HandleToNum(paramPtr, paramPtr->params[1]);
        offsetLeft = (int) HandleToNum(paramPtr, paramPtr->params[2]);
        HandleToPstr(fontName, paramPtr->params[3]);
        GetFNum(fontName, &myFontNum);
        break;
  }
/*
  Make the dialog manager display the string.
  Dialog 107 is already set up correctly for this call.
*/
ParamText(displayStr, "", "", "");

/*
  Use SetDaFont to establish a font for the dialog
*/
SetDAFont(myFontNum);

/*
  Look in the resource fork for dialog 107 and return a handle if found.
  Make it the uppermost window.  The dialog is still invisible at this point.
*/
myDialogPtr = GetNewDialog(dialogID, (Ptr) 0, (WindowPtr) -1);

/*
  Move the dialog to its correct screen position before showing it.
  If the user hasn't supplied a location, center the dialog within
  the card window.  Then make the dialog window the active window and
  make it visible.
*/
MoveWindow(myDialogPtr, offsetLeft + cardWindowLoc.h,
           offsetTop + cardWindowLoc.v, TRUE);
ShowWindow(myDialogPtr);

/*
  Make the dialog window the current port and make the OK button the
  default by drawing a 3-pixel line around it.  Use the constant "OK"
  for the item number when getting the rect.
*/
SetPort(myDialogPtr);
PenSize(lineSize, lineSize);
GetDItem(myDialogPtr, OK, &itemType, &tempHandle, &ctlRect);
InsetRect(&ctlRect, gapBetween, gapBetween);
FrameRoundRect(&ctlRect, edgeCurve, edgeCurve);
```

continued...

...from previous page

```
/*
    Before we make the dialog modal, flush events so pending key and mouse
    events won't put the dialog away too early.  Once modal, hit test for
    a click of the OK button.
*/
FlushEvents((int) everyEvent, (int) 0);
do
    {
        ModalDialog((Ptr) 0, &itemHit);
    }
while (itemHit != OK);

/*
    When the user clicks the OK button, it's time to clean up and restore
    the port and penstate.
*/
DisposDialog(myDialogPtr);
SetDAFont(0);                       /* reset to system font for future dialogs */
SetPort(savePort);
SetPenState(&savePen);

return;
}


int GetLocOfCardWindow(paramPtr, loc)
    XCmdBlockPtr    paramPtr;
    Point           *loc;
{
    Handle  hndl;
    char    str[256];

    strcpy(str, "item 1 of rect of card window");
    hndl = EvalExpr(paramPtr, (StringPtr) ToPstr(str));
    if (paramPtr->result == noErr)
        {
            loc->h = HandleToNum(paramPtr, hndl);
            DisposHandle(hndl);

            strcpy(str, "item 2 of rect of card window");
            hndl = EvalExpr(paramPtr, (StringPtr) ToPstr(str));
            if (paramPtr->result == noErr)
                {
```

continued...

...from previous page

```
                loc->v = HandleToNum(paramPtr, hndl);
                DisposHandle(hndl);
                return(noErr);
            }
        }
    paramPtr->returnValue = (Handle) CopyStrToHand("Can't get rect of card window");
    return((int) errorFlag);
}


short GetParamCount(paramPtr, str)
    XCmdBlockPtr   paramPtr;
    char           *str;
{
    short    count;

    count = paramPtr->paramCount;
    if ((count > maxParamCount) || (count < minParamCount))
        {
            paramPtr->returnValue = (Handle) CopyStrToHand(str);
            return(errorFlag);
        }
    return(count);
}


/*
    This utility function allocates heapspace and copies a string into it.
*/
Handle CopyStrToHand(str)
    char *str;
{
    Handle   newHndl;

    newHndl = (Handle) NewHandle((long) strlen(str) + 1);
    strcpy((char *)(*newHndl), str);
    return(newHndl);
}
```

continued...

...from previous page

```
/*
   This function makes a callback to HyperCard to convert a string to an
   unsigned long integer.  It takes a handle to a C string as an argument.
*/
long HandleToNum(paramPtr, hndl)
   XCmdBlockPtr  paramPtr;
   Handle        hndl;
{
   char  str[32];
   long  num;

   strcpy(str, *hndl);
   num = StrToLong(paramPtr, (Str31 *) ToPstr(str));
   return(num);
}


/*
   This utility function copies the string pointed to by a handle into
   a character array, then converts the C string to a Pascal string.
   Note that the C string is overwritten by the Pascal string.
*/
void HandleToPstr(str, hndl)
   Str255  str;
   Handle  hndl;
{
   strcpy((char *) str, *hndl);
   ToPstr((char *) str);
}


/*
   This utility function converts a Pascal string to a C string.
   Note that the Pascal string is overwritten in the process.
*/
char *ToCstr(str)
   char *str;
{
   unsigned char length, i;

   length = str[0];
   for (i = 0; i < length; ++i)         /* Shift string 1 byte to the left */
      str[i] = str[i+1];
   str[length] = 0;                     /* Put zero-terminator after string */
   return(str);
}
```

continued...

...from previous page

```
/*
   This utility function converts a C string to a Pascal string.
   Note that the C string is overwritten in the process.
*/
char *ToPstr(str)
   char *str;
{
   unsigned char length, i;

   for (i = 0, length = 0; str[i] != 0; ++i)     /* Find end of string */
      ++length;
   while (i--)                                    /* Shift string 1 byte to right */
      str[i+1] = str[i];
   str[0] = length;                               /* Put string length in 1st byte */
   return(str);
}
```

HINTS AND TIPS

- For clarity, use constants in place of numbers.

- Give your variables names that reflect their content or function, which will help you remember (or figure out) what's going on when you review your code a year from now.

- XCMD's and XFCN's differ from normal Macintosh programming code; they are not required to have a main event loop. XCMD's and XFCN's are an excellent environment in which to learn the various facets of Macintosh programming without worrying about the requirements of creating a normal application.

- XCMD's and XFCN's don't retain information from one call to another; however, there are tricks you can use to accomplish this task. See Chapter 5 for more details.

- If your Macintosh is low on memory, you might want to make the user-specified font non-purgeable so it won't be thrown away before you have a chance to use it.

- If you are designing an XCMD or XFCN that uses features specific to the Macintosh II, be sure to check the type of computer you are running on before your XCMD or XFCN continues.

- When programming XCMD's and XFCN's, you should write the code first and then optimize for speed and efficiency. You may find that your first pass at the code is adequate, which could save a lot of unnecessary coding time.

- When using File Manager calls, use the information in Volume 4 of *Inside Macintosh*. The File Manager information in Volume 3 is no longer valid.

SUMMARY

In this chapter, you began to use what you learned in Chapters 1 through 3. You found that with even a simple XCMD such as Dialog, there are many design issues that must be addressed before the coding process can begin. You also examined the twists and turns of designing and coding.

While you may not agree with some of the conclusions or paths chosen during the design phase, you should strive to maintain a balance between features, ease of use, and elegance when creating any XCMD or XFCN. The code of an XCMD or XFCN is much like the code for any other Macintosh program. The real difference is in how you treat the code.

You should now have a clear understanding of the use of the glue routines, call back interface, and ROM routines in the creation and coding of an XCMD. The creation of an XFCN follows the same rules. As discussed in Chapter 2, the only real difference between an XCMD and an XFCN is in the resource type and the way in which values are returned.

In the next chapter, you will learn some tactics for debugging your XCMD's and XFCN's, and you will pick up some tips and tricks.

CHAPTER 5

DEBUGGING AND RELATED INFORMATION

Bill Atkinson, the inventor of HyperCard, when asked what he did for a living, once replied "I create bugs." No program or programmer is perfect. Errors can creep into your code no matter how careful you are. Finding the bugs and stomping them out can be a real challenge and is as much an art form as programming. Debugging is one of those things that machines have trouble with but people seem to do really well. It involves guessing, intuition, flashes of brilliance, and sometimes a lot of luck.

There is no prescribed method for debugging a program. And even after you have discovered the bug, there are countless ways to fix it. The method you use will be uniquely your own. It will flow from your own creative and problem-solving abilities. This chapter does not presume to teach you the art or practice of debugging, but it does offer hints, tips, stumbling blocks, and the experience of others.

The first part of this chapter discusses removing bugs from your code. The second part discusses getting around some of the bugs in HyperCard.

MAKING SURE THE XCMD OR XFCN IS ATTACHED TO THE STACK

Once you have written and compiled an XCMD or XFCN, it is time to try it out. If you are like most people, you will hurry to launch HyperCard, bring the message box up, type in the name and parameters to call your XCMD or XFCN, and press the Return key. If you are very lucky, your XCMD or XFCN will work perfectly the first time. If you are like most programmers, however, some kind of error will occur.

One of the more common error messages is "Can't understand animate" (or whatever the name of your XCMD or XFCN was). If you get a similar error message, you or your compiler forgot to attach it to the stack you are using.

To remedy the situation, you can use ResEdit (available from most Macintosh user groups) or a similar resource editor to move the XCMD or XFCN to the correct stack. If you want it to be accessible from any stack, attach it to your Home stack; otherwise, attach the XCMD or XFCN to the stack in which it will be used.

Note: Some language compilers (including MPW) allow you to specify the file to which your code resource can be attached. If your compiler does not let you attach your XCMD or XFCN directly to a stack, you can use ResEdit or a similar resource editor to copy and paste the XCMD or XFCN to the stack of your choice. To protect existing stacks from damage, you should first attach untested XCMD's and XFCN's to a junk stack. You can move them to permanent stacks after you get the bugs out.

LOOKING FOR ERRORS

When you first try a new XCMD or XFCN, watch it closely to see how it behaves. This will give you some early feedback on the health of the XCMD or XFCN. For example, an XCMD to write to a field might leave the field empty or fill it with garbage characters. In a more extreme example, your XCMD or XFCN might drop into the debugger (if you have one installed) or display the all-too-familiar system bomb.

Once you have the XCMD or XFCN up and running, give it a thorough test. Pretend you are a novice user. Deliberately set out to break your XCMD or XFCN in any way you can. You should include things like mixing up the parameters, violating the range boundaries, using the wrong data type, stripping necessary quotes, or passing parameters that make no sense.

Even if your XCMD or XFCN stands up to torture tests, it can still have problems. The next three sections will help you identify different kinds of bugs and specific things to watch out for and will give you some tips on preventing some of the more common bugs.

Note: One torture test your XCMD or XFCN should be able to stand up to is heap scramble—the ability of a debugger to constantly rearrange and compact the heap. XCMD's and XFCN's with memory-management problems usually fail the heap scramble test. See your specific debugger for information on this feature.

Fatal Errors

When an XCMD or XFCN drops into the debugger, it indicates a gross error. Following are some examples of gross errors:

- Initializing the grafPort.
- Disposing of a handle and then trying to access it.
- Disposing of a handle that HyperCard still needs.
- Accessing a handle that points to a purged object.
- Forgetting to unlock or dispose of your handles before returning to HyperCard.
- Setting the contents of a field to greater than 30,000 characters.
- Setting the contents of a script to greater than 30,000 characters.
- Forgetting to restore the port before returning to HyperCard.
- Writing more bytes to a handle than the size of the handle permits.

The best way to find gross errors is to step through your code, using a source level debugger such as the one found in LightSpeed Pascal (available from Think Technologies); this way, you can spot the specific point at which the error occurs. If you do not have access to a source-level debugger, you must step through the 68000 commands—one at a time—examining memory and the individual registers while looking for problems.

Note: Because HyperCard makes a copy of your XCMD or XFCN and locks it on the heap, you cannot use the symbols feature of your compiler to aid your debugging efforts.

Fatal Error Debugging Hints and Tips

- In versions of HyperCard through 1.1, if you supply more than 16 parameters to an XCMD or XFCN, HyperCard will crash.

- Any error in a SendCardMessage call back causes all future SendCardMessage calls to fail. This is a bug with no solution in versions of HyperCard through 1.1.

- Unlock and dispose of all handles at the end of your XCMD or XFCN. In long XCMD's or XFCN's, it is helpful to keep a written list of the handles and pointers you must dispose of before you exit.

- Always measure the length of zero-terminated text before you write it to a field or script, to avoid exceeding the 30,000 character limit. (You can use the StringLength glue routine discussed in Chapter 3 for the measurement).

- Never include a statement in your XCMD or XFCN that starts with INIT (for example, InitPort, InitMenus, or InitDialogs).

- Always restore HyperCard's state before exiting your XCMD or XFCN.

- Never dispose of a handle that HyperCard still needs. One of the most common ways to do this is shown in the following example:

```
paramPtr^.returnValue := myHandle; {don't do this!}
DisposHandle(myHandle);
```

In this example, the paramPtr^.returnValue field is being set. The contents of the handle have not yet been passed. HyperCard still needs those contents. If you dispose of the handle on the next call, HyperCard will crash. (HyperCard disposes of the handle for you.)

Obvious Errors

Obvious errors are the type of bugs you look at and think, "Oops!" They usually occur as a result of a silly error on your part or a problem in one of your algorithms.

Examples of this type of bug might include the following:

- Missing data in a field
- Garbage in a field
- Range errors
- Parameter errors
- Incorrect values sent or received
- ROM call errors
- Wrong menu items displayed
- Truncated or reversed data
- Wrong font in HyperCard's dialogs
- Failures in your routines and procedures

Obvious Error Hints and Tips

- Flush mouse events before displaying a dialog.

- Move parameter handles high on the heap, and lock them before using them. (To help prevent heap fragmentation, it is a good idea to lock the handle only as long as you need it to be locked.)

- Do proper range and parameter checking.

- Whenever a ROM call returns an error, develop a routine to handle the error.

- Pascal arrays start with element 1, but C arrays start with element 0.

- If your XCMD or XFCN is not passing the message along the inheritance path, make sure you are setting the passFlag field of the XCmdBlock record to TRUE.

- When converting between Pascal strings and C strings, keep in mind that Pascal strings start with a length byte and C strings end with a zero byte.

- Never pass a Pascal string to a routine that requires a zero-terminated string, and vice-versa.

Subtle Errors

Subtle errors usually appear at random and are generally not reproducible. They can also be cumulative in nature. For example, an XCMD that forgets to dispose of handles returned by glue routines will eat chunks of the heap over a period of time, making HyperCard display an out-of-memory error.

Following are some examples of subtle errors to watch out for:

- Diminishing heap space
- Failure to pass heap scramble
- Random garbage in your output
- Occasional drops into the debugger
- Update problems that come and go
- Unknown beeps

Subtle Error Hints and Tips

- Dispose of handles that have been allocated by glue routines. The glue routines that allocate handles are as follows:

  EvalExpr
  PasToZero
  GetGlobal
  GetFieldByName
  GetFieldByNum
  GetFieldByID

- Use the HyperTalk function *the heapspace* before and after a call to your XCMD or XFCN to determine if it is leaving anything on the heap. If the *after value* is different from the *before value*, take another look at your memory management procedures.

- As a debugging aid, you should also call your XCMD or XFCN within a long HyperTalk repeat loop. Use the HyperTalk function *the heapspace* within the loop to spot any diminishing heap problems.

- If your compiler supports symbols and your XCMD causes an unknown beep, set your debugger to break on the ROM routine Sysbeep (for Mascbug, you can do this by entering the debugger, typing AB Sysbeep <return>, and then typing G <return> to resume execution of your program).

- If your XCMD or XFCN beeps, it might be trying to Set or Get a HyperTalk global variable that does not exist.

OVERCOMING OBSTACLES IN HYPERCARD

Few things cause more frustration than needing to have your XCMD or XFCN do something that the external interface does not support or needing to have your XCMD or XFCN do something that does not work because of bugs. This section deals with overcoming two common problems with HyperCard's external interface. These problems are brought about by the need to perform the following tasks:

1. Making a global variable from within an XCMD or XFCN.
2. Saving information that your XCMD or XFCN can reference during a later call.

Techniques for solving both of these problems are shown in separate sections that follow. Because HyperCard's external interface is not designed to perform either of these tasks, what you will find can only be described as a "hack."

> **Note:** In versions of HyperCard greater than 1.1, the SetGlobal glue routine automatically creates a global variable for you (see Chapter 3).

Making a Global Variable

You would think that creating a global variable from within an XCMD or XFCN would be easy. It should be as easy as using one of the glue routines to send a card message back to HyperTalk (SendCardMessage ('global var')).

Instead, creating a HyperTalk global variable from within an XCMD in versions of HyperCard through 1.1 requires a somewhat convoluted procedure.

Because HyperTalk handlers can create globals, you must create an object and then add a handler to its script that creates one or more globals. After the handler is in place, you can invoke it with the SendCardMessage glue routine. Following is a step-by-step approach:

1. Use the SendCardMessage glue routine to create a new field object (the scripts of fields are easier to set, as you will see later in this section). You will want to lock the screen so the user cannot see what you are doing. For example,

```
SendCardMessage('set lockscreen to true'); {to keep user from viewing the process}
SendCardMessage('domenu "new field"'); {create a new field}
```

> **Note:** You could use the script of any object. For example, background scripts are generally smaller than card or stack scripts, and they are always around. The problem with using them is that if anything goes wrong within your XCMD or XFCN, you could destroy existing scripts.

2. Next, put the following handler into the field, substituting your own global variable names for var1,var2,var3, and so on (do not forget to put return characters in front of the first line and at the end of the first and second lines). Putting the text for the handler into the field will make it easier to set the script of that field.

```
On MakeGlobal
    global var1,var2,var3,var4,var5
End MakeGlobal
```

For example,

```
SendCardMessage('put "On MakeGlobal" & return into last card field');
SendCardMessage(CONCAT('put "global ',myGlobName,'" after last card field'));
SendCardMessage('put return & "End MakeGlobal" after last card field');
```

By putting the comma-separated list of HyperTalk global variable names in the variable *myGlobname*, you make it easy to change them in the future.

> **Note:** it is a good idea to choose unusual variable names such as GlobalGooberGoo so you do not accidentally overwrite an existing HyperTalk global variable.

3. Use the SendCardMessage routine to set the script of the field, using the contents of the field. For example,

```
SendCardMessage('set script of last card field to last card field');
```

4. Use the SendCardMessage routine to send a MakeGlobal message directly to the field. When the field receives the MakeGlobal message, it will invoke the MakeGlobal handler, creating the global variables. Once the globals are created, you can access them using the Get and Set Global glue routines. For example,

```
SendCardMessage('send "makeglobal" to last card field');
```

5. The only task that remains is to get rid of the field and clean up. You can use the SendCardMessage glue routine to select and clear the field, select the browse tool, and unlock the screen. For example,

```
SendCardMessage('click at loc of last card field'); {to select it }
SendCardMessage('domenu "clear field"'); {to delete it}
SendCardMessage('choose browse tool'); {creating the field left you in field tool}
SendCardMessage('set lockscreen to false');
```

Turning It into a Procedure

The previous example would be even more useful if you turned it into a procedure that could be called whenever you wanted to create a HyperTalk global variable. The procedure might take a single argument of type Str255 to represent the names of the global variables to be created. (You could use a comma-separated list when specifying more than one global —for example, 'var1,var2,var3'.)

The procedure that follows is named MakeGlobal. You should consider adding it to the XCmdGlue file as one of your own library routines:

For the Pascal Programmer

```
PROCEDURE MakeGlobal(myGlobName: Str255); {needs comma separated global names}
   BEGIN
       SendCardMessage('set lockscreen to true');
       SendCardMessage('domenu "new field"');
       SendCardMessage('put "on makeglobal" & return into last card field');
       SendCardMessage(CONCAT('put "global ',myGlobName,'" after last card field'));
       SendCardMessage('put return & "end makeglobal" after last card field');
       SendCardMessage('set script of last card field to last card field');
       SendCardMessage('send "makeglobal" to last card field');
       SendCardMessage('click at loc of last card field');
       SendCardMessage('domenu "clear field"');
       SendCardMessage('choose browse tool');
       SendCardMessage('set lockscreen to false');
   END; {MakeGlobal}
```

For the C Programmer

```
/*
   This function, via a series of SendCardMessage callbacks,
   creates a global variable with the specified name.
*/
void MakeGlobal(paramPtr, name)
   XCmdBlockPtr paramPtr;
   char         *name;
{
   Str255   message;

   mySendCardMessage(paramPtr, "set lockScreen to true");
   mySendCardMessage(paramPtr, "doMenu \"New Field\"");
   mySendCardMessage(paramPtr,"put \"on makeglobal\" & return into last card field")
   strcpy(message, "put \"global ");
   strcat(message, name);
   strcat(message, "\" & return after last card field");
   mySendCardMessage(paramPtr, (char *) message);
   mySendCardMessage(paramPtr,
       "put return & \"end makeglobal\" & return after last card field");
```

continued...

...from previous page

```
   mySendCardMessage(paramPtr, "set script of last card field to last card field");
   mySendCardMessage(paramPtr, "send \"makeglobal\" to last card field");
   mySendCardMessage(paramPtr, "click at the loc of last card field");
   mySendCardMessage(paramPtr, "doMenu \"Clear Field\"");
   mySendCardMessage(paramPtr, "choose browse tool");
   mySendCardMessage(paramPtr, "set lockScreen to false");
}


/*
   This cover routine does the conversion to a pascal string and calls
   SendCardMessage with the message.
*/
void mySendCardMessage(paramPtr, str)
   XCmdBlockPtr paramPtr;
   char         *str;
{
   Str255 message;

   strcpy(message, str);
   ToPstr((char *) message);
   SendCardMessage(paramPtr, message);
}
```

Saving Information Between Calls

Sometimes, you will want to save a handle between calls to an XCMD or XFCN or to pass a handle from one XCMD or XFCN to another. Because there is no defined way of doing this, you must create your own way.

One way to pass a handle is to store the decimal value of the master pointer of the handle in a HyperTalk global variable and retrieve it when you need it. (You can also save the value of your variables in this way.)

The technique for performing this task involves moving the handle as high on the heap as possible, locking it, and making it unpurgeable. You can then save the decimal value of the master pointer in a HyperTalk global variable (created with the MakeGlobal routine shown in the last section) and retrieve it on the next call to your XCMD or XFCN.

Saving the Handle

Following is how you might save a handle for later use:

```
MoveHHi(myHandle); {move the handle out of the way and lock it down}
Hlock(myHandle);
HNoPurge(myHandle);
MakeGlobal('myOldSavedHandle'); {create a global to store the handle in}
tempStr := LongToStr(ORD(myHandle^)); {get the decimal value of the master pointer}
SetGlobal('myOldSavedHandle',PasToZero(tempStr)); {the master pointer is now saved}
```

The master pointer to the handle is now stored in the HyperTalk global variable *myOldSavedHandle*. You can either create a global variable from a script ahead of time, or you can create one on the fly using the MakeGlobal procedure shown earlier in this chapter.

Note: saving a handle in this manner can cause heap fragmentation.

Recovering the Handle

Reverse the process when you want to recover the handle by using the contents of the HyperTalk global variable—and some ROM magic—to restore it:

```
tempHandle := GetGlobal('myOldSavedHandle'); {retrieve the master pointer}
ZeroToPas(tempHandle^,tempStr); {put it into a string for conversion}
myRestoredHandle := RecoverHandle(POINTER(StrToLong(tempStr)));
```

Note: after you have finished with the various handles, be sure to dispose of them.

HINTS AND TIPS

- Another way to save information between calls to your XCMD or XFCN is to create a resource with the information you want to save in the stack to which the XCMD or XFCN is attached.

- Use constants in place of numbers to make debugging your code easier. For example, the word maxParamCount tells you a lot more than the number 3 does.

- In C, a common error is leaving the additional equal sign off in an equate. In C, an equal sign (=) is specified by two equal signs (==).

- Handles to the parameters passed with your XCMD or XFCN are not locked. Always lock a parameter handle before dereferencing it.

- If your XCMD runs too fast on a Mac II, use the output of the Environs ROM routine (actually loaded into RAM) to tell you when it needs to be slowed (see the Machine XCMD in Chapter 2).

- Menu icons must be numbered between 256 and 511 to appear in the menu bar.

- The glue routines do very little error checking. Any error made in the SendCardMessage and SendHCMessage glue routines might cause all future calls to those routines to be ignored.

- Use the returnValue field of the XCmdBlock record to pass the value of your program's variables or other information back to HyperTalk. To pass more than one value, concatenate them into a comma-separated list.

- When you gray a menu item out on a Mac II, command-key equivalents are still active.

- The only thing passed into an XCMD or XFCN is a pointer to the XCmdBlock record.

- HyperCard treats the contents of all variables as zero-terminated strings. Make sure that any strings you pass back to HyperCard are zero-terminated.

- If your compiler does not allow you to use embedded strings (MPW C has this problem), put the string into a STR-type resource, and use the GetResource ROM routine to retrieve it.

- When using color in your XMCD's, use the old color routines (ForeColor, BackColor and ColorBit) if you want your XCMD or XFCN to be compatible with all models of the Macintosh.

- Call StillDown before GrowWindow to ensure proper tracking of the grow box in windows.

- Call MoveHHi before locking a handle to help prevent heap fragmentation.

- To change a HyperCard text file into a Macwrite file, assign it the file type WORD and give it the creator MACA.

- Do not try to write your code and optimize it all in one step. Get your XCMD or XFCN working first; then, optimize it for speed or efficiency.

SUMMARY

In this chapter, you learned some common ways that bugs can creep into your code and how to avoid them. You learned about testing and tracking down a bug, and you picked up some debugging tips along the way.

In addition, you learned how to create a HyperTalk global from an XCMD or XFCN and how to save information on the heap between calls to your XCMD or XFCN.

In the next and final chapter, you will find 20 coded and ready-to-compile XCMD's and XFCN's that accomplish everything from adding menu bars to sorting fields.

CHAPTER 6

READY-TO-USE XCMD'S AND XFCN'S

In this chapter, you will find 20 ready-to-use XCMD's and XFCN's shown in both Pascal and C. Because different compilers require that different information and directives be imbedded in the source code, you should make the appropriate modifications before compiling and linking the XCMD's or XFCN's. (The code is in MPW Pascal and LightSpeedC format).

Each XCMD or XFCN in this chapter is accompanied by a brief description and one or more HyperTalk examples showing how to use it from within a script.

Following is a list and brief description of the XCMD's and XFCN's in this chapter:

- HardCopy (prints the contents of a field, variable, the selection, or a string).
- EjectDisk (ejects a disk from any floppy drive)
- SetGlobal (sets the contents of one or many global variables at once)
- NewMenuBar (lets you create your own menu bar)
- RestoreMenuBar (restores menu bars saved by NewMenuBar)
- PopMenu (creates a pop-up menu on the fly)
- AddMenu (lets you add as many menus to the current menu bar as will fit)
- ResMenu (displays a menu of one resource type: like "XCMD" or "FONT")
- ClearMenu (clears menus added using AddMenu and ResMenu)
- ModifyMenuItem (lets you modify the text, icon, mark, and highlight of a menu item)
- SmartSum (quickly and intelligently sums fields and lists)
- GetEvent (returns a pending event, optionally letting you flush it from the queue)
- QuickSort (sorts the contents of a field, variable, or the selection)
- CopyRes (copies resources between stacks—including XCMD's and XFCN's)
- GetDiskVol (returns the name of the currently mounted disk volume)
- TalkString (uses the Macintalk speech drivers to speak a word or phrase)
- GetPathName (displays the standard file dialog, returning a pathname to the file chosen)
- SetWindowName (sets the title of the card window—works best with a Mac II)
- FontReal (lets you know whether a font and size are available)
- DeleteFile (deletes a disk file)

Note: You must supply the parameters in the order shown for each XCMD or XFCN in this chapter.

HardCopy

The HardCopy command prints the contents of a string or container. Appropriate containers are fields, variables, the message box, and the selection. You can specify the font, font size, a simple font style (see below), and auto-page numbering; you can optionally display a dialog that allows you to choose the page range and number of copies. HardCopy will print to an ImageWriter or LaserWriter printer and supports print spooling.

Quick Reference

HardCopy card field 1,geneva,10,bold,true,dialog

Parameters

HardCopy takes six parameters:

Parameter 1: the container to be printed.
Parameter 2: the name of the font to use when printing
Parameter 3: the point size of the font to use when printing
Parameter 4: style: plain, bold, italic, underline, outline, shadow, expand, or condense
Parameter 5: a flag for page numbering (TRUE = on, FALSE = off)
Parameter 6: the word "dialog" (displays a job dialog—can be used in parameter position 2 through 6)

The default values for omitted parameters are as follows:

Default for parameter 1: none—this parameter must be supplied
Default for parameter 2: font: geneva
Default for parameter 3: font size: 12 pt
Default for parameter 4: font style: plain
Default for parameter 5: auto-numbering: false
Default for parameter 6: dialog: not displayed

Examples

HardCopy field "myFieldName"
HardCopy card field 1 & card field 2,dialog
HardCopy myVar,chicago,48,dialog
HardCopy the selection,elvish,5,shadow,false
HardCopy "This string"

Tips

If you want HardCopy to print evenly spaced columns, concatenate the information into a variable and use a monospaced font—such as Monaco or Courier—when printing.

For the Pascal Programmer

```
{$R-}
( *
   © 1988 by Gary Bond
   All Rights Reserved

   HardCopy -- a Hypercard XCMD that prints the contents of a string, field, variable,
               the selection or the message box.

   Form:  HardCopy  "Container",fontName,fontSize,fontStyle,pageNum[true/false],dialog

   Container: Includes strings, variables, the selection etc.
   Font: can be any font name available - defaults to geneva
   Size: point size - defaults to 12pt
   Style:  Bold,Italic,outline,shadow,plain,underline,condense,extend
   Numbering: automatic if set to true - none if set to false
   Dialog: when specified, provides a job dialog

   Example: HardCopy  field  1,geneva,14,bold,false,dialog
```

continued...

...from previous page

Note: compound styles like underline-shadow-italic aren't supported.

To compile and link this file using MPW Pascal, select the following lines and press the ENTER key

---

```
pascal HardCopy.p
link -o "HD:Hypercard:Home" -rt XCMD=1503 -sn Main=HardCopy HardCopy.p.o ∂
{MPW}Libraries:Interface.o -m ENTRYPOINT ∂
{MPW}PLibraries:PasLib.o -m ENTRYPOINT

* )

{$S HardCopy } { Segment name must be the same as the command name. }

UNIT DummyUnit;

INTERFACE

USES MemTypes, QuickDraw, OSIntf, ToolIntf, MacPrint, PasLibIntf, HyperXCmd;

PROCEDURE ENTRYPOINT(paramPtr: XCmdPtr);

IMPLEMENTATION

TYPE  Str31  =  String[31];

PROCEDURE HardCopy(paramPtr: XCmdPtr);        FORWARD;

PROCEDURE ENTRYPOINT(paramPtr: XCmdPtr);

  BEGIN
    HardCopy(paramPtr);
  END;

PROCEDURE HardCopy(paramPtr: XCmdPtr);
```

continued...

...from previous page

```
CONST left = 25;
      top = 20;
      right = 525;
      bottom = 700;
      pageBottom = 724;
      pageCenter = 275;
      minParamCount = 1 ;
      maxParamCount = 6 ;


VAR   str:                Str255;
      txtStyle:           Str255;
      savePort:           GrafPtr;
      myPtr:              Ptr;
      myEditRecord:       TEHandle;
      hPrint:             THPrint;
      pPrPort:            TPPrPort;
      prStatus:           TPrStatus;
      err:                Boolean;
      dlog:               Boolean;
      pNum:               Boolean;
      myPrRect:           Rect;
      size:               LongInt;
      txtSize:            Integer;
      txtFont:            Integer;
      myJustification:    Integer;
      pageSize:           Integer;
      charsThisPage:      Integer;
      pageCount:          Integer;
      i :                 Integer; {document loop}
      j :                 Integer; {numb of copies loop}
      sumChars:           Integer;
```

{$I XCmdGlue.inc } {includes the glue routines}

continued...

...from previous page

```
PROCEDURE Fail(errStr: Str255); {Exit returning an error message}
  BEGIN
    PrClose;
    SetPort(savePort); {restore the port}
    DisposHandle(Handle(hPrint));
    HUnlock(paramPtr^.params[1]);
    HPurge(paramPtr^.params[1]);
    paramPtr^.returnValue := PasToZero(errStr); {load the result}
    EXIT(HardCopy); {leave the XCMD}
  END;

PROCEDURE CheckParamCount; {checks for the correct parameter count}

  VAR numParams: Integer;

  BEGIN
    numParams := paramPtr^.paramCount; {store the number of parameters passed}
    IF ((numParams < minParamCount) OR (numParams > maxParamCount))
    THEN Fail('Form: HardCopy "Text",Name,Size,Style,pNum[true/false],dialog');
  END; {CheckParamCount}

PROCEDURE GetStyle; {lets you set simple styles}
  BEGIN
    TextFace([]); {set default for if they err}
    IF EqualString('bold',txtStyle,FALSE,FALSE) THEN TextFace([bold]);
    IF EqualString('italic',txtStyle,FALSE,FALSE) THEN TextFace([italic]);
    IF EqualString('underline',txtStyle,FALSE,FALSE) THEN TextFace([underline]);
    IF EqualString('outline',txtStyle,FALSE,FALSE) THEN TextFace([outline]);
    IF EqualString('shadow',txtStyle,FALSE,FALSE) THEN TextFace([shadow]);
    IF EqualString('condense',txtStyle,FALSE,FALSE) THEN TextFace([condense]);
    IF EqualString('extend',txtStyle,FALSE,FALSE) THEN TextFace([extend]);
    IF EqualString('plain',txtStyle,FALSE,FALSE) THEN TextFace([]);
  END; {end GetStyle}
```

continued...

...from previous page

```
BEGIN {main}
  CheckParamCount; {must be between 1 and 6}
  InitCursor; {don't want I-beam cursor for job dialogs}
  sumChars := 0; {initialize it}
  txtFont := 3; {default value of geneva}
  txtSize := 12; {default value of 12pt.}
  txtStyle := 'plain'; {default style}
  myJustification := teJustLeft; {default justification}
  dlog := FALSE; {set default for dialog to not shown}
  pNum := FALSE; {set auto page numbering off as the default}

  IF paramPtr^.paramcount >= 2 THEN
    BEGIN
      ZeroToPas(paramPtr^.params[2]^,str);
      IF EqualString('Dialog',str,FALSE,FALSE) {allow job dialogs here}
      THEN dlog := TRUE
      ELSE GetFNum(str,txtFont); {if not a dialog then try to convert font name}
      IF txtFont = 0 THEN txtFont := 3; {set it to geneva if they err}
    END;

  IF paramPtr^.paramcount >= 3 THEN
    BEGIN
      ZeroToPas(paramPtr^.params[3]^,str);
      IF EqualString('Dialog',str,FALSE,FALSE)
      THEN dlog := TRUE  {allow job dialogs here}
      ELSE txtSize := StrToNum(str); {if not a dialog then try to convert font name}
      IF txtSize = 0 THEN txtSize := 12; {set it to 12pt if they err}
    END;

  IF paramPtr^.paramcount >= 4 THEN
    BEGIN
      ZeroToPas(paramPtr^.params[4]^,str);
      IF EqualString('Dialog',str,FALSE,FALSE)
      THEN dlog := TRUE
      ELSE txtStyle := str; {allow dialog otherwise set text style}
    END;
```

continued...

...from previous page

```
IF paramPtr^.paramcount >= 5 THEN
  BEGIN
    ZeroToPas(paramPtr^.params[5]^,str);
    IF EqualString('Dialog',str,FALSE,FALSE)
    THEN dlog := TRUE
    ELSE pNum := StrToBool(str); {correct for bad value passed}
    IF paramPtr^.result <> 0 THEN pNum := StrToBool('FALSE');
  END;

IF paramPtr^.paramcount = 6 THEN dlog := TRUE;

MoveHHi(paramPtr^.params[1]); {this will move so lock it down}
Hlock(paramPtr^.params[1]);
HNoPurge(paramPtr^.params[1]); {overly conservative}
GetPort(savePort); {save the current port and restore after printing}
PrOpen; {prepare the print manager for use}
Handle(hPrint) := NewHandle(SizeOf(TPrint));
PrintDefault(hPrint); {get printer resource file defaults}
err := PrValidate(hPrint); {insure compatibility with current print drivers}
size := StringLength(paramPtr^.params[1]^); {check size of print stuff}
IF (size > 32000)
THEN Fail('Can only print 32000 characters at a time');
IF (size = 0) THEN Fail('Nothing to print');

IF dlog THEN IF NOT PrJobDialog(hPrint) THEN Fail('Print job cancelled');
SendCardMessage('set cursor to 4'); {put up the watch cursor using HC}

TextFont(txtFont); {set the font of the printout}
TextSize(txtSize); {set the point size of the printout}
GetStyle; {select the correct style or default to plain}
SetRect(myPrRect,left,top,right,bottom); {set size of rectangle to draw text into}
myEditRecord := TeNew(myPrRect,myPrRect); {allocate a new edit record}
TESetText(paramPtr^.params[1]^,size,myEditRecord);
{-----calculate number of pages and lines per page-----}
pageSize := TRUNC((bottom-top)/myEditRecord^^.lineHeight)-1; {calc lines/page}
pageCount := TRUNC(myEditRecord^^.nLines/pageSize); {calc number of pages}
IF ((myEditRecord^^.nLines/pageSize) > TRUNC(myEditRecord^^.nLines/pageSize))
THEN pageCount := pageCount + 1; {account for a partially full last page}

pPrPort := PrOpenDoc(hPrint,NIL,NIL);  {open a new printing grafport}
```

continued...

...from previous page

```
FOR j := 1 TO (hPrint^^.prJob.iCopies) DO BEGIN {number of copies in job dialog}
  sumChars := 0; {reset total chars to print}
FOR i := 1 TO pageCount DO
  BEGIN {for loop}
    PrOpenPage(pPrPort,NIL); {begin a new page for printing}
    TextFont(txtFont); {must set the font of printout for each page}
    TextSize(txtSize); {must set the point size of printout for each page}
    GetStyle; {must set style of printout for each page}

    charsThisPage := (myEditRecord^^.lineStarts[(pageSize * i)+1])-sumChars-1;
    IF i = pageCount THEN charsThisPage := (size-sumChars); {last page}
    EraseRect(myPrRect); {clear the space before drawing into the port}
    myPtr := paramPtr^.params[1]^; {get ptr to text to draw}
    IF i >1
    THEN myPtr := Pointer(ORD(myPtr)+(sumChars+1)); {advance the pointer}
    TextBox(myPtr,charsThisPage,myPrRect,myJustification); {draw the text}

    IF pNum THEN {do the page numbering}
      BEGIN
        MoveTo(pageCenter,pageBottom); {add the page number}
        TextFont(20); {Set 12 pt times as the font for the page number}
        TextSize(12);
        TextFace([]);
        DrawString(NumToStr(i));
      END; {pNum}
    sumChars := (sumChars + charsThisPage); {keep running total of chars printed}
    PrClosePage(pPrPort); {print & then cycle to next page}
  END; {for i loop (document)}
END; {for j loop (copies)}

PrCloseDoc(pPrPort); {close this document}
```

continued...

...from previous page

```
{--If document was spooled, print it now. Includes Best and Faster Imagewriter--}
IF (hPrint^^.prJob.bjDocLoop = bSpoolLoop)
THEN PrPicFile(hPrint,NIL,NIL,NIL,prStatus);

PrClose; {clean-up and leave}
HUnlock(paramPtr^.params[1]);
HPurge(paramPtr^.params[1]);
SetPort(savePort); {restore the port}
DisposHandle(Handle(hPrint));
TEDispose(myEditRecord);
END; {main}

END. {HardCopy}
```

For the C Programmer

```
/*
  © 1988 by Gary Bond
  All Rights Reserved

  Translated to C by Sioux Lacy

  HardCopy:     a Hypercard XCMD that prints the contents of a string, field,
                variable, the selection or the message box.

  Form:         HardCopy "Container", fontName, fontSize, fontStyle,
                pageNumbers[true/false], dialog

  Container:    Includes strings, variables, the selection etc.
  Font:         can be any font name available - defaults to geneva
  Size:         point size - defaults to 12 pt
  Style:        bold,italic,outline,shadow,plain,underline,condense,extend
  Numbering:    automatic if set to true|none if set to false
  Dialog:       when specified, provides job and print dialogs

  Example: HardCopy field 1, geneva, 14, bold, false, dialog

  _____

  Compile and link this file with the MacTraps, string, PrLink libraries
*/
```

continued...

...from previous page

```
/*
   Includes
   Note that these header files are for LightspeedC development.
   Substitute the files that are appropriate for your compiler.
*/
#include <MacTypes.h>
#include <PrintMgr.h>
#include <FontMgr.h>
#include <TextEdit.h>
#include <QuickDraw.h>
#include "HyperXCmd.h"

/*
   LightspeedC Prototypes
*/
pascal   void main(XCmdBlockPtr);
void     SetStyle(Str255 *);
short    GetParamCount(XCmdBlockPtr, char *);
void     PrintFail(XCmdBlockPtr, char *, THPrint);
Handle   CopyStrToHand(char *);
void     HandleToPstr(Str255, Handle);
char     *ToPstr(char *);

/*
   Defined Constants
*/
#define  minParamCount  (short)           1
#define  maxParamCount  (short)           6
#define  left           (int)             25
#define  top            (int)             20
#define  right          (int)             525
#define  bottom         (int)             700
#define  pageBottom     (int)             724
#define  pageCenter     (int)             275
#define  errorFlag      (short)           -1
#define  EOS            (unsigned char)   0
#define  NIL            (Handle)          0


pascal void    main(paramPtr)
   XCmdBlockPtr paramPtr;
{
   short int     paramCount;
   short int     paramNum;
   Str255        str;
   Str255        txtStyle;
```

continued...

...from previous page

```
int         txtSize;
int         txtFont;
int         txtJustify;
Ptr         txtPointer;
Boolean     dialog;
Boolean     autoPageNum;
GrafPtr     savePort;
THPrint     printHndl;
TPPrPort    printPort;
TPrStatus   printStatus;
Rect        printRect;

TEHandle    myEditRecord;
TEPtr       myEditPtr;
int         numCopies;
int         pageCount;
int         thisPage;
int         linesPerPage;
int         linesPrinted;
long        charsToPrint;
long        charsThisPage;
long        charsPrinted;

paramCount = GetParamCount(paramPtr,
    "Form: HardCopy \"Container\", fontName, size, style pageNumbers[T/F], dialog");
if (paramCount == errorFlag)
    return;

/*
    Initialize cursor because I-beam is inappropriate for dialogs
    Set up defaults for font, size, style, justification, dialog
    and page numbering.

    Programming note:
    The Pascal string literals in the calls to EqualString and strncpy
    consist of a length byte followed by the characters of the string.
    strncpy can be used for Pascal strings as well as C strings since
    it copies for a specified number of characters or until a terminating
    0 is encountered.  Be certain that the number of chars specified
    includes the length byte.
*/
InitCursor();
txtFont = 3;                                    /* Geneva */
txtSize = 12;                                   /* 12 point */
strncpy((char *)txtStyle, "\5plain", (int) 6);  /* plain style */
txtJustify = teJustLeft;                        /* justification flush left */
dialog = FALSE;                                 /* dialog not shown */
autoPageNum = FALSE;                            /* auto page numbering */
```

continued...

...from previous page

```
for (paramNum = 2; paramNum <= paramCount; paramNum++)
    {
        /*
        Get the parameter
        If it matches the string "dialog", then user wants a dialog
        */
        HandleToPstr(str, paramPtr->params[paramNum-1]);
        if (EqualString("\6dialog", str, FALSE, FALSE))
            dialog = TRUE;
        else
            {
                switch (paramNum)
                    {
                        case 2:    /* Assume it's a font name */
                            GetFNum(str, &txtFont);
                            if (txtFont == 0)
                                txtFont = 3;  /* If error, set to Geneva */
                            break;
                        case 3:    /* Assume it's a font size */
                            txtSize = (int) StrToLong(paramPtr, (Str31 *) &str);
                            if (txtSize == 0)
                                txtSize = 12; /* If error, set to 12 point */
                            break;
                        case 4:    /* Assume it's a text style */
                            strncpy((char *)txtStyle, str, (int) str[0]+1);
                            break;
                        case 5:    /* Assume it's a flag for auto page numbering */
                            if (EqualString("\4true", str, FALSE, FALSE))
                                autoPageNum = TRUE;
                            break;
                    }
            }
    }
MoveHHi(paramPtr->params[0]);
HLock(paramPtr->params[0]);
txtPointer = *(paramPtr->params[0]);
GetPort(&savePort);

/*
    Prepare the print manager for use
    Get printer resource file defaults
    Ensure compatibility with current print drivers
*/
PrOpen();
printHndl = (THPrint) NewHandle(sizeof(TPrint));
PrintDefault(printHndl);
PrValidate(printHndl);
```

continued...

...from previous page

```
charsToPrint = (long) strlen(txtPointer);
if (charsToPrint > 32000)
    {
        PrintFail(paramPtr, "Can only print 32000 characters at a time", printHndl);
        return;
    }
else if (charsToPrint == 0)
    {
        PrintFail(paramPtr, "Nothing to print", printHndl);
        return;
    }

if (dialog)
    if (PrJobDialog(printHndl) == FALSE)
        {
            PrintFail(paramPtr, "Print job cancelled", printHndl);
            return;
        }
strcpy((char *) str, "set cursor to 4");
SendCardMessage(paramPtr, (StringPtr) ToPstr((char *) str));

/*
    Set the textfont, point size, style, size of rectangle to draw text into
    Allocate a new edit record for text edit
*/
TextFont(txtFont);
TextSize(txtSize);
SetStyle(&txtStyle);
SetRect(&printRect, left, top, right, bottom);
myEditRecord = TENew(&printRect, &printRect);
TESetText(txtPointer, (long) charsToPrint, myEditRecord);

/*
    Calculate number of pages and lines per page
    Account for a partially full last page
*/
HLock(myEditRecord);
myEditPtr = *myEditRecord;
linesPerPage = ((bottom - top) / myEditPtr->lineHeight ) - 1;
pageCount = myEditPtr->nLines / linesPerPage;
if (myEditPtr->nLines % linesPerPage != 0)
    pageCount++;
HUnlock(myEditRecord);
```

continued...

...from previous page

```
/*
   Open a grafPort for printing
   Get number of copies to print
   Print calculated number of pages for each
*/
printPort = PrOpenDoc(printHndl, NIL, NIL);

numCopies = ((*printHndl)->prJob).iCopies;
while (numCopies--)
    {
        charsPrinted = (long) 0;
        linesPrinted = 0;
        for (thisPage = 1; thisPage <= pageCount; thisPage++)
            {
                /*
                   Need to set up text parameters for this page
                   Calculate number of characters for this page
                */
                PrOpenPage(printPort, NIL);
                TextFont(txtFont);
                TextSize(txtSize);
                SetStyle(&txtStyle);
                if (thisPage == pageCount)
                    charsThisPage = (charsToPrint - charsPrinted);    /* last page */
                else
                    charsThisPage = (*myEditRecord)->lineStarts[linesPrinted +
                        linesPerPage] - charsPrinted;

                EraseRect(&printRect);
                TextBox(txtPointer, charsThisPage, &printRect, txtJustify);

                txtPointer += charsThisPage;
                charsPrinted += charsThisPage;
                linesPrinted += linesPerPage;

                if (autoPageNum)
                    {
                        /*
                            Switch to 12 pt. Geneva for page numbers
                        */
                        MoveTo(pageCenter, pageBottom);
                        TextFont(3);
                        TextSize(12);
                        SetStyle((Str255 *) "\5plain");
                        LongToStr(paramPtr, (long) thisPage, (Str31 *) &str);
                        DrawString(str);
                    }
                PrClosePage(printPort);
            }
    }
```
        continued...

...from previous page

```
/*
    Close this document
    If document was spooled, print it now.
    Includes Best and Faster Imagewriter
*/
PrCloseDoc(printPort);

if ((*printHndl)->prJob.bJDocLoop == bSpoolLoop)
    PrPicFile(printHndl, NIL, NIL, NIL, &printStatus);

/*
    Clean up: unlock handle, restore the port
    Dispose of the print handle and the edit record
*/
PrClose();
HUnlock(paramPtr->params[0]);
SetPort(savePort);
DisposHandle(printHndl);
TEDispose(myEditRecord);

    return;
}


/*
    This function sets the text style to a specified style
    Note that the Pascal string literals in the calls to EqualString
    consist of a length byte followed by the characters of the string.
*/
void SetStyle(str)
    Str255 *str;
{
    if (EqualString("\4bold", str, FALSE, FALSE))
        TextFace((Style) bold);
    else if (EqualString("\6italic", str, FALSE, FALSE))
        TextFace((Style) italic);
    else if (EqualString("\9underline", str, FALSE, FALSE))
        TextFace((Style) underline);
    else if (EqualString("\7outline", str, FALSE, FALSE))
        TextFace((Style) outline);
    else if (EqualString("\6shadow", str, FALSE, FALSE))
        TextFace((Style) shadow);
    else if (EqualString("\8condense", str, FALSE, FALSE))
        TextFace((Style) condense);
    else if (EqualString("\6extend", str, FALSE, FALSE))
        TextFace((Style) extend);
    else
        TextFace((Style) 0);
}
```

continued...

...from previous page

```
/*
   This function checks to see if the correct number of params were received.
   And writes an error message into the returnValue if they were not.
*/
short GetParamCount(paramPtr, str)
   XCmdBlockPtr paramPtr;
   char         *str;
{
   short    count;

   count = paramPtr->paramCount;
   if ((count > maxParamCount) || (count < minParamCount))
      {
         paramPtr->returnValue = (Handle) CopyStrToHand (str);
         return(errorFlag);
      }
   return(count);
}



/*
   This function gets a handle and copies the error string it receives into the heap
   for return to HyperCard.
*/
void PrintFail(paramPtr, str, hndl)
   XCmdBlockPtr  paramPtr;
   char          *str;
   THPrint       hndl;
{
   HUnlock(paramPtr->params[0]);
   DisposHandle(hndl);
   paramPtr->returnValue = (Handle) CopyStrToHand(str);
   return;
}



/*
   This utility function allocates heapspace and copies a string into it.
*/
Handle CopyStrToHand(str)
   char *str;
{
   Handle    newHndl;

   newHndl = (Handle) NewHandle((long) strlen(str) + 1);
   strcpy((char *)(*newHndl), str);
   return(newHndl);
}
```

continued...

...from previous page

```
/*
   This utility function copies the string pointed to by a handle into
   a character array, then converts the C string to a Pascal string.
   Note that the C string is overwritten by the Pascal string.
*/
void HandleToPstr(str, hndl)
   Str255   str;
   Handle   hndl;
{
   strcpy((char *) str, *hndl);
   ToPstr((char *) str);
}


/*
   This utility function converts a C string to a Pascal string.
   Note that the C string is overwritten in the process.
*/
char *ToPstr(str)
   char *str;
{
   unsigned char length, i;

   for (i = 0, length = 0; str[i] != 0; ++i)     /* Find end of string */
      ++length;
   while (i--)                                    /* Shift string 1 byte to right */
      str[i+1] = str[i];
   str[0] = length;                               /* Put string length in 1st byte */
   return(str);
}
```

EjectDisk

The EjectDisk command ejects, flushes, and unmounts a floppy disk from the specified floppy drive.

Quick Reference

EjectDisk driveNumber

Parameters

EjectDisk takes one parameter:

Parameter 1: The drive number (1-3) of the disk to be ejected.

There are no default values for omitted parameters.

Examples

EjectDisk 1
EjectDisk 2
EjectDisk 3

Tips

You should include the full range of drives (1–3) for this XCMD because the Macintosh SE can include two internal floppy drives *and* one external floppy drive.

For the Pascal Programmer

```
{$R-}
( *
  © 1988 by Gary Bond
  All Rights Reserved

  EjectDisk -- a Hypercard XCMD that unmounts, flushes and ejects a floppy volume

  Form: EjectDisk number 1-3

  Example: EjectDisk 1

  Note:  The range for floppy drives is 1-3 since the MacSE can have 2 internal
         and 1 external floppy operating at once
```

continued...

...from previous page

To compile and link this file using MPW Pascal, select the following lines and press the ENTER key

---

```
pascal EjectDisk.p
link -o "HD:Hypercard:Home" -rt XCMD=1504 -sn Main=EjectDisk EjectDisk.p.o ∂
{MPW}Libraries:Interface.o -m ENTRYPOINT ∂
{MPW}PLibraries:PasLib.o -m ENTRYPOINT

* )

{$S EjectDisk }  {Segment name must be the same as the command name}

UNIT DummyUnit;

INTERFACE

USES MemTypes, QuickDraw, OSIntf, ToolIntf, PasLibIntf, HyperXCmd;

PROCEDURE ENTRYPOINT(paramPtr: XCmdPtr);

IMPLEMENTATION

TYPE  Str31 = String[31];

PROCEDURE EjectDisk(paramPtr: XCmdPtr);        FORWARD;

  PROCEDURE ENTRYPOINT(paramPtr: XCmdPtr);

    BEGIN
      EjectDisk(paramPtr);
    END;

  PROCEDURE EjectDisk(paramPtr: XCmdPtr);

  CONST  maxParamCount = 1;
         fileSystemError = 1;
         driveNumberError = 2;
```

continued...

...from previous page

```
VAR   str:          Str255;
      volName:      Str255;
      err:          Integer;
      vRefNum:      Integer;
      drvNum:       Integer;
      freeBytes:    LongInt;


{$I XCmdGlue.inc } {Includes the glue routines}


  PROCEDURE CheckParamCount; {Checks for the correct parameter count}
    BEGIN
      IF (paramPtr^.paramcount <> maxParamCount) THEN
        BEGIN {Exit loading the result if no filename or incorrect parameters supplied}
          IF paramPtr^.paramcount = 0 THEN str := 'Disk Number Parameter Missing'
          ELSE str := 'Incorrect Parameter Count';
          paramPtr^.returnValue := PasToZero(str); {This call loads the result}
          EXIT(EjectDisk); {Leave the XCMD}
        END; {If begin}
    END; {CheckParamCount begin}


  PROCEDURE ErrorCheck(error: Integer); {Checks for file system errors}
    BEGIN
      CASE error OF
        1 : BEGIN
            CASE err OF {Set the appropriate error message for the result}
              bdNamErr: str := 'Bad Volume Name';
              extFSErr: str := 'External File System';
              ioErr:  str := 'I/O Error';
              nsDrvErr: str := 'No Such Drive';
              nsvErr: str := 'No Such Volume';
              paramErr:  str := 'No Default Volume';
            OTHERWISE str := CONCAT('Unknown Error: ',NumToStr(err));
            END; {Case err}
            paramPtr^.returnValue := PasToZero(str);  {Return the error in the result}
            EXIT(EjectDisk); {Exit the XCMD}
          END; {Begin 1:}
        2 : BEGIN
            IF ((drvNum < 0) OR (drvNum > 3)) THEN
```

continued...

...from previous page

```
        BEGIN {Range check the drive number}
          str := 'Incorrect Drive Number';
          paramPtr^.returnValue := PasToZero(str);
          EXIT(EjectDisk);
        END;
      END; {Begin 2:}
    END; {Case error}
  END; {ErrorCheck begin}

BEGIN {main}
  CheckParamCount; {See if the caller supplied the correct number of parameters}
  ZeroToPas(paramPtr^.params[1]^,str); {Get the disk number from the caller}
  drvNum := StrToNum(str); {Convert it to an integer}
  ErrorCheck(DriveNumberError); {Check it for legal drive number}
  err := GetVInfo(drvNum,@volName,vRefNum,freeBytes); {Get vol for eject call}
  IF err <> noErr THEN ErrorCheck(fileSystemError);
  err := Eject(@volName,vRefNum);  {Kick the disk out}
  IF err <> noErr THEN ErrorCheck(fileSystemError);
  err := UnmountVol (@volName,vRefNum); {Now do a finder dismount}
  IF err <> noErr THEN ErrorCheck(fileSystemError);
END; {main}

END. {EjectDisk}
```

For the C Programmer

```
/*
  © 1988 by Gary Bond
  All Rights Reserved

  Translated to C by Sioux Lacy

  EjectDisk:   a Hypercard XCMD that unmounts, flushes and ejects a floppy volume

  Form:        EjectDisk number 1-3

  Example:     EjectDisk 1

  Note:        The range for floppy drives is 1-3 since the MacSE can have 2
               internal and 1 external floppy operating at once
```

continued...

...from previous page

```
   Compile and link this file with the MacTraps and string libraries
*/


/*
   Includes
   Note that these header files are for LightspeedC development.
   Substitute the files that are appropriate for your compiler.
*/
#include <MacTypes.h>
#include <FileMgr.h>
#include "HyperXCmd.h"

/*
   LightspeedC Prototypes
*/
pascal   void  main(XCmdBlockPtr);
Boolean  ErrorCheck(XCmdBlockPtr, int, int);
Handle   ConcatErrorStr(XCmdBlockPtr, char *, int);
Handle   CopyStrToHand(char *);
char     *ToCstr(char *);
char     *ToPstr(char *);


/*
   Defined Constants
*/

#define  requiredParamCount   (short) 1
#define  fileSystemError      (int) 1
#define  driveNumberError     (int) 2


pascal   void  main(paramPtr)
   XCmdBlockPtr   paramPtr;
{
   Str255       volName;
   char         str[32];
   int          err;
   int          vRefNum;
   int          drvNum;
   long         freeBytes;
```

continued...

...from previous page

```
    if (paramPtr->paramCount != requiredParamCount)
        {
            if (paramPtr->paramCount == 0)
                paramPtr->returnValue = (Handle)
                    CopyStrToHand("Disk Number Parameter Missing");
            else
                paramPtr->returnValue = (Handle)
                    CopyStrToHand("Incorrect Parameter Count");
            return;
        }
    /*
        Get the drive number from the parameter block
    */
    strcpy(str, *(paramPtr->params[0]));
    drvNum = (int) StrToLong(paramPtr, (Str31 *) ToPstr(str));

    if (ErrorCheck(paramPtr, driveNumberError, drvNum))
        return;              /* If not legal drive number, exit */

    err = GetVInfo(drvNum, volName, &vRefNum, &freeBytes);
    if (err == noErr)
        {
            err = Eject(volName, vRefNum);  /* Eject the disk */
            if (err == noErr)
                err = UnmountVol(volName, vRefNum);  /* Do a finder dismount */
        }
    if (err != noErr)
        {
            ErrorCheck(paramPtr, fileSystemError, err);
            return;           /* If something went wrong, return message */
        }
    return;    /* If everything went OK, the result will be empty */
}


/*
    Check for file system or drive number errors
*/
Boolean ErrorCheck(paramPtr, errorType, errorNumber)
    XCmdBlockPtr  paramPtr;
    int           errorType;
    int           errorNumber;
{
    switch (errorType)
        {
```

continued...

...from previous page

```
        case fileSystemError:
            switch (errorNumber)
                {
                case noErr:
                    return(FALSE);          /* No error occurrred */
                    break;
                case bdNamErr:
                    paramPtr->returnValue = (Handle) CopyStrToHand("Bad Volume Name");
                    break;
                case extFSErr:
                    paramPtr->returnValue = (Handle)
                        CopyStrToHand("External File System");
                    break;
                case ioErr:
                    paramPtr->returnValue = (Handle) CopyStrToHand("I/O Error");
                    break;
                case nsDrvErr:
                    paramPtr->returnValue = (Handle) CopyStrToHand("No Such Drive");
                    break;
                case nsvErr:
                    paramPtr->returnValue = (Handle) CopyStrToHand("No Such Volume");
                    break;
                case paramErr:
                    paramPtr->returnValue = (Handle) CopyStrToHand("No Default Volume
                    break;
                default:
                    paramPtr->returnValue = (Handle) ConcatErrorStr(paramPtr,
                        "Unknown Error:", errorNumber);
                    break;
                }
            return(TRUE); /* A file system error has occurred */
            break;

        case driveNumberError:
            if ((errorNumber < 0) || (errorNumber > 3))      /* Range check the drive
                number */
                {
                paramPtr->returnValue = (Handle) CopyStrToHand
                    ("Incorrect Drive Number");
                return(TRUE); /* The drive number is invalid */
                }
            else
                return(FALSE);          /* No error has occurred */
            break;
        }
    }


/*

    continued...
```

...from previous page

This function concatenates an integer converted to a string onto a given error message. For consistency, it returns the handle and allows the caller to assign it to paramPtr->returnValue.

```
*/
Handle ConcatErrorStr(paramPtr, errorString, errorNumber)
   XCmdBlockPtr   paramPtr;
   char           *errorString;
   int            errorNumber;
{
   Str31    str1, str2;

   strcpy(str1, errorString);
   LongToStr(paramPtr, (long) errorNumber, &str2);
   ToCstr((char *) str2);
   strcat(str1, str2);
   return((Handle) CopyStrToHand((char *) str1));
}


/*
   This utility function allocates heapspace and copies a string into it.
*/
Handle CopyStrToHand(str)
   char *str;
{
   Handle   newHndl;

   newHndl = (Handle) NewHandle((long) strlen(str) + 1);
   strcpy((char *) (*newHndl), str);
   return(newHndl);
}


/*
   This utility function converts a Pascal string to a C string.
   Note that the Pascal string is overwritten in the process.
*/
char *ToCstr(str)
   char *str;
{
   unsigned char length, i;

   length = str[0];
   for (i = 0; i < length; ++i)         /* Shift string 1 byte to the left */
      str[i] = str[i+1];
   str[length] = 0;                     /* Put zero-terminator after string */
   return(str);
}
```

continued...

...from previous page

```
/*
   This utility function converts a C string to a Pascal string.
   Note that the C string is overwritten in the process.
*/
char *ToPstr(str)
   char *str;
{
   unsigned char length, i;

   for (i = 0, length = 0; str[i] != 0; ++i)     /* Find end of string */
      ++length;
   while (i--)                                    /* Shift string 1 byte to right */
      str[i+1] = str[i];
   str[0] = length;                               /* Put string length in 1st byte */
   return(str);
}
```

SetGlobal

The SetGlobal command allows you to set the contents of one or more HyperTalk global variables to the value supplied in the first parameter.

Quick Reference

SetGlobal valueToSet,"comma separated list of variable names"

Parameters

SetGlobal takes two parameters:

Parameter 1: The value to use when changing the variables. Supports all HyperTalk constants, functions, and containers.

Parameter 2: A quoted, comma-separated list of HyperTalk global variable names (local variables don't work). Each variable will be set to the value supplied in parameter 1.

Examples

SetGlobal empty,"myGlobal,anotherVar,selectedBit,PhilWyman,DavidLeffler"
SetGlobal zero,"var1,var2,var3"
SetGlobal the time,"varA,varB,varC,varD"
SetGlobal card field 1,"who,what,when,where,why,how"
SetGlobal myVar,"zip,zap,zop"

Tips

You must use a quoted list when passing HyperTalk variable names, or HyperTalk will pass the values of the variables instead. A side benefit of this requirement is that you can specify as many variable names as you can fit into the 255-character limit.

For the Pascal Programmer

```
{$R-}
( *
  © 1988 by Gary Bond
  All Rights Reserved

  SetGlobal --  a Hypercard XCMD that sets the comma separated list of global variables
                to a single value.

  Form: value to set,"comma separated list of global names"

  Example:  SetGlobal  empty,"var1,var2,var3,var4,var5"

  Note: If you don't put the global variable names in quotes, the values of the variables
  will be passed instead of the variable names.

  _____

  To compile and link this file using MPW Pascal, select the following lines and press
  the ENTER key
  _____
```

continued...

...from previous page

```
pascal SetGlobal.p
link -o "HD:Hypercard:Home" -rt XCMD=1505 -sn Main=SetGlobal SetGlobal.p.o ∂
{MPW}PLibraries:PasLib.o -m ENTRYPOINT∂
{MPW}Libraries:Interface.o -m ENTRYPOINT

* )

{$S SetGlobal } {Segment name must be the same as the command name}

UNIT DummyUnit;

INTERFACE

USES MemTypes, QuickDraw, OSIntf, ToolIntf, PasLibIntf, PackIntf, HyperXCmd;

PROCEDURE ENTRYPOINT(paramPtr: XCmdPtr);

IMPLEMENTATION

TYPE  Str31  =  String[31];

PROCEDURE SetGlobal(paramPtr: XCmdPtr);        FORWARD;

PROCEDURE ENTRYPOINT(paramPtr: XCmdPtr);

  BEGIN
    SetGlobal(paramPtr);
  END;

  PROCEDURE SetGlobal(paramPtr: XCmdPtr);

    CONST minParamCount = 2;

    VAR  myValue:       Str255;
         count:         Integer;
         i :            Integer;
         varNames:      ARRAY[1..50] OF  Str31;
         myHandle:      Handle;
         myScanPtr:     Ptr;
         exitLoop:      Boolean;
```

continued...

...from previous page

```
{$I XCmdGlue.inc } {Includes the glue routines}

   PROCEDURE Fail(errStr: Str255); {Exit returning an error message}
     BEGIN
       paramPtr^.returnValue := PasToZero(errStr); {load the result}
       EXIT(SetGlobal); {Leave the XCMD}
     END; {Fail}

   PROCEDURE CheckParamCount; {checks for the correct parameter count}

     VAR numParams: Integer;

     BEGIN
       numParams := paramPtr^.paramCount; {store the number of parameters passed}
       IF (numParams <> minParamCount)
       THEN Fail('Form: SetGlobal value to set,"comma separated list of global names"');
     END; {CheckParamCount}

   FUNCTION CollectToComma(VAR scanPtr: Ptr): Str255;

     TYPE Str1 = String[1];

     VAR exitLoop:   Boolean;
         tempStr:    Str1;
         collectStr: Str255;

     BEGIN {CollectToComma}
       exitLoop := FALSE; {set to enter loop}
       tempStr[0] := chr(1); {make a 1 character pascal string}
       collectStr := ''; {initialize it}
       REPEAT {look for comma or end of string}
       IF ((scanPtr^ = $2C) OR (scanPtr^ = $0)) THEN exitLoop := TRUE
       ELSE {gather the characters one at a time if comma or zero not found}
         BEGIN
           tempStr[1] := chr(scanPtr^); {convert 1 character}
           collectStr := CONCAT(collectStr,tempStr); {make a string of characters}
           scanPtr := POINTER(ORD(scanPtr)+1); {advance the pointer 1 position}
           END;
```

continued...

...from previous page

```
      UNTIL exitLoop = TRUE;
      CollectToComma := collectStr; {return  the  result  of  the  function  call}
   END; {CollectToComma}


BEGIN {main}
   CheckParamCount; {only need value and quoted list of names}
   count := 0; {initialize the counter}
   exitLoop := TRUE; {initialize the loop's starting value}
   MoveHHi(paramPtr^.params[2]); {relocate to prevent fragmentation}
   Hlock(paramPtr^.params[2]); {insure no movement while working}
   HNoPurge(paramPtr^.params[2]); {overly conservative}
   myScanPtr := paramPtr^.params[2]^; {copy the master pointer}

   WHILE exitLoop DO {collect the comma separated names and stuff them into an array}
     BEGIN
       count := count + 1; {increment the index var for the array}
       varNames[count] := CollectToComma(myScanPtr); {get next name into array}
       IF myScanPtr^ = 0 THEN exitLoop := FALSE {at end of the zero string?}
       ELSE
         BEGIN
           myScanPtr := Pointer(ORD(myScanPtr)+1); {inc pointer past the comma}
           IF myScanPtr^ = 0 THEN exitLoop := FALSE; {exit if end of zero string}
         END;
       IF count >= 50 THEN exitLoop := FALSE; {can't overrun the array}
     END; {while loop}

   ZeroToPas(paramPtr^.params[1]^,myValue); {get the value to be set}
   myHandle := PasToZero(myValue); {convert the value for SetGlobal}
   FOR i := 1 to count DO SetGlobal(varNames[i],myHandle); {set each global}
   disposHandle(myHandle); {don't need this anymore}
   HUnlock(paramPtr^.params[2]); {HC disposes of this}
   HPurge(paramPtr^.params[2]); {last  of  the  clean-up}
   END; {main}


END. {SetGlobal}
```

For the C Programmer

```
/*
   © 1988 by Gary Bond
   All Rights Reserved
   Translated to C by Sioux Lacy

   SetGlobal:    a Hypercard XCMD that sets the comma separated list of global
                 variables to a single value.

   Form:         value to set,"comma separated list of global names"

   Example:      SetGlobal empty,"var1,var2,var3,var4,var5"

   Note:         If you don't put the global variable names in quotes, the values
                 of the variables will be passed instead of the variable names.

   -----------------------------------------------
   Compile and link this file with the MacTraps and string libraries
*/


/*
   Includes
   Note that these header files are for LightspeedC development.
   Substitute the files that are appropriate for your compiler.
*/
#include    <MacTypes.h>
#include    "HyperXCmd.h"

/*
   LightspeedC Prototypes
*/
pascal    void main(XCmdBlockPtr);
char      *CollectToComma(char *, char *);
short     CheckParamCount(XCmdBlockPtr, char *);
Handle    CopyStrToHand(char *);
char      *ToPstr(char *);


/*
   Defined Constants
*/
#define  requiredParamCount    (short) 2
#define  maxGlobals            (short) 50
#define  errorFlag             (short) -1
#define  EOS                   (unsigned char) 0
```

continued...

235

...from previous page

```
pascal void    main(paramPtr)
    XCmdBlockPtr paramPtr;
{
    int    count, i;
    char   globalName[256];
    char   *myScanPtr;

    if (CheckParamCount(paramPtr,
        "Form: SetGlobal value, \"comma separated list of global names\"") == errorFla
        return;

    MoveHHi(paramPtr->params[1]);
    HLock(paramPtr->params[1]);
    myScanPtr = *(paramPtr->params[1]);

    /*
        Extract the name of each global from the comma-separated list.
        Use SetGlobal to assign the value to the global.
        Check for end-of-string (means end of list) & move pointer past comma.
    */
    for (count = 0; count < maxGlobals; count++)
        {
            myScanPtr = CollectToComma(myScanPtr, globalName);
            SetGlobal(paramPtr, (StringPtr) ToPstr(globalName), paramPtr->params[0]);
            if (*myScanPtr++ == EOS)
                break;
        }
    HUnlock(paramPtr->params[1]);
    return;
}


/*
    This function copies characters from one string to another until it
    finds either a comma, or end-of-string. It returns the pointer into
    the target string.
*/
char *CollectToComma(targetStr, subStr)
    char   *targetStr;
    char   *subStr;
{
    while ((*targetStr != ',') && (*targetStr != EOS))
        *subStr++ = *targetStr++;

    *subStr = EOS;
    return(targetStr);
}
```

continued...

...*from previous page*

```
/*
   This function checks to see if the correct number of params were received.
   And writes an error message into the returnValue if they were not.
*/
short CheckParamCount(paramPtr, str)
   XCmdBlockPtr paramPtr;
   char         *str;
{
   short    count;

   count = paramPtr->paramCount;
   if (count != requiredParamCount)
      {
         paramPtr->returnValue = (Handle) CopyStrToHand(str);
         return(errorFlag);
      }
   return(count);
}


/*
   This utility function allocates heapspace and copies a string into it.
*/
Handle CopyStrToHand(str)
   char *str;
{
   Handle   newHndl;

   newHndl = (Handle) NewHandle((long) strlen(str) + 1);
   strcpy((char *)(*newHndl), str);
   return(newHndl);
}


/*
   This utility function converts a C string to a Pascal string.
   Note that the C string is overwritten in the process.
*/
char *ToPstr(str)
   char *str;
{
   unsigned char length, i;

   for (i = 0, length = 0; str[i] != 0; ++i)    /* Find end of string */
      ++length;
   while (i--)                                  /* Shift string 1 byte to right */
      str[i+1] = str[i];
   str[0] = length;                             /* Put string length in 1st byte */
   return(str);
}
```

NewMenuBar

The NewMenuBar command displays the Apple symbol at the left edge of an empty menu bar. (Use the XCMD RestoreMenuBar to restore the menu bar saved by NewMenuBar.)

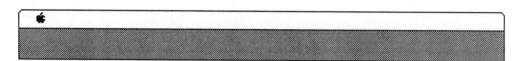

Figure 6.1

The result of the NewMenuBar command.

Quick Reference

NewMenuBar "Name of first item in Apple menu"

Parameters

NewMenuBar takes one parameter:

Parameter 1: The name of the "About" menu item (the first menu item in the Apple menu).

The default values for omitted parameters are as follows:

Default for parameter 1: "My About"

Examples

NewMenuBar "Sioux Lacy's About"
NewMenuBar "About My Program"
NewMenuBar myVar
NewMenuBar card field id 7
NewMenuBar the selection

Tips

The current menu bar can be restored with the RestoreMenuBar XCMD detailed later in this chapter.

Note: You can add menus to the new menu bar, using the AddMenu and ResMenu XCMD's detailed later in this chapter.

For the Pascal Programmer

```
{$R-}
( *
© 1988 by Gary Bond
All Rights Reserved

NewMenuBar -- An XCMD that clears and saves the current menu bar. The new menu
              bar is drawn with an Apple menu.

Form: NewMenuBar "The name of the about menu Item"

Example: NewMenuBar "Gary's About"

Note: NewMenuBar creates a global and uses it to store the handle to the old menubar.
Use the RestoreMenuBar XCMD to release the memory and restore the menu bar to the
state before calling NewMenuBar.
```

To compile and link this file using MPW Pascal, select the following lines and press the ENTER key

---

```
pascal NewMenuBar.p
link -o "HD:Hypercard:Home" -rt XCMD=1506 ∂
-sn Main=NewMenuBar NewMenuBar.p.o ∂
{MPW}PLibraries:PasLib.o -m ENTRYPOINT
```

continued...

...from previous page

```
* )

{$S NewMenuBar} {Segment name must be the same as the command name}

UNIT DummyUnit;

INTERFACE

USES MemTypes, QuickDraw, OSIntf, ToolIntf, PasLibIntf, HyperXCmd;

PROCEDURE ENTRYPOINT(paramPtr: XCmdPtr);

IMPLEMENTATION

TYPE Str31 = String[31];

PROCEDURE NewMenuBar(paramPtr: XCmdPtr);        FORWARD;

   PROCEDURE ENTRYPOINT(paramPtr: XCmdPtr);

     BEGIN
       NewMenuBar(paramPtr);
     END;

   PROCEDURE NewMenuBar(paramPtr: XCmdPtr);

     CONST  AppleID = 300;
            minParamCount = 1;

     VAR    appleTitle:       Str255;
            aboutText:        Str255;
            tempStr:          Str255;
            oldMenuHandle:    Handle;
            appleMenu:        MenuHandle;

{$I XCmdGlue.inc } {includes the glue routines}

   PROCEDURE Fail(errStr: Str255); {Exit returning an error message}
```

continued...

...from previous page

```
    BEGIN
      paramPtr^.returnValue := PasToZero(errStr); {load the result}
      EXIT(NewMenuBar); {leave the XCMD}
    END; {Fail}


  PROCEDURE CheckParamCount; {checks for the correct parameter count}

    VAR numParams: Integer;

    BEGIN
      numParams := paramPtr^.paramCount; {store the number of parameters passed}
      IF (numParams <> minParamCount)
      THEN Fail('Form: NewMenuBar "Your About Name"');
    END; {CheckParamCount}

  BEGIN {main}
    CheckParamCount; {see if the about name is there}
    ZeroToPas(paramPtr^.params[1]^,aboutText);
    IF aboutText = '' THEN aboutText := ' '; {or ROM chokes}
    ClearMenuBar; {then clear it for new menus}
    appleTitle := '@';
    appleTitle[1] := CHR(AppleMark); {prepare apple symbol for apple menu}
    appleMenu := NewMenu(AppleID,appleTitle);
    IF appleMenu = NIL THEN Fail('Unable to get Apple menu handle');
    AppendMenu(appleMenu,aboutText);
    InsertMenu(appleMenu,0);
    DrawMenuBar;
  END; {main}


END. {NewMenuBar}
```

For the C Programmer

```
/*
   © 1988 by Gary Bond
   All Rights Reserved

   Translated to C by Sioux Lacy

   NewMenuBar:  An XCMD that saves the current menu bar, and replaces it with
                your custom menu bar.  The new menu bar is drawn with an Apple
                title.

   Form:    NewMenuBar "The name of the about menu Item"

   Example: NewMenuBar "Gary's About"

   Note:    NewMenuBar replaces HyperCard's menubar with its own custom menu.
            Use the RestoreMenuBar XCMD to restore the HyperCard menuBar.

            Be aware that new users may rely on certain HyperCard menu items,
            like "Go Home" and may feel lost without them.  So it is a good
            idea to intercept "doMenu Home" in your stack script, and call your
            RestoreMenuBar XCMD at that time.

   ─────────────────────────────────────────────────────────────────────

   Compile and link this file with the MacTraps and string libraries
*/


/*
   Includes
   Note that these header files are for LightspeedC development.
   Substitute the files that are appropriate for your compiler.
*/
#include    <MacTypes.h>
#include    <MenuMgr.h>
#include    "HyperXCmd.h"

/*
   LightspeedC Prototypes
*/
pascal    void main(XCmdBlockPtr);
short     CheckParamCount(XCmdBlockPtr, char *);
void      Fail(XCmdBlockPtr, char *);
Handle    CopyStrToHand(char *);
void      HandleToPstr(Str255, Handle);
char      *ToCstr(char *);
char      *ToPstr(char *);
```

continued...

...from previous page

```
/*
   Defined Constants
*/
#define  requiredParamCount   (short)    1
#define  errorFlag            (short)   -1
#define  NIL                  (Handle)   0
#define  EOS                  (unsigned char) 0
#define  myMenuID             (int)    300
#define  afterCurrentMenus    (int)      0


pascal void    main(paramPtr)
   XCmdBlockPtr paramPtr;
{
     Str255       appleTitle;
     Str255       myMenuList;
   MenuHandle     myMenuHandle;

   if (CheckParamCount(paramPtr, "Form: NewMenuBar \"Your About Name\"") == errorFlag)
     return;

   /*
      Clear menuBar for new menus
      Prepare the Apple symbol for the Apple menu
      Get a new menu handle, and insert it in the Apple menu
   */
   ClearMenuBar();
   appleTitle[0] = 1;            /* Make a Pascal string of apple symbol */
   appleTitle[1] = appleMark;

   /*
      Get text for the new menu's options
      If received an empty string, convert it to single space character,
      Pascal-format string.
   */
   HandleToPstr(myMenuList, paramPtr->params[0]);
   if (myMenuList[0] == EOS)
     strcpy(myMenuList, "\1 ");

   /*
      Create a new menu.  If failure, exit
      Add menuList to the new menu
      Add the menu to the ones in the menuBar
      Draw the menuBar
   */
```

continued...

...from previous page

```
    if ((myMenuHandle = NewMenu(myMenuID, appleTitle)) == (MenuHandle) NIL)
        {
            Fail(paramPtr, "Unable to allocate new menu");
            return;
        }
    AppendMenu(myMenuHandle, myMenuList);
    InsertMenu(myMenuHandle, afterCurrentMenus);
    DrawMenuBar();

    return;
}


/*
    This function checks to see if the correct number of params were received.
    And writes an error message into the returnValue if they were not.
*/
short CheckParamCount(paramPtr, str)
    XCmdBlockPtr paramPtr;
    char         *str;
{
    short    count;

    count = paramPtr->paramCount;
    if (count != requiredParamCount)
        {
            paramPtr->returnValue = (Handle) CopyStrToHand (str);
            return(errorFlag);
        }
    return(count);
}


/*
    This function gets a handle and copies the error string it receives into the heap
    for return to HyperCard.
*/
void Fail(paramPtr, str)
    XCmdBlockPtr  paramPtr;
    char          *str;
{
```

continued...

...from previous page

```
   paramPtr->returnValue = (Handle) CopyStrToHand(str);
   return;
}


/*
   This utility function allocates heapspace and copies a string into it.
*/
Handle CopyStrToHand(str)
   char *str;
{

   Handle   newHndl;

   newHndl = (Handle) NewHandle((long) strlen(str) + 1);
   strcpy((char *)(*newHndl), str);
   return(newHndl);
}


/*
   This function makes a callback to HyperCard to convert a string to an
   unsigned long integer.  It takes a handle to a C string as an argument.
*/
long HandleToNum(paramPtr, hndl)
   XCmdBlockPtr   paramPtr;
   Handle         hndl;
{
   char  str[32];
   long  num;

   strcpy(str, *hndl);
   num = StrToLong(paramPtr, (Str31 *) ToPstr(str));
   return(num);
}


/*
   This utility function copies the string pointed to by a handle into
   a character array, then converts the C string to a Pascal string.
   Note that the C string is overwritten by the Pascal string.
*/
void HandleToPstr(str, hndl)
   Str255   str;
   Handle   hndl;
{
   strcpy((char *) str, *hndl);
   ToPstr((char *) str);
}
```

continued...

...from previous page

```
/*
   This utility function converts a Pascal string to a C string.
   Note that the Pascal string is overwritten in the process.
*/
char *ToCstr(str)
   char *str;
{
   unsigned char length, i;

   length = str[0];
   for (i = 0; i < length; ++i)        /* Shift string 1 byte to the left */
      str[i] = str[i+1];
   str[length] = 0;                    /* Put zero-terminator after string */
   return(str);
}


/*
   This utility function converts a C string to a Pascal string.
   Note that the C string is overwritten in the process.
*/
char *ToPstr(str)
   char *str;
{
   unsigned char length, i;

   for (i = 0, length = 0; str[i] != 0; ++i)    /* Find end of string */
      ++length;
   while (i--)                                  /* Shift string 1 byte to right */
      str[i+1] = str[i];
   str[0] = length;                             /* Put string length in 1st byte */
   return(str);
}
```

RestoreMenuBar

The RestoreMenuBar command restores the menu bar previously saved by New-MenuBar.

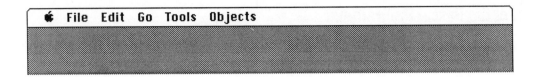

Figure 6.2

The result of the RestoreMenuBar command.

Quick Reference

RestoreMenuBar

Parameters

RestoreMenuBar takes no parameters.

Examples

RestoreMenuBar

Tips

Restore the menu bar on closeStack to ensure that HyperCard's menus will be restored as you leave the stack.

For the Pascal Programmer

```
{$R-}
( *
    © 1988 by Gary Bond
    All Rights Reserved

    RestoreMenuBar -- An XCMD that restores a menu bar saved by the NewMenuBar
                        XCMD.

    Form: RestoreMenuBar "The name of the about menu Item"
    Example: RestoreMenuBar

    Note: RestoreMenuBar restores only the last saved menu bar.
```

To compile and link this file using MPW Pascal, select the following lines and press the ENTER key

```
    pascal RestoreMenuBar.p
    link -o "HD:Hypercard:Home" -rt XCMD=1507 ∂
    -sn Main=RestoreMenuBar RestoreMenuBar.p.o -m ENTRYPOINT

* )

{$S RestoreMenuBar} {Segment name must be the same as the command name}

UNIT DummyUnit;

INTERFACE

USES MemTypes, QuickDraw, OSIntf, ToolIntf, PasLibIntf, HyperXCmd;

PROCEDURE ENTRYPOINT(paramPtr: XCmdPtr);

IMPLEMENTATION

TYPE  Str31 = String[31];
```

continued...

...from previous page

```
PROCEDURE RestoreMenuBar(paramPtr: XCmdPtr);        FORWARD;

  PROCEDURE ENTRYPOINT(paramPtr: XCmdPtr);

    BEGIN
      RestoreMenuBar(paramPtr);
    END;

  PROCEDURE RestoreMenuBar(paramPtr: XCmdPtr);

    CONST minParamCount = 0;

{$I XCmdGlue.inc } {Includes the Glue routines}

  PROCEDURE Fail(errStr: Str255); {Exit returning an error message}
    BEGIN
      paramPtr^.returnValue := PasToZero(errStr); {load the result}
      EXIT(RestoreMenuBar); {leave the XCMD}
    END; {Fail}

  PROCEDURE CheckParamCount; {checks for the correct parameter count}

    VAR numParams: Integer;

    BEGIN
      numParams := paramPtr^.paramCount; {store the number of parameters passed}
      IF (numParams <> minParamCount)
      THEN Fail('Form: RestoreMenuBar');
    END; {CheckParamCount}

  BEGIN {main}
    CheckParamCount; {friendly feedback}
    ClearMenuBar; {gets rid of all the menus that are up}
    SendCardMessage('choose brush tool');
    SendCardMessage('choose browse tool'); {this is safest way in HC ver > 1.1}
  END; {main}

END. {RestoreMenuBar}
```

For the C Programmer

```
/*
    © 1988 by Gary Bond
    All Rights Reserved

    Translated to C by Sioux Lacy

    RestoreMenuBar: An XCMD that restores a menu bar saved by the NewMenuBar XCMD.

    Form:           RestoreMenuBar

    Example:        RestoreMenuBar

    Note:           RestoreMenuBar restores the HyperCard menuBar, returning the stac
                    to the browse tool.
    ──────────────────────────────────────────────────────────────────
    Compile and link this file with the MacTraps and string libraries
*/


/*
    Includes
    Note that these header files are for LightspeedC development.
    Substitute the files that are appropriate for your compiler.
*/
#include <MacTypes.h>
#include <MenuMgr.h>
#include "HyperXCmd.h"

/*
    LightspeedC Prototypes
*/
pascal   void main(XCmdBlockPtr);
void     MySendCardMessage(XCmdBlockPtr, char *);
short    CheckParamCount(XCmdBlockPtr, char *);
void     Fail(XCmdBlockPtr, char *);
Handle   CopyStrToHand(char *);
char     *ToPstr(char *);


/*
```

continued...

...from previous page

```
   Defined Constants
*/
#define  requiredParamCount  (short)    0
#define  errorFlag           (short)   -1
#define  NIL                 (Handle)   0
#define  myMenuID             (int)    300


pascal void    main(paramPtr)
   XCmdBlockPtr paramPtr;
{
   MenuHandle  myMenuHandle;

   if (CheckParamCount(paramPtr, "Form: ClearMenu MenuID") == errorFlag)
      return;

   ClearMenuBar();
   MySendCardMessage(paramPtr, "choose brush tool");
   MySendCardMessage(paramPtr, "choose browse tool");

   return;
}



/*
   This cover routine does the conversion to a pascal string and calls
   SendCardMessage with the message.
*/
void MySendCardMessage(paramPtr, str)
   XCmdBlockPtr paramPtr;
   char         *str;
{
   Str255 message;

   strcpy(message, str);
   ToPstr((char *) message);
   SendCardMessage(paramPtr, message);
}
```

continued...

...from previous page

```
/*
   This function checks to see if the correct number of params were received.
   And writes an error message into the returnValue if they were not.
*/
short CheckParamCount(paramPtr, str)
   XCmdBlockPtr paramPtr;
   char        *str;
{
   short   count;

   count = paramPtr->paramCount;
   if (count != requiredParamCount)
      {
         paramPtr->returnValue = (Handle) CopyStrToHand (str);
         return(errorFlag);
      }
   return(count);
}


/*
   This utility function allocates heapspace and copies a string into it.
*/
Handle CopyStrToHand(str)
   char *str;
{
   Handle  newHndl;

   newHndl = (Handle) NewHandle((long) strlen(str) + 1);
   strcpy((char *)(*newHndl), str);
   return(newHndl);
}


/*
   This utility function converts a C string to a Pascal string.
   Note that the C string is overwritten in the process.
*/
char *ToPstr(str)
   char *str;
{
   unsigned char length, i;

   for (i = 0, length = 0; str[i] != 0; ++i)     /* Find end of string */
      ++length;
   while (i--)                                    /* Shift string 1 byte to right */
      str[i+1] = str[i];
   str[0] = length;                               /* Put string length in 1st byte */
   return(str);
}
```

PopMenu

The PopMenu function displays a pop-up menu at the location specified and returns an integer representing the number of the chosen menu item. If no menu item was chosen, PopMenu returns zero. The location at which the menu is displayed can be specified by individual top and left coordinates or by a comma-separated point (100,78).

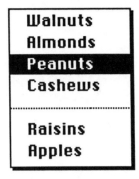

Figure 6.3

The result of the PopMenu function.

Quick Reference

PopMenu(top,left,"menuList")
PopMenu(point,"menuList")

Parameters

PopMenu takes up to three parameters:

Parameter 1: Point or top coordinate to use when displaying the menu (if only two parameters are supplied, the first is assumed to be a point).

Parameter 2: Left coordinate or menuList.

Parameter 3: MenuList (you must separate menu items with semicolons).

PopMenu supports the following meta functions:

! followed by a character, precedes (marks) the item in the menu with that character
< followed by B,I,U,O,S sets the character style of that item
/ followed by a character, associates a keyboard equivalent with the item
(disables the item
- hyphen followed by (inserts a grayed out line

Examples

put PopMenu(the mouseloc,"item1;item2;item3") into menuChoice
IF PopMenu(100,45,"item1;(-;item2<B;item3!√") is 5 THEN doProcFive

Tips

PopMenu works best in a MouseDown handler at the card level.

For the Pascal Programmer

```
{$R-}
( *
  © 1988 by Gary Bond
  All Rights Reserved

  PopMenu -- a Hypercard XFCN that displays a pop-up menu at a user specified
            location.

  PopMenu supports the meta functions:

  ! Followed by a character, marks the item with that character
  < Followed by B,I,U,O,S sets the character style of that item
  / Followed by a character, associates a keyboard equivalent with the item
  ( Disables the item
  - Hypen followed by ( inserts a grayed out line

  Form: PopMenu Top,Left,"Menu List"

  Example: PopMenu 100,100,"Choice 1;Choice 2;(-;New Stuff"
```

continued...

...from previous page

Note: The selected menu item returns an integer representing the menu item chosen as a result of this function. PopMenu will work with two parameters if the user supplies a valid, comma separated point in place of the top,left coordinates.

To compile and link this file using MPW Pascal, select the following lines and press the ENTER key

---

```
pascal PopMenu.p
link -o "HD:Hypercard:Home" -rt XFCN=1508 -sn Main=PopMenu PopMenu.p.o ∂
{MPW}Libraries:Interface.o -m ENTRYPOINT ∂
{MPW}PLibraries:PasLib.o -m ENTRYPOINT

* )

{$S PopMenu } {Segment name must be the same as the command name}

UNIT DummyUnit;

INTERFACE

USES MemTypes, QuickDraw, OSIntf, ToolIntf, PasLibIntf, HyperXCmd;

PROCEDURE ENTRYPOINT(paramPtr: XCmdPtr);

IMPLEMENTATION

TYPE  Str31 = String[31];

PROCEDURE PopMenu(paramPtr: XCmdPtr);        FORWARD;

  PROCEDURE ENTRYPOINT(paramPtr: XCmdPtr);

  BEGIN
    PopMenu(paramPtr);
  END;
```

continued...

...from previous page

```
PROCEDURE PopMenu(paramPtr: XCmdPtr);

  CONST  MenuID = 200;
         minParamCount = 2;
         maxParamCount = 3;

  VAR  menuList:      Str255;
       tempStr:       Str255;
       offsetLeft:    Integer;
       offsetTop:     Integer;
       windLeft:      Integer;
       windTop:       Integer;
       choice:        Integer;
       myScanPtr:     Ptr;
       myHandle:      Handle;
       myMenuHandle:  MenuHandle;

{$I XCmdGlue.inc} {Includes the glue routines}

  PROCEDURE Fail(errStr: Str255); {Exit returning an error message}
    BEGIN
      paramPtr^.returnValue := PasToZero(errStr); {load the result}
      EXIT(PopMenu); {leave the XCMD}
    END; {Fail}

  PROCEDURE CheckParamCount; {checks for the correct parameter count}

    VAR numParams: Integer;

    BEGIN
      numParams := paramPtr^.paramCount; {store the number of parameters passed}
      IF ((numParams < minParamCount) OR (numParams > maxParamCount))
      THEN Fail('Form: PopMenu Top,Left,"Menu List"');
    END; {CheckParamCount}

  PROCEDURE GetLocOfCardWindow; {gets the left and top edges of the card window}

    VAR  tempStr:     Str255;
         tempHandle:  Handle;
```

continued...

...from previous page

```
BEGIN {use call backs to get current window loc}
  tempHandle := EvalExpr('Item 1 of rect of card window'); {left edge}
  ZeroToPas(tempHandle^,tempStr); {convert to a string and then an integer}
  windLeft := StrToNum(tempStr); {now have left edge of card window}
  disposHandle(tempHandle); {don't need this any longer}
  tempHandle := EvalExpr('Item 2 of rect of card window'); {top edge}
  ZeroToPas(tempHandle^,tempStr); {convert to a string and then an integer}
  windTop := StrToNum(tempStr); {now have top edge of card window}
  disposHandle(tempHandle); {don't need this any longer}
END; {GetLocOfCardWindow}

FUNCTION CollectToComma(VAR scanPtr: Ptr): Str255;

  TYPE Str1  =  String[1];

  VAR  exitloop:     BOOLEAN;
       tempStr:      Str1;
       collectStr:   Str255;

  BEGIN
    exitloop := FALSE;
    tempStr[0]  :=  chr(1);
    collectStr := '';
    REPEAT
    IF ((scanPtr^ = $2C) OR (scanPtr^ = 0)) THEN exitloop := TRUE
    ELSE
      BEGIN
        tempStr[1]  :=  chr(scanPtr^);
        collectStr  :=  Concat(collectStr,tempStr);
        scanPtr  :=  Pointer(ORD(scanPtr)+1);
        END;
    UNTIL exitloop = TRUE;
    CollectToComma := collectStr;
  END; {collectToComma}

BEGIN {main}
  CheckParamCount; {no more than 3 and no less than 2}
  InitCursor; {so user can't choose menu with I-beam}
  GetLocOfCardWindow;
```

continued...

...from previous page

```
IF paramPtr^.paramCount = 2 THEN {user supplied a point}
  BEGIN
    ZeroToPas(paramPtr^.params[1]^,tempStr);
    MoveHHi(paramPtr^.params[1]); {don't want it going anywhere}
    Hlock(paramPtr^.params[1]);
    HNoPurge(paramPtr^.params[1]);
    myScanPtr := paramPtr^.params[1]^; {make a local copy}
    tempStr := CollectToComma(myScanPtr); {get the left coordinate}
    offsetLeft := StrToNum(tempStr); {store it for later use}
    myScanPtr := Pointer(ORD(myScanPtr)+1); {move pointer past the comma}
    tempStr := CollectToComma(myScanPtr); {get the top coordinate}
    offsetTop := StrToNum(tempStr); {store it for later use}
    HUnlock(paramPtr^.params[1]);   {clean-up}
    HPurge(paramPtr^.params[1]);
    ZeroToPas(paramPtr^.params[2]^,menuList); {menu list}
  END; {if paramCount = 2}

IF paramPtr^.paramCount = 3 THEN {user supplied a top,left}
  BEGIN
    ZeroToPas(paramPtr^.params[1]^,tempStr); {top}
     offsetTop := StrToNum(tempStr);
    ZeroToPas(paramPtr^.params[2]^,tempStr); {left}
    offsetLeft := StrToNum(tempStr);
    ZeroToPas(paramPtr^.params[3]^,menuList); {menu list}
  END; {if paramCount=3}

myMenuHandle := NewMenu(MenuID,''); {create a new menu list}
AppendMenu(myMenuHandle,menuList); {add the popup stuff to it}
InsertMenu(myMenuHandle,-1);
choice :=
PopUpMenuSelect(myMenuHandle,(offsetTop+windTop),(offsetLeft+windLeft),1);
DeleteMenu(MenuID); {don't need it after a choice was made}
DisposeMenu(myMenuHandle);
paramPtr^.returnValue := PasToZero(NumToStr(LoWord(choice))); {return item}
END; {main}

END. {PopMenu}
```

For the C Programmer

```
/*
   © 1988 by Gary Bond
   All Rights Reserved

   Translated to C by Sioux Lacy

   PopMenu:    a Hypercard XFCN that displays a pop-up menu at a user
               specified location.

   Form:       PopMenu Top, Left, "Menu List"

   Example:    PopMenu 100, 100, "Choice 1;Choice 2;(-;New Stuff"

   Note:       The selected menu item returns an integer representing the
               menu item chosen as a result of this function. PopMenu will
               work with two parameters if the user supplies a valid, comma
               separated point in place of the top,left coordinates.

   PopMenu supports the meta functions:

   ! Followed by a character, marks the item with that character
   < Followed by B,I,U,O,S sets the character style of that item
   / Followed by a character, associates a keyboard equivalent with the item
   ( Disables the item
   - Hypen followed by ( inserts a grayed out line
   _____

   Compile and link this file with the MacTraps and string libraries
*/


/*
   Includes
   Note that these header files are for LightspeedC development.
   Substitute the files that are appropriate for your compiler.
*/
#include <MacTypes.h>
#include <MenuMgr.h>
#include "HyperXCmd.h"

/*
   LightspeedC Prototypes
*/
pascal   void main(XCmdBlockPtr);
int      GetLocOfCardWindow(XCmdBlockPtr, Point *);
char     *CollectToComma(char *, char *);
short    GetParamCount(XCmdBlockPtr, char *);
```

continued...

...from previous page

```
void      Fail(XCmdBlockPtr, char *);
Handle    CopyStrToHand(char *);
long      HandleToNum(XCmdBlockPtr, Handle);
void      HandleToPstr(Str255, Handle);
char      *ToCstr(char *);
char      *ToPstr(char *);


/*
   Defined Constants
*/
#define minParamCount      (short)           2
#define maxParamCount      (short)           3
#define menuID             (short)           200
#define errorFlag          (short)           -1
#define EOS                (unsigned char)   0
#define NIL                (Handle)          0
#define lowWordMask        (long)            0x0000FFFF


pascal void    main(paramPtr)
   XCmdBlockPtr paramPtr;
{
   short         numParams;
   char          *scanPtr;
   char          tempStr[32];
   long          selection;
   Str255        menuList;
   MenuHandle    myMenuHandle;
   Handle        myHandle;
   int           offsetLeft;
   int           offsetTop;
   Point         cardWindowLoc;

   if ((numParams = GetParamCount(paramPtr,
      "Form: PopMenu Top, Left, \"Menu List\"")) == errorFlag)
      return;

   InitCursor();      /* So user can't choose menu with I-beam */
   if ((GetLocOfCardWindow(paramPtr, &cardWindowLoc)) == errorFlag)
      return;

   if (numParams == 2)    /* User supplied a "point" instead of top, left */
      {
         MoveHHi(paramPtr->params[0]);
         HLock(paramPtr->params[0]);
         scanPtr = (char *) *(paramPtr->params[0]);
```

continued...

...from previous page

```
        scanPtr = CollectToComma(scanPtr, tempStr);
        offsetLeft = (int) StrToNum(paramPtr, (Str31 *) ToPstr(tempStr));
        ++scanPtr;                              /* Move past the comma */
        scanPtr = CollectToComma(scanPtr, tempStr);
        offsetTop = (int) StrToNum(paramPtr, (Str31 *) ToPstr(tempStr));

        HUnlock(paramPtr->params[0]);
        HandleToPstr(menuList, paramPtr->params[1]);
    }

else if (numParams == 3) /* User specified position as top, left */
    {
        offsetTop = (int) HandleToNum(paramPtr, paramPtr->params[0]);
        offsetLeft = (int) HandleToNum(paramPtr, paramPtr->params[1]);
        HandleToPstr(menuList, paramPtr->params[2]);
    }

/*
    Create a new menu (with no name).
    (If failure, exit to HyperCard.)
    Add the popup list to the menu.
*/
if ((myMenuHandle = NewMenu(menuID, "")) == (MenuHandle) NIL)
    {
        Fail(paramPtr, "Unable to allocate new menu");
        return;
    }
AppendMenu(myMenuHandle, menuList);
InsertMenu(myMenuHandle, (int) -1);

/*
    Let the user make a selection.
    Then the menu isn't needed any longer, delete it.
    Return the number of the item that was selected to HyperCard.
*/
selection = (long) PopUpMenuSelect(myMenuHandle,
    (offsetTop + cardWindowLoc.h), (offsetLeft + cardWindowLoc.v), 1);
DeleteMenu(menuID);
DisposeMenu(myMenuHandle);
NumToStr(paramPtr, (long) (selection & lowWordMask), (Str31 *) &tempStr);
paramPtr->returnValue = (Handle) CopyStrToHand(ToCstr((char *) tempStr));

return;
}
```

continued...

...from previous page

```
int GetLocOfCardWindow(paramPtr, loc)
   XCmdBlockPtr   paramPtr;
   Point          *loc;
{
   Handle   hndl;
   char     str[256];

   strcpy(str, "item 1 of rect of card window");
   hndl = EvalExpr(paramPtr, (StringPtr) ToPstr(str));
   if (paramPtr->result == noErr)
      {
         loc->h = HandleToNum(paramPtr, hndl);
         DisposHandle(hndl);

         strcpy(str, "item 2 of rect of card window");
         hndl = EvalExpr(paramPtr, (StringPtr) ToPstr(str));
         if (paramPtr->result == noErr)
            {
               loc->v = HandleToNum(paramPtr, hndl);
               DisposHandle(hndl);
               return(noErr);
            }
      }
   paramPtr->returnValue = (Handle) CopyStrToHand("Can't get rect of card window");
   return((int) errorFlag);
}


/*
   This function copies characters from one string to another until it
   finds either a comma, or end-of-string. It returns the pointer into
   the target string.
*/
char *CollectToComma(targetStr, subStr)
   char *targetStr;
   char *subStr;
{
   while ((*targetStr != ',') && (*targetStr != EOS))
      *subStr++ = *targetStr++;

   *subStr = EOS;
   return(targetStr);
}
```

continued...

...from previous page

```
/*
   This function checks to see if the correct number of params were received.
   And writes an error message into the returnValue if they were not.
*/
short GetParamCount(paramPtr, str)
   XCmdBlockPtr paramPtr;
   char         *str;
{
   short    count;

   count = paramPtr->paramCount;
   if ((count > maxParamCount) || (count < minParamCount))
      {
         paramPtr->returnValue = (Handle) CopyStrToHand(str);
         return(errorFlag);
      }
   return(count);
}


/*
   This function gets a handle and copies the error string it receives into
   the heap for return to HyperCard.
*/
void Fail(paramPtr, str)
   XCmdBlockPtr  paramPtr;
   char          *str;
{
   paramPtr->returnValue = (Handle) CopyStrToHand(str);
   return;
}


/*
   This utility function allocates heapspace and copies a string into it.
*/
Handle CopyStrToHand(str)
   char *str;
{
   Handle   newHndl;

   newHndl = (Handle) NewHandle((long) strlen(str) + 1);
   strcpy((char *)(*newHndl), str);
   return(newHndl);
}
```

continued...

...from previous page

```
/*
   This function makes a callback to HyperCard to convert a string to an
   unsigned long integer.  It takes a handle to a C string as an argument.
*/
long HandleToNum(paramPtr, hndl)
   XCmdBlockPtr   paramPtr;
   Handle         hndl;
{
   char  str[32];
   long  num;

   strcpy(str, *hndl);
   num = StrToLong(paramPtr, (Str31 *) ToPstr(str));
   return(num);
}


/*
   This utility function copies the string pointed to by a handle into
   a character array, then converts the C string to a Pascal string.
   Note that the C string is overwritten by the Pascal string.
*/
void HandleToPstr(str, hndl)
   Str255  str;
   Handle  hndl;
{
   strcpy((char *) str, *hndl);
   ToPstr((char *) str);
}


/*
   This utility function converts a Pascal string to a C string.
   Note that the Pascal string is overwritten in the process.
*/
char *ToCstr(str)
   char *str;
{
   unsigned char length, i;

   length = str[0];
   for (i = 0; i < length; ++i)      /* Shift string 1 byte to the left */
      str[i] = str[i+1];
   str[length] = 0;                  /* Put zero-terminator after string */
   return(str);
}
```

continued...

...from previous page

```
/*
   This utility function converts a C string to a Pascal string.
   Note that the C string is overwritten in the process.
*/
char *ToPstr(str)
   char *str;
{
   unsigned char length, i;

   for (i = 0, length = 0; str[i] != 0; ++i)      /* Find end of string */
      ++length;
   while (i--)                                     /* Shift string 1 byte to right */
      str[i+1] = str[i];
   str[0] = length;                                /* Put string length in 1st byte */
   return(str);
}
```

AddMenu

The AddMenu command appends a single menu to the end of HyperCard's menu bar. You can add as many menus as will fit in the menu bar. (When you add more than one menu, each must have a different menuID number.)

> **Note:** Use the ClearMenu XCMD (detailed later in this chapter) to remove menus added with AddMenu. You can also use the ModifyMenuItem XCMD (also detailed later in this chapter) to change a menu item's text, icon, mark, and highlight.

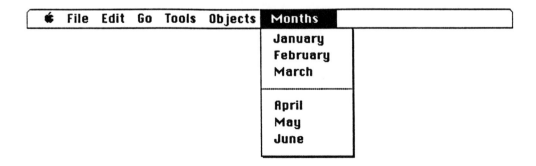

Figure 6.4

The result of the AddMenu command.

Quick Reference

AddMenu "MenuName",MenuID,"MenuList"

Parameters

AddMenu takes three parameters:

Parameter 1: The name that will appear in the menu bar.
Parameter 2: A unique number greater than 200 that will represent this menu.
Parameter 3: A double-quoted, semicolon-separated list of items that are to appear in the menu.

There are no default values for omitted parameters.

AddMenu supports the following meta functions:

! followed by a character marks the item with that character
< followed by B,I,U,O,S sets the character style of that item:
B: Bold
I: Italic
U: Underline
O: Outline
S: Shadow
/ followed by a character creates a keyboard equivalent
(disables an item
(- inserts a grayed out line

Examples

AddMenu "File",500,"Open File/O;Close File;(-;Save/S;Save As..."
AddMenu "Credit Cards",501,"Chevron;Macys;Visa;American Express"
AddMenu "Months:,502,"January;February;March;April;May;June"

Tips

You can use AddMenu with NewMenuBar to create a custom menu bar. Menu items chosen from the new menus are sent to HyperCard as DoMenu messages and can be trapped with a DoMenu handler in the card, background, or stack script.

For the Pascal Programmer

```
{$R-}
( *
  © 1988 by Gary Bond
  All Rights Reserved

  AddMenu -- a Hypercard XCMD that appends a menu to the existing menu bar
             and sends the selected menu item as a doMenu message. As many menus
             can be added as there is space; each must have a different
             menuID.

  Form: AddMenu "MenuName",MenuID,MenuList

  Example: AddMenu "MenuName",MenuID,"one/o;two;(-;three;four"

  Note: You need the ClearMenu XCMD to dispose of the menu item.

  AddMenu supports the meta functions:

  ! Followed by a character, marks the item with that character
  < Followed by B,I,U,O,S sets the character style of that item:
        B: Bold
        I: Italic
        U: Underline
        O: Outline
        S: Shadow
  / Followed by a character, creates a keyboard equivalent
  ( Disables an item
```

continued...

...from previous page

(- Inserts a grayed out line

To compile and link this file using MPW Pascal, select the following lines and press the ENTER key

---

```
pascal Addmenu.p
link -o "HD:Hypercard:Home" -rt XCMD=1509 -sn Main=AddMenu Addmenu.p.o ∂
{MPW}PLibraries:PasLib.o -m ENTRYPOINT

* )

{$S AddMenu} {Segment name must be the same as the command name}

UNIT DummyUnit;

INTERFACE

USES MemTypes, QuickDraw, OSIntf, ToolIntf, PasLibIntf, HyperXCmd;

PROCEDURE ENTRYPOINT(paramPtr: XCmdPtr);

IMPLEMENTATION

TYPE  Str31 = String[31];

PROCEDURE AddMenu(paramPtr: XCmdPtr);        FORWARD;

  PROCEDURE ENTRYPOINT(paramPtr: XCmdPtr);

    BEGIN
      AddMenu(paramPtr);
    END;

  PROCEDURE AddMenu(paramPtr: XCmdPtr);

    CONST minParamCount = 3;
    VAR  menuList:        Str255;
```

continued...

...from previous page

```
          menuName:        Str255;
          tempStr:         Str255;
          menuID:          LongInt;
          myMenuList:      Handle;
          myMenuHandle:    MenuHandle;

{$I XCmdGlue.inc } {Includes the glue routines}

  PROCEDURE Fail(errStr: Str255); {Exit returning an error message}

    BEGIN
      paramPtr^.returnValue := PasToZero(errStr); {load the result}
      EXIT(AddMenu); {Leave the XCMD}
    END; {Fail}


  PROCEDURE CheckParamCount; {checks for the correct parameter count}

    VAR numParams: Integer;

    BEGIN
      numParams := paramPtr^.paramCount; {store the number of parameters passed}
      IF (numParams <> minParamCount)
      THEN Fail('Form: AddMenu "MenuName",MenuNumber,MenuList');
    END; {CheckParamCount}

  BEGIN {main}
    CheckParamCount; {make sure there's enough parameters}
    ZeroToPas(paramPtr^.params[1]^,menuName); {convert the menu name}
    ZeroToPas(paramPtr^.params[2]^,tempStr);
    menuID := StrToLong(tempStr); {convert the menu number}
    IF menuID <= 0 THEN Fail('Zero and negative numbers not allowed');
    ZeroToPas(paramPtr^.params[3]^,menuList); {convert the menu list}
    IF menuList = " THEN menuList := ' '; {make a null list work correctly}
    myMenuHandle := NewMenu(MenuID,menuName); {create a new menu item}
    IF myMenuHandle = NIL THEN Fail('Unable to get menu handle');
    AppendMenu(myMenuHandle,menuList); {adds menuList to end of menu}
    InsertMenu(myMenuHandle,0); {adds the menu to the end of the menu list}
    DrawMenuBar; {draw the menu bar with the new menu}
  END; {main}

END. {AddMenu}
```

For the C Programmer

```
/*
   © 1988 by Gary Bond
   All Rights Reserved

   Translated to C by Sioux Lacy

   AddMenu:        a Hypercard XCMD that appends a menu to the existing menu bar
                   and sends the selected menu item as a doMenu message. As many
                   menus can be added as there is space. Each must have a
                   different menuID.

   Form:           AddMenu "MenuName", MenuID, "MenuList"

   Example:        AddMenu "MenuName", MenuID, "one/o;two;(-;three;four"

   Note:           You need the ClearMenu XCMD to dispose of the menu.
                   Be sure to separate the menu options with semi-colons.

   AddMenu supports the meta functions:

   ! Followed by a character, marks the item with that character
   < Followed by B,I,U,O,S sets the character style of that item:
       B: Bold
       I: Italic
       U: Underline
       O: Outline
       S: Shadow
   / Followed by a character, creates a keyboard equivalent
   ( Disables an item
   (- Inserts a grayed out line

   ---------------------------------------------
   Compile and link this file with the MacTraps and string libraries
*/


/*
   Includes
   Note that these header files are for LightspeedC development.
   Substitute the files that are appropriate for your compiler.
*/
#include <MacTypes.h>
#include <MenuMgr.h>
#include "HyperXCmd.h"
```

continued...

...from previous page

```
/*
   LightspeedC Prototypes
*/
pascal    void main(XCmdBlockPtr);
short     CheckParamCount(XCmdBlockPtr, char *);
void      Fail(XCmdBlockPtr, char *);
Handle    CopyStrToHand(char *);
long      HandleToNum(XCmdBlockPtr, Handle);
void      HandleToPstr(Str255, Handle);
char      *ToCstr(char *);
char      *ToPstr(char *);


/*
   Defined Constants
*/
#define requiredParamCount  (short)          3
#define errorFlag           (short)         -1
#define EOS                 (unsigned char)  0    /* end of string */
#define NIL                 (Handle)         0
#define afterCurrentMenus   (int)            0


pascal void    main(paramPtr)
   XCmdBlockPtr paramPtr;
{
   Str255          menuList;
   Str255          menuName;
   int             menuID;
   MenuHandle      myMenuHandle;

   if (CheckParamCount(paramPtr,"Form: AddMenu Name,Num,List") == errorFlag)
      return;

   /*
      Get the 1st param: the menu name
      CheckParamCount ensures 3 parameters.
   */
   HandleToPstr(menuName, paramPtr->params[0]);
   menuID = (int) HandleToNum(paramPtr, paramPtr->params[1]);
   if (menuID <= 0)
      {
         Fail(paramPtr, "Zero and negative menu IDs not allowed");
         return;
      }
   HandleToPstr(menuList, paramPtr->params[2]);
```

continued...

...from previous page

```
/*
    Convert empty string to single space character,
    Pascal-format string.
*/
if (menuList[0] == EOS)
    strcpy(menuList, "\1 ");
/*
    Create a new menu
    If failure, exit
*/
if ((myMenuHandle = NewMenu(menuID, menuName)) == (MenuHandle) NIL)
    {
        Fail(paramPtr, "Unable to allocate new menu");
        return;
    }
/*
    Add menuList to the new menu
    Add the menu to the ones in the menuBar
    Draw the menuBar
*/
AppendMenu(myMenuHandle, menuList);
InsertMenu(myMenuHandle, afterCurrentMenus);
DrawMenuBar();

    return;
}


/*
    This function checks to see if the correct number of params were received.
    And writes an error message into the returnValue if they were not.
*/
short CheckParamCount(paramPtr, str)
    XCmdBlockPtr paramPtr;
    char        *str;
{
    short   count;

    count = paramPtr->paramCount;
    if (count != requiredParamCount)
        {
            paramPtr->returnValue = (Handle) CopyStrToHand(str);
            return(errorFlag);
        }
    return(count);
}
```

continued...

...from previous page

```
/*
   This function gets a handle and copies the error string it receives into the
      heap for return to HyperCard.
*/
void Fail(paramPtr, str)
   XCmdBlockPtr   paramPtr;
   char           *str;
{
   paramPtr->returnValue = (Handle) CopyStrToHand(str);
   return;
}


/*
   This utility function allocates heapspace and copies a string into it.
*/
Handle CopyStrToHand(str)
   char *str;
{
   Handle   newHndl;

   newHndl = (Handle) NewHandle((long) strlen(str) + 1);
   strcpy((char *)(*newHndl), str);
   return(newHndl);
}


/*
   This function makes a callback to HyperCard to convert a string to an
   unsigned long integer.  It takes a handle to a C string as an argument.
*/
long HandleToNum(paramPtr, hndl)
   XCmdBlockPtr   paramPtr;
   Handle         hndl;
{
   char  str[32];
   long  num;

   strcpy(str, *hndl);
   num = StrToLong(paramPtr, (Str31 *) ToPstr(str));
   return(num);
}
```

continued...

...*from previous page*

```
/*
   This utility function copies the string pointed to by a handle into
   a character array, then converts the C string to a Pascal string.
   Note that the C string is overwritten by the Pascal string.
*/
void HandleToPstr(str, hndl)
   Str255   str;
   Handle   hndl;
{
   strcpy((char *) str, *hndl);
   ToPstr((char *) str);
}



/*
   This utility function converts a Pascal string to a C string.
   Note that the Pascal string is overwritten in the process.
*/
char *ToCstr(str)
   char *str;
{
   unsigned char length, i;

   length = str[0];
   for (i = 0; i < length; ++i)        /* Shift string 1 byte to the left */
      str[i] = str[i+1];
   str[length] = 0;                    /* Put zero-terminator after string */
   return(str);
}



/*
   This utility function converts a C string to a Pascal string.
   Note that the C string is overwritten in the process.
*/
char *ToPstr(str)
   char *str;
{
   unsigned char length, i;

   for (i = 0, length = 0; str[i] != 0; ++i)    /* Find end of string */
      ++length;
   while (i--)                                  /* Shift string 1 byte to right */
      str[i+1] = str[i];
   str[0] = length;                             /* Put string length in 1st byte */
   return(str);
}
```

ResMenu

The ResMenu command appends a menu of available resources of a given type to HyperCard's menu bar. (For example, ResMenu "Fonts",500,"FONT" would display a menu of all of your on-line fonts). Acceptable resource types include FONT, ICON, snd, XCMD, XFCN, and so on.

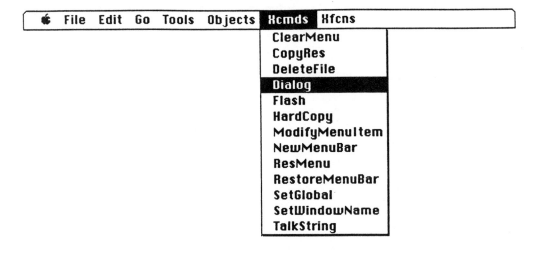

Figure 6.5

The result of the ResMenu command.

> **Note:** Use the ClearMenu XCMD (detailed later in this chapter) to remove a menu added with ResMenu. You can also use the ModifyMenuItem XCMD (also detailed later in this chapter) to change a menu item's text, icon, mark, and highlight.

Quick Reference

ResMenu "MenuName",MenuID,"Resource Type"

Parameters

ResMenu takes three parameters:

Parameter 1: The name you want to appear in HyperCard's menu bar.
Parameter 2: A unique number to be used in identifying this menu.
Parameter 3: The resource type exactly as you see it in the resource fork (this parameter is case-sensitive and should never contain more than four letters)

Examples

```
ResMenu  "Xcmd's",600,"XCMD"
ResMenu  "Xfcn's",799,"XFCN"
ResMenu  "Sounds",601,"snd "
ResMenu  "Fonts",602,"FONT"
ResMenu  "ICONS",603,"ICON"
```

Tips

When you choose a menu item from a menu added with ResMenu, it is sent as a DoMenu message to HyperCard. To intercept and act on the message, you must include a DoMenu message handler in your card, background, or stack script.

For the Pascal Programmer

```
{$R-}
( *
  © 1988 by Gary Bond
  All Rights Reserved

  ResMenu --  An XCMD that appends a menu of the specified resource type
              to the existing menu bar.

  Form: ResMenu MenuName,MenuID,Resource Type

  Example: ResMenu "Sounds",555,"snd "
```

   continued...

...from previous page

Note: Use the ClearMenu XCMD to get rid of menus created with the ResMenu XCMD.

To compile and link this file using MPW Pascal, select the following lines and press the ENTER key

---

```
pascal ResMenu.p
link -o "HD:Hypercard:Home" -rt XCMD=1510 -sn Main=ResMenu ResMenu.p.o ∂
-m ENTRYPOINT
```

*)

```
{$S ResMenu} {Segment name must be the same as the command name}

UNIT DummyUnit;

INTERFACE

USES MemTypes, QuickDraw, OSIntf, ToolIntf, HyperXCmd;

PROCEDURE ENTRYPOINT(paramPtr: XCmdPtr);

IMPLEMENTATION

TYPE Str31  =  String[31];

PROCEDURE ResMenu(paramPtr: XCmdPtr);        FORWARD;

  PROCEDURE ENTRYPOINT(paramPtr: XCmdPtr);

    BEGIN
      ResMenu(paramPtr);
    END;

  PROCEDURE ResMenu(paramPtr: XCmdPtr);

    CONST minParamCount = 3;
```

continued...

...from previous page

```
VAR     menuName:      Str255;
        tempStr:       Str255;
        resName:       ResType;
        menuID:        LongInt;
        i :            Integer;
        myMenuHandle:  MenuHandle;

{$I XCmdGlue.inc } {Includes the glue routines}

  PROCEDURE Fail(errStr: Str255);  {Exit returning an error message}

    BEGIN
      paramPtr^.returnValue := PasToZero(errStr); {load the result}
      EXIT(ResMenu); {leave the XCMD}
    END; {Fail}


  PROCEDURE CheckParamCount; {checks for the correct parameter count}

    VAR numParams: Integer;

    BEGIN
      numParams := paramPtr^.paramCount; {store the number of parameters passed}
      IF (numParams <> minParamCount)
      THEN Fail('Form: ResMenu "MenuName",MenuNumber,"Resource Type"');
    END; {CheckParamCount}

BEGIN {main}
  CheckParamCount; {make sure there's enough parameters}
  ZeroToPas(paramPtr^.params[1]^,menuName); {convert the menu name}
  ZeroToPas(paramPtr^.params[2]^,tempStr);
  menuID := StrToLong(tempStr); {convert the menu number}
  IF menuID <= 0 THEN Fail('Zero and negative numbers not allowed');
  ZeroToPas(paramPtr^.params[3]^,tempStr); {convert the resource type}
  FOR i := 1 to 4 DO resName[i] := tempStr[i]; {move string to packed array}
  myMenuHandle := NewMenu(MenuID,menuName); {create a new menu item}
  IF myMenuHandle = NIL THEN Fail('Unable to get menu handle');
  AddResMenu(myMenuHandle,resName); {append resource items to new menu}
  InsertMenu(myMenuHandle,0); {adds the menu to the end of the menu list}
  DrawMenuBar; {draw the menu bar with the new menu}
END; {main}


END. {ResMenu}
```

For the C Programmer

```
/*
   © 1988 by Gary Bond
   All Rights Reserved

   Translated to C by Sioux Lacy

   ResMenu:   An XCMD that appends a menu of the specified resource type
              to the existing menu bar.

   Form:      ResMenu MenuName, MenuID, ResourceType

   Example:   ResMenu "Sounds", 555, "snd "

   Note:      Use ClearMenu to get rid of menus created with the ResMenu XCMD.
   _____

   Compile and link this file with the MacTraps and string libraries
*/


/*
   Includes
   Note that these header files are for LightspeedC development.
   Substitute the files that are appropriate for your compiler.
*/
#include <MacTypes.h>
#include <MenuMgr.h>
#include "HyperXCmd.h"

/*
   LightspeedC Prototypes
*/
pascal   void   main(XCmdBlockPtr);
void     HandleToBytes(char *, Handle);
short    CheckParamCount(XCmdBlockPtr, char *);
void     Fail(XCmdBlockPtr, char *);
Handle   CopyStrToHand(char *);
long     HandleToNum(XCmdBlockPtr, Handle);
void     HandleToPstr(Str255, Handle);
char     *ToPstr(char *);
```

continued...

...from previous page

```
/*
   Defined Constants
*/
#define requiredParamCount  (short)           3
#define errorFlag           (short)          -1
#define NIL                 (Handle)          0
#define EOS                 (unsigned char)   0    /* end of string */
#define afterCurrentMenus   (int) 0

pascal void    main(paramPtr)
   XCmdBlockPtr paramPtr;
{
   Str255          menuName;
   ResType         resName;
   int             menuID;
   MenuHandle      myMenuHandle;

   if (CheckParamCount
      (paramPtr, "Form: ResMenu \"MenuName\",MenuNumber,\"ResourceType\"")
      == errorFlag)
      return;


   HandleToPstr(menuName, paramPtr->params[0]);
   menuID = (int) HandleToNum(paramPtr, paramPtr->params[1]);
   if (menuID <= 0)
      {
         Fail(paramPtr, "Zero and negative menu IDs not allowed");
         return;
      }
   HandleToBytes((char *) &resName, paramPtr->params[2]);
   /*
      Create a new menu
      If failure, exit
   */
   if ((myMenuHandle = NewMenu(menuID, menuName)) == (MenuHandle) NIL)
      {
         Fail(paramPtr, "Unable to allocate new menu");
         return;
      }
   /*
      Append resource items to new menu
      Add the menu to the end of the menu list
      Draw the menuBar
   */
   AddResMenu(myMenuHandle, (ResType) resName);
   InsertMenu(myMenuHandle, afterCurrentMenus);
   DrawMenuBar();
```

continued...

...from previous page

```
        return;
}


/*
    This function copies the string pointed to by a handle into an array
    of bytes.  It does not copy the terminating 0.
*/
void HandleToBytes(array, hndl)
    char      *array;
    Handle    hndl;
{
    char *ptr;

    HLock(hndl);
    ptr = *hndl;
    while (*ptr != EOS)
        *array++ = *ptr++;
    HUnlock(hndl);
}


/*
    This function checks to see if the correct number of params were received.
    And writes an error message into the returnValue if they were not.
*/
short CheckParamCount(paramPtr, str)
    XCmdBlockPtr paramPtr;
    char         *str;
{
    short    count;

    count = paramPtr->paramCount;
    if (count != requiredParamCount)
        {
            paramPtr->returnValue = (Handle) CopyStrToHand(str);
            return(errorFlag);
        }
    return(count);
}


/*
    This function gets a handle and copies the error string it receives into the
    heap for return to HyperCard.
*/
```

continued...

...from previous page

```
void Fail(paramPtr, str)
   XCmdBlockPtr   paramPtr;
   char           *str;
{
   paramPtr->returnValue = (Handle) CopyStrToHand(str);
   return;
}


/*
   This utility function allocates heapspace and copies a string into it.
*/
Handle CopyStrToHand(str)
   char *str;
{
   Handle   newHndl;

   newHndl = (Handle) NewHandle((long) strlen(str) + 1);
   strcpy((char *)(*newHndl), str);
   return(newHndl);
}


/*
   This function makes a callback to HyperCard to convert a string to an
   unsigned long integer.  It takes a handle to a C string as an argument.
*/
long HandleToNum(paramPtr, hndl)
   XCmdBlockPtr   paramPtr;
   Handle         hndl;
{
   char  str[32];
   long  num;

   strcpy(str, *hndl);
   num = StrToLong(paramPtr, (Str31 *) ToPstr(str));
   return(num);
}


/*
   This utility function copies the string pointed to by a handle into
   a character array, then converts the C string to a Pascal string.
   Note that the C string is overwritten by the Pascal string.
*/
```

continued...

...from previous page

```
void HandleToPstr(str, hndl)
   Str255   str;
   Handle   hndl;
{
   strcpy((char *) str, *hndl);
   ToPstr((char *) str);
}


/*
   This utility function converts a C string to a Pascal string.
   Note that the C string is overwritten in the process.
*/
char *ToPstr(str)
   char *str;
{
   unsigned char length, i;

   for (i = 0, length = 0; str[i] != 0; ++i)     /* Find end of string */
      ++length;
   while (i--)                                    /* Shift string 1 byte to right */
      str[i+1] = str[i];
   str[0] = length;                               /* Put string length in 1st byte */
   return(str);
}
```

ClearMenu

The ClearMenu command removes a menu from HyperCard's menu bar. The menu to be removed must be specified by its menu ID number.

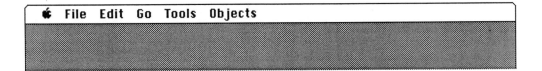

Figure 6.6

The result of the ClearMenu command.

Quick Reference

ClearMenu MenuID

Parameters

ClearMenu takes one parameter:

Parameter 1: The menu ID number of the menu to be removed.

Examples

ClearMenu 500
ClearMenu 324
ClearMenu 107

Tips

If you want to clear any of HyperCard's normal menus, look in HyperCard's resource fork for the MenuID number of the menu you want to clear.

For the Pascal Programmer

```
{$R-}
( *
  © 1988 by Gary Bond
  All Rights Reserved

  ClearMenu -- a Hypercard XCMD that removes a menu added with the AddMenu XCMD.

  Form: ClearMenu MenuID

  Example: ClearMenu 500

  Note: You must use ClearMenu to get rid of added menu items - even after they've been
  erased from the menu bar by Hypercard.
```

continued...

...from previous page

To compile and link this file using MPW Pascal, select the following lines and press the ENTER key

---

```
pascal ClearMenu.p
link -o "HD:Hypercard:Home" -rt XCMD=1511 ∂
-sn Main=ClearMenu ClearMenu.p.o -m ENTRYPOINT
```

*)

{$S ClearMenu} {Segment name must be the same as the command name}

UNIT DummyUnit;

INTERFACE

USES MemTypes, QuickDraw, OSIntf, ToolIntf, HyperXCmd;

PROCEDURE ENTRYPOINT(paramPtr: XCmdPtr);

IMPLEMENTATION

TYPE Str31 = String[31];

PROCEDURE ClearMenu(paramPtr: XCmdPtr);   FORWARD;

  PROCEDURE ENTRYPOINT(paramPtr: XCmdPtr);

BEGIN
   ClearMenu(paramPtr);
END;

  PROCEDURE ClearMenu(paramPtr: XCmdPtr);

   CONST minParamCount = 1;

   VAR tempStr: Str255;
        menuID: LongInt;
        myMenuHandle: MenuHandle;
```

*continued...*
```

...from previous page

```
{$I XCmdGlue.inc } {Includes the glue routines}

  PROCEDURE Fail(errStr: Str255); {Exit returning an error message}

    BEGIN
      paramPtr^.returnValue := PasToZero(errStr); {load the result}
      EXIT(ClearMenu); {Leave the XCMD}
    END; {Fail}

  PROCEDURE CheckParamCount; {checks for the correct parameter count}

    VAR numParams: Integer;

    BEGIN
      numParams := paramPtr^.paramCount; {store the number of parameters passed}
      IF (numParams <> minParamCount)
      THEN Fail('Form: ClearMenu MenuID');
    END; {CheckParamCount}

  BEGIN {main}
    CheckParamCount; {make sure there's enough parameters}
    ZeroToPas(paramPtr^.params[1]^,tempStr);
    menuID := StrToLong(tempStr); {get and store the ID}
    IF menuID <= 0 THEN Fail('Zero and negative numbers not allowed');
    myMenuHandle := GetMHandle(MenuID); {disposeMenu needs a handle}
    IF myMenuHandle = NIL THEN Fail('Cannot find that menu item');
    deleteMenu(MenuID); {must remove it from the menu list before deleting}
    disposeMenu(myMenuHandle); {delete the menu item}
    DrawMenuBar; {draw the menu bar without the item}
  END; {main}

END. {ClearMenu}
```

For the C Programmer

```
/*
    © 1988 by Gary Bond
    All Rights Reserved

    Translated to C by Sioux Lacy

    ClearMenu:      a Hypercard XCMD that removes a menu added with the AddMenu XCMD

    Form:           ClearMenu MenuID

    Example:        ClearMenu 500

    Note:           You must use ClearMenu to get rid of added menus -
                    even after they've been erased from the menu bar by HyperCard.

    ───────────────────────────────────────────────────────────────────

    Compile and link this file with the MacTraps and string libraries
*/


/*
    Includes
    Note that these header files are for LightspeedC development.
    Substitute the files that are appropriate for your compiler.
*/
#include <MacTypes.h>
#include <MenuMgr.h>
#include "HyperXCmd.h"

/*
    LightspeedC Prototypes
*/
pascal  void main(XCmdBlockPtr);
short   CheckParamCount(XCmdBlockPtr, char *);
void    Fail(XCmdBlockPtr, char *);
Handle  CopyStrToHand(char *);
long    HandleToNum(XCmdBlockPtr, Handle);
char    *ToPstr(char *);


/*
    Defined Constants
*/
#define requiredParamCount  (short)    1
#define errorFlag           (short)   -1
#define NIL                 (Handle)   0
```

continued...

...from previous page

```
pascal void    main(paramPtr)
   XCmdBlockPtr paramPtr;
{
   int         menuID;
   MenuHandle  myMenuHandle;

   if (CheckParamCount(paramPtr, "Form: ClearMenu MenuID") == errorFlag)
      return;

   /*
      Get the only param: the menu ID
      Return error string if menu ID is not valid
   */
   menuID = (int) HandleToNum(paramPtr, paramPtr->params[0]);
   if (menuID <= 0)
      {
         Fail(paramPtr, "Zero and negative menu IDs not allowed");
         return;
      }
   /*
      Get menuHandle associated with menuID
      Remove menu from the list
      Dispose of its handle
      Draw the menuBar without the menu
   */
   if ((myMenuHandle = GetMHandle(menuID)) == (MenuHandle) NIL)
      {
         Fail(paramPtr, "Cannot find that menu");
         return;
      }
   DeleteMenu(menuID);
   DisposeMenu(myMenuHandle);
   DrawMenuBar();

   return;
}


/*
   This function checks to see if the correct number of params were received.
   And writes an error message into the returnValue if they were not.
*/
short CheckParamCount(paramPtr, str)
   XCmdBlockPtr paramPtr;
   char        *str;
{
   short    count;
```

continued...

...from previous page

```
    count = paramPtr->paramCount;
    if (count != requiredParamCount)
        {
            paramPtr->returnValue = (Handle) CopyStrToHand (str);
            return(errorFlag);
        }
    return(count);
}


/*
    This function gets a handle and copies the error string it receives into the
heap
    for return to HyperCard.
*/
void Fail(paramPtr, str)
    XCmdBlockPtr   paramPtr;
    char           *str;
{
    paramPtr->returnValue = (Handle) CopyStrToHand(str);
    return;
}


/*
    This utility function allocates heapspace and copies a string into it.
*/
Handle CopyStrToHand(str)
    char *str;
{
    Handle   newHndl;

    newHndl = (Handle) NewHandle((long) strlen(str) + 1);
    strcpy((char *)(*newHndl), str);
    return(newHndl);
}


/*
    This function makes a callback to HyperCard to convert a string to an
    unsigned long integer.  It takes a handle to a C string as an argument.
*/
long HandleToNum(paramPtr, hndl)
    XCmdBlockPtr   paramPtr;
    Handle         hndl;
{
    char   str[32];
    long   num;
```

continued...

...from previous page

```
    strcpy(str, *hndl);
    num = StrToLong(paramPtr, (Str31 *) ToPstr(str));
    return(num);
}


/*
    This utility function converts a C string to a Pascal string.
    Note that the C string is overwritten in the process.
*/
char *ToPstr(str)
    char *str;
{
    unsigned char length, i;

    for (i = 0, length = 0; str[i] != 0; ++i)        /* Find end of string */
        ++length;
    while (i--)                                       /* Shift string 1 byte to right */
        str[i+1] = str[i];
    str[0] = length;                                  /* Put string length in 1st byte */
    return(str);
}
```

ModifyMenuItem

The ModifyMenuItem command allows you to change the text, icon, mark (√ or other mark), and highlight (gray or black) of any menu item in any menu.

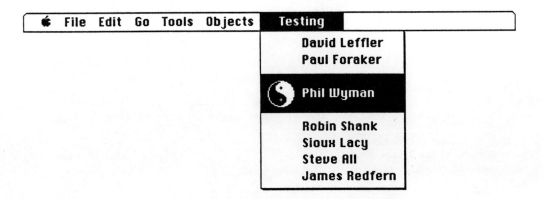

Figure 6.7

The result of the ModifyMenuItem command

Quick Reference

ModifyMenuItem MenuID,MenuItem,VisFlag,Mark,Icon,Text

Parameters

ModifyMenuItem takes six parameters:

Parameter 1: A number used to identify the menu in which an item is to be modified.
Parameter 2: The number of the menu item you want to modify (the first item in a menu is number one—lines or menu choices that are grayed in a menu count as one menu item).
Parameter 3: Pass FALSE if you want the item to be inactive (grayed) or TRUE if you want it to be active (black).
Parameter 4: The ASCII value of the mark you want to place to the left of the specified menu item (such as a check mark).
Parameter 5: Number of the icon (257-511) you want displayed to the left of the menu item. Use HyperTalk's constant EMPTY to remove an icon from a menu.
Parameter 6: Changes the text of the specified menu item. (The user interface guidelines recommend doing this sparingly; it has a tendency to confuse the user.)

The default values for omitted parameters are as follows:

Default for parameter 1: Must be supplied—no default.
Default for parameter 2: Must be supplied—no default.
Default for parameter 3: Must be supplied—defaults to inactive (grayed out).
Default for parameter 4: Optional—defaults to no change. Pass empty to remove the mark.
Default for parameter 5: Optional—defaults to no change. Pass empty to remove the icon.
Default for parameter 6: Optional—no default.

Examples

ModifyMenuItem 500,3,TRUE -- enable a menu item
ModifyMenuItem 799,7,FALSE -- disable a menu item
ModifyMenuItem 343,4,TRUE,CharToNum("√") -- check a menu item
ModifyMenuItem 343,4,TRUE,empty -- uncheck a menu item
ModifyMenuItem 555,1,TRUE,empty,300 -- show an icon next to menu item 1
ModifyMenuItem 555,1,TRUE,empty,300 -- remove an icon
ModifyMenuItem 555,2,TRUE,CharToNum("√"),309 --show icon & check item
ModifyMenuItem 865,10,TRUE,empty,empty,"New Text" --change item text
ModifyMenuItem 865,10,TRUE,CharToNum("√"),309,"Ankh" -- change it all

Tips

• You can determine the menuID numbers for HyperCard's menus from HyperCard's resource fork, using Resedit or a similar resource editor.

• An easy way to specify the mark is with HyperTalk's CharToNum function as follows:

CharToNum("√")

• You can use ResEdit or any other resource editor to renumber existing icons so they fall within the correct range (257-511).

> **Note:** when using icons, only the name of the menu item is sent as a doMenu message; the name of the icon is not sent.

For the Pascal Programmer

{$R-}
(*
© 1988 by Gary Bond
All Rights Reserved

ModifyMenuItem -- a Hypercard XCMD that lets you change the text, icon, mark and visibility of the specified menu item. You must know the menuID and item number of the menu item.

continued...

...from previous page

Form: ModifyMenuItem MenuID,MenuItem,VisFlag,Mark,Icon,Text

Example: ModifyMenuItem 500,3,TRUE,NumToChar(65),200,"My New Text"

Note: The last 3 parameters may be optionally omitted. You ca use the HyperTalk constant 'empty' to remove a mark or icon.

To compile and link this file using MPW Pascal, select the following lines and press the ENTER key

---

```
pascal ModifyMenuItem.p
link -o "HD:Hypercard:Home" -rt XCMD=1512 -sn ∂
Main=ModifyMenuItem ModifyMenuItem.p.o ∂
{MPW}PLibraries:PasLib.o -m ENTRYPOINT
```

*)

{$S ModifyMenuItem} {Segment name must be the same as the command name}

UNIT DummyUnit;

INTERFACE

USES MemTypes, QuickDraw, OSIntf, ToolIntf, PasLibIntf, HyperXCmd;

PROCEDURE ENTRYPOINT(paramPtr: XCmdPtr);

IMPLEMENTATION

TYPE Str31 = String[31];

PROCEDURE ModifyMenuItem(paramPtr: XCmdPtr);   FORWARD;

  PROCEDURE ENTRYPOINT(paramPtr: XCmdPtr);

    BEGIN
      ModifyMenuItem(paramPtr);
    END;

  continued...

...from previous page

```
PROCEDURE ModifyMenuItem(paramPtr: XCmdPtr);

   CONST  minParamCount = 3;
          maxParamCount = 6;

   VAR  tempStr:        Str255;
        menuText:       Str255;
        markChar:       Char;
        menuID:         LongInt;
        menuItem:       LongInt;
        iconNum:        LongInt;
        myMark:         LongInt;
        visFlag:        Boolean;
        myMenuHandle:   MenuHandle;

{$I XCmdGlue.inc } {Includes the glue routines}

   PROCEDURE Fail(errStr: Str255); {Exit returning an error message}

      BEGIN
        paramPtr^.returnValue := PasToZero(errStr); {load the result}
        EXIT(ModifyMenuItem); {Leave the XCMD}
      END; {Fail}

   PROCEDURE CheckParamCount; {checks for the correct parameter count}

      VAR numParams: Integer;

      BEGIN
        numParams := paramPtr^.paramCount; {store the number of parameters passed}
        IF ((numParams < minParamCount) OR (numParams > maxParamCount))
        THEN Fail('Form: ModifyMenuItem MenuId,MenuItem,VisFlag,Mark,Icon,Text');
      END; {CheckParamCount}

BEGIN {main}
  CheckParamCount; {make sure there's enough parameters}
  ZeroToPas(paramPtr^.params[1]^,tempStr);
  menuId := StrToNum(tempStr); {convert the ID number}
  ZeroToPas(paramPtr^.params[2]^,tempStr);
```

continued...

...from previous page

```
menuItem := StrToNum(tempStr); {convert the item number}
ZeroToPas(paramPtr^.params[3]^,tempStr);
visFlag := StrToBool(tempStr); {convert the visible boolean - TRUE = visible}
myMenuHandle := GetMHandle(MenuId); {get a handle to the menu being changed}

CASE paramPtr^.paramCount OF
  3: {menuID,menuItem,visFlag}
    BEGIN
      IF VisFlag THEN EnableItem(myMenuHandle,menuItem)
      ELSE DisableItem(myMenuHandle,menuItem);
    END; {case 3}
  4: {menuID,menuItem,visFlag,mark}
    BEGIN
      IF VisFlag THEN EnableItem(myMenuHandle,menuItem)
      ELSE DisableItem(myMenuHandle,menuItem);
      ZeroToPas(paramPtr^.params[4]^,tempStr);
      myMark := StrToNum(tempStr); {convert character to use as a mark}
      markChar := CHR(myMark);
      SetItemMark(myMenuHandle,MenuItem,markChar);
    END; {case 4}
  5: {menuID,menuItem,visFlag,mark,Icon} {icon number must be 257-511}
    BEGIN
      IF VisFlag THEN EnableItem(myMenuHandle,menuItem)
      ELSE DisableItem(myMenuHandle,menuItem);
      ZeroToPas(paramPtr^.params[4]^,tempStr);
      myMark := StrToNum(tempStr); {convert character to use as a mark}
      markChar := CHR(myMark);
      SetItemMark(myMenuHandle,MenuItem,markChar);
      ZeroToPas(paramPtr^.params[5]^,tempStr);
      IF tempStr = '' THEN iconNum := 0 {turn it off is passes an EMPTY}
      ELSE BEGIN
        iconNum := StrToNum(tempStr);
        IF ((iconNum < 257) OR (iconNum > 511))
        THEN Fail('Icon numbers must be in the range 257-511');
      END;
      SetItemIcon(myMenuHandle,menuItem,iconNum);
    END; {case 5}
  6: {menuID,menuItem,visFlag,mark,Icon,Text}
```

continued...

...from previous page

```
      BEGIN{case 6}
        IF VisFlag THEN EnableItem(myMenuHandle,menuItem)
        ELSE DisableItem(myMenuHandle,menuItem);
        ZeroToPas(paramPtr^.params[4]^,tempStr);
        myMark := StrToNum(tempStr); {convert character to use as a mark}
        markChar := CHR(myMark);
        SetItemMark(myMenuHandle,MenuItem,markChar);
        ZeroToPas(paramPtr^.params[5]^,tempStr);
        IF tempStr = '' THEN iconNum := 0 {turn it off is passes an EMPTY}
        ELSE BEGIN
          iconNum := StrToNum(tempStr);
          IF ((iconNum < 257) OR (iconNum > 511))
          THEN Fail('Icon numbers must be in the range 257-511');
        END; {else}
        SetItemIcon(myMenuHandle,menuItem,iconNum);
        ZeroToPas(paramPtr^.params[6]^,menuText);
        IF (menuText = '') THEN Fail('Menu text must not be empty');
        SetItem(myMenuHandle,menuItem,menuText);
      END; {case 6}
    END; {case}
  END; {main}

END. {ModifyMenuItem}
```

For the C Programmer

```
/*
    © 1988 by Gary Bond
    All Rights Reserved

    Translated to C by Sioux Lacy

    ModifyMenuItem:    a Hypercard XCMD that lets you change the text, icon, mark
                       and visibility of the specified menu item.  You must know
                       the menuID
                       and item number of the menu item.

    Form:              ModifyMenuItem MenuID, MenuItem,  VisFlag, Mark, Icon, Text

    Example:           ModifyMenuItem 500, 3, TRUE, NumToChar(65), 200, "My New
                       Text"

    Note:              The last 3 parameters may be optionally omitted. You can use
                       the HyperTalk constant 'empty' to remove a mark or icon.
    ─────────────────────────────────────────────────────────────────────────
    Compile and link this file with the MacTraps and string libraries
*/


/*
    Includes
    Note that these header files are for LightspeedC development.
    Substitute the files that are appropriate for your compiler.
*/
#include <MacTypes.h>
#include <MenuMgr.h>
#include "HyperXCmd.h"

/*
    LightspeedC Prototypes
*/
pascal    void main(XCmdBlockPtr);
short     GetParamCount(XCmdBlockPtr, char *);
void      Fail(XCmdBlockPtr, char *);
Handle    CopyStrToHand(char *);
Boolean   HandleToBool(XCmdBlockPtr, Handle);
long      HandleToNum(XCmdBlockPtr, Handle);
void      HandleToPstr(Str255, Handle);
char      *ToCstr(char *);
char      *ToPstr(char *);
```

continued...

...from previous page

```
/*
   Defined Constants
*/
#define  minParamCount      (short)            3
#define  maxParamCount      (short)            6
#define  errorFlag          (short)           -1
#define  EOS                (unsigned char)    0
#define  NIL                (Handle)           0
#define  afterCurrentMenus  (int)              0


pascal void   main(paramPtr)
   XCmdBlockPtr paramPtr;
{
   Str255       menuText;
   char         markChar;
   int          menuID;
   int          menuItem;
   int          myMark;
   Byte         iconNum;
   Boolean      visFlag;
   MenuHandle   myMenuHandle;
   short        paramCount;

   if ((paramCount = GetParamCount(paramPtr,
      "Form: ModifyMenuItem Id,Item,VisFlag,Mark,Icon,Text")) == errorFlag)
      return;

   /*
      Get the 1st 3 parameters: the menuID, menuItem, visibility flag
      Get a handle to the menu being changed.
   */
   menuID = (int) HandleToNum(paramPtr, paramPtr->params[0]);
   if (menuID <= 0)
      {
         Fail(paramPtr, "Zero and negative menu IDs not allowed");
         return;
      }
   menuItem = (int) HandleToNum(paramPtr, paramPtr->params[1]);
   visFlag = (Boolean) HandleToBool(paramPtr, paramPtr->params[2]);
   myMenuHandle = GetMHandle(menuID);
   if (visFlag == TRUE)
      EnableItem(myMenuHandle, menuItem);
   else
      DisableItem(myMenuHandle, menuItem);
```

continued...

...from previous page

```
switch (paramCount)
    {
        case 6: /* menuID, menuItem, visFlag, mark, icon, text */
            HandleToPstr(menuText, paramPtr->params[5]);
            if (menuText[0] == 0)
                {
                    Fail(paramPtr, "Menu text must not be empty");
                    return;
                }
            SetItem(myMenuHandle, menuItem, menuText);
            /* Note that there is no break here. Fall thru to the next case is
               intentional */

        case 5: /* menuID, menuItem, visFlag, mark, icon */
            iconNum = (int) HandleToNum(paramPtr, paramPtr->params[4]);
            if ((iconNum < 257) || (iconNum > 511))
                {
                    Fail(paramPtr, "Icon numbers must be in the range 257 - 511");
                    return;
                }
            SetItemIcon(myMenuHandle, menuItem, iconNum);
            /* Note that there is no break here. Fall thru to the next case is
               intentional */

        case 4: /* menuID, menuItem,visFlag, mark */
            markChar = (char) **(paramPtr->params[3]);
            SetItemMark(myMenuHandle, menuItem, markChar);
            break;
    }
    return;
}
```

continued...

...from previous page

```
/*
    This function checks to see if the correct number of params were received.
    And writes an error message into the returnValue if they were not.
*/
short GetParamCount(paramPtr, str)
    XCmdBlockPtr paramPtr;
    char          *str;
{
    short     count;

    count = paramPtr->paramCount;
    if ((count > maxParamCount) || (count < minParamCount))
        {
            paramPtr->returnValue = (Handle) CopyStrToHand(str);
            return(errorFlag);
        }
    return(count);
}



/*
    This function gets a handle and copies the error string it receives into the
        heap for return to HyperCard.
*/
void Fail(paramPtr, str)
    XCmdBlockPtr   paramPtr;
    char           *str;
{
    paramPtr->returnValue = (Handle) CopyStrToHand(str);
    return;
}
```

continued...

...from previous page

```
/*
   This utility function allocates heapspace and copies a string into it.
*/
Handle CopyStrToHand(str)
   char *str;
{
   Handle   newHndl;

   newHndl = (Handle) NewHandle((long) strlen(str) + 1);
   strcpy((char *)(*newHndl), str);
   return(newHndl);
}


/*
   This function makes a callback to HyperCard to convert a string to an
   boolean (true/false).  It takes a handle to a C string as an argument.
*/
Boolean HandleToBool(paramPtr, hndl)
   XCmdBlockPtr   paramPtr;
   Handle         hndl;
{
   Str31      str;

   HandleToPstr(str, hndl);
   return(StrToBool(paramPtr, &str));
}


/*
   This function makes a callback to HyperCard to convert a string to an
   unsigned long integer.  It takes a handle to a C string as an argument.
*/
long HandleToNum(paramPtr, hndl)
   XCmdBlockPtr   paramPtr;
   Handle         hndl;
{
   char  str[32];
   long  num;

   strcpy(str, *hndl);
   num = StrToLong(paramPtr, (Str31 *) ToPstr(str));
   return(num);
}
```

continued...

...from previous page

```
/*
   This utility function copies the string pointed to by a handle into
   a character array, then converts the C string to a Pascal string.
   Note that the C string is overwritten by the Pascal string.
*/
void HandleToPstr(str, hndl)
   Str255   str;
   Handle   hndl;
{
   strcpy((char *) str, *hndl);
   ToPstr((char *) str);
}


/*
   This utility function converts a Pascal string to a C string.
   Note that the Pascal string is overwritten in the process.
*/
char *ToCstr(str)
   char *str;
{
   unsigned char length, i;

   length = str[0];
   for (i = 0; i < length; ++i)        /* Shift string 1 byte to the left */
      str[i] = str[i+1];
   str[length] = 0;                    /* Put zero-terminator after string */
   return(str);
}


/*
   This utility function converts a C string to a Pascal string.
   Note that the C string is overwritten in the process.
*/
char *ToPstr(str)
   char *str;
{
   unsigned char length, i;

   for (i = 0, length = 0; str[i] != 0; ++i)    /* Find end of string */
      ++length;
   while (i--)                                  /* Shift string 1 byte to right */
      str[i+1] = str[i];
   str[0] = length;                             /* Put string length in 1st byte */
   return(str);
}
```

SmartSum

The SmartSum function returns the sum of its arguments. SmartSum is intelligent; if there is more than one argument (up to 16), SmartSum adds each separately. If there is only one argument, SmartSum searches for commas and—if found—parses the comma-separated items (up to 255 characters) and then adds them (if it doesn't find a comma, it parses the return-separated items and adds them).

Quick Reference

SmartSum(value1,value2,value3....value16) -- up to 16 parameters
SmartSum("comma separated list of values") -- up to 255 characters

Parameters

SmartSum takes up to 16 parameters:

Parameter 1:   comma or RETURN separated list of values to sum (includes any container).
Parameter 2-16: values to sum.

Examples

SmartSum(card field 3)
SmartSum(Var)
SmartSum(the selection)
SmartSum(1,2,3,4,5) -- individual parameters
SmartSum("45.12,649,14.95,9,12.50") -- quoted list

Tips

Due to a bug in the external interface, HyperCard will crash if you supply more than 16 parameters to this or any other XCMD or XFCN in versions of HyperCard through 1.1.

For the Pascal Programmer

```
{$R-}
( *
  © 1988 by Gary Bond
  All Rights Reserved

     SmartSum -- a Hypercard XFCN that intelligently sums its arguments. If there's more
                 than one argument, SmartSum adds each separately. If there's only one
                 argument, SmartSum looks for a comma - if found it parses the comma
                 separated items and adds them.  If no comma was found, it parses the
                 return separated items and adds them.

     Form:  SmartSum([container|parameter  list])

     Example:   SmartSum(card field 3)
                SmartSum(Var)
                SmartSum(the  selection)
                SmartSum(1,2,3)
                SmartSum("12.95,14.95,24.95")

  Note:  When adding individual parameters, the limit imposed by the external interface
  is 16.
```

To compile and link this file using MPW Pascal, select the following lines and press
the ENTER key

```
pascal SmartSum.p
link -o "HD:Hypercard:Home" -rt XFCN=1513 ∂
-sn Main=SmartSum SmartSum.p.o ∂
{MPW}PLibraries:PasLib.o -m ENTRYPOINT ∂
{MPW}Libraries:Interface.o -m ENTRYPOINT

* )

{$S SmartSum } {Segment name must be the same as the command name}

UNIT DummyUnit;

INTERFACE
```

continued...

...from previous page

USES MemTypes, QuickDraw, OSIntf, ToolIntf, PasLibIntf, PackIntf, HyperXCmd;

PROCEDURE ENTRYPOINT(paramPtr: XCmdPtr);

IMPLEMENTATION

TYPE Str31 = String[31];

PROCEDURE SmartSum(paramPtr: XCmdPtr);   FORWARD;

  PROCEDURE ENTRYPOINT(paramPtr: XCmdPtr);

  BEGIN
    SmartSum(paramPtr);
  END;

  PROCEDURE SmartSum(paramPtr: XCmdPtr);

```
    VAR  tempStr:    Str255;
         container:  Str255;
         scanPtr:    Ptr;
         count:      Integer;
         i :         Integer;
         commaLoc:   Integer;
         total :     Extended;
         exitLoop:   Boolean;
```

{$I XCmdGlue.inc } {includes the glue routines}

  PROCEDURE Fail(errStr: Str255); {Exit returning an error message}

  BEGIN
    paramPtr^.returnValue := PasToZero(errStr); {load the result}
    EXIT(SmartSum); {leave the XFCN}
  END; {Fail}

  FUNCTION CollectToComma(VAR scanPtr: Ptr): Str255;

continued...

...from previous page

```
TYPE Str1 = String[1];

VAR  exitLoop:  Boolean;
     tempStr:   Str1;
     collectStr: Str255;


BEGIN {CollectToComma}
  exitLoop := FALSE; {set to enter loop}
  tempStr[0] := chr(1); {make a 1 character pascal string}
  collectStr := ''; {initialize it}
  REPEAT {look for comma or end of string}
  IF ((scanPtr^ = $2C) OR (scanPtr^ = $0)) THEN exitLoop := TRUE
  ELSE {gather the characters one at a time if comma or zero not found}
    BEGIN
      tempStr[1] := chr(scanPtr^); {convert 1 character}
      collectStr := CONCAT(collectStr,tempStr); {make a string of characters}
      scanPtr := POINTER(ORD(scanPtr)+1); {advance the pointer 1 position}
      END;
  UNTIL exitLoop = TRUE;
  CollectToComma := collectStr; {return the result of the function call}
END; {CollectToComma}

BEGIN {main}
  IF (paramPtr^.paramCount > 16) THEN Fail('Only 16 parameters allowed');
  total := 0; {reset the total}
  IF (paramPtr^.paramCount > 1) THEN {do a list sum}
    BEGIN
      FOR count := 1 TO (paramPtr^.paramCount) DO
        BEGIN
          ZeroToPas(paramPtr^.params[count]^,tempStr);
          total := total + StrToExt(tempStr); {add them as we go}
          END;
    END {if paramCount}

ELSE {Otherwise do a container sum - but parse for a comma}

  BEGIN {container parse}
    MoveHHi(paramPtr^.params[1]); {dont want this moving while we parse}
    HLock(paramPtr^.params[1]);
```

continued...

...from previous page

```
HNoPurge(paramPtr^.params[1]);
ZeroToPas(paramPtr^.params[1]^,container); {get the container}
IF Pos(',',container) <> 0 THEN {if there's a comma then parse the list}
  BEGIN {parse comma}
    exitLoop := TRUE; {initialize the loop starting value}
    scanPtr := paramPtr^.params[1]^; {make a local copy}

    WHILE exitLoop DO {collect and add comma separated values}
      BEGIN
        tempStr := CollectToComma(scanPtr); {get next value}
        total := total + StrToExt(tempStr); {add them up}
        IF scanPtr^ = 0 THEN exitLoop := FALSE {end of the zero string?}
        ELSE
          BEGIN
            scanPtr := Pointer(ORD(scanPtr)+1); {incr past comma}
            IF scanPtr^ = 0 THEN exitLoop := FALSE; {end of zero string?}
          END;
      END; {while loop}
  END {parse comma}

ELSE {if no comma then it must be a normal container}

  BEGIN {else}
    count := 1; {initialize the count}
    scanPtr := paramPtr^.params[1]^; {initialize the pointer}
    exitloop := TRUE; {initialize the loop conditional}

    WHILE exitLoop DO {add the lines}
      BEGIN {while}
        ReturnToPas(scanPtr,tempStr); {collect to next return}
        total := total + StrToExt(tempStr);
        ScanToReturn(scanPtr); {look for following return}
        IF scanPtr^ = 0 THEN exitLoop := FALSE; {end of zero string?}
        scanPtr := Pointer(ORD(scanPtr)+1); {incr past return}
        IF scanPtr^ = 0 THEN exitLoop := FALSE; {end of zero string?}
      END; {while}
  END {else}

END; {if}
HUnLock(paramPtr^.params[1]); {clean-up}
```

continued...

...from previous page

```
    HPurge(paramPtr^.params[1]);
    paramPtr^.returnValue := PasToZero(ExtToStr(total)); {return the total}
  END; {main}


END. {SmartSum}
```

For the C Programmer

```
/*
    © 1988 by Gary Bond
    All Rights Reserved

    Translated to C by Sioux Lacy

    SmartSum:    a Hypercard XFCN that intelligently sums its arguments. If there's
                 more than one argument, SmartSum adds each separately. If there's
                 only one argument, SmartSum looks for a comma - if found it parses
                 the comma-separated items and adds them.  If no comma was found, it
                 parses the return separated items and adds them.

    Form:        SmartSum([container|parameter list])

    Example:     Sum(card field 3)
                 Sum(Var)
                 Sum(the selection)
                 Sum(1,2,3)
                 Sum(CommaList)

    Note:        When adding individual parameters, the limit imposed by the external
                 interface is 16.
    _____

    Compile and link this file with the MacTraps and string libraries
*/


/*
    Includes
    Note that these header files are for LightspeedC development.
    Substitute the files that are appropriate for your compiler.
*/
#include    <MacTypes.h>
#include    "HyperXCmd.h"
```

continued...

...from previous page

```
/*
   LightspeedC Prototypes
*/
pascal   void main(XCmdBlockPtr);
char     *CollectToSpec(char *, char *, char);
void     Fail(XCmdBlockPtr, char *);
Handle   CopyStrToHand(char *);
void     HandleToPstr(Str255, Handle);
char     *ToCstr(char *);
char     *ToPstr(char *);


/*
   Defined Constants
*/
#define  EOS           (unsigned char) 0
#define  returnChar     (char) 0x0d
#define  commaChar      (char) 0x2c


pascal void    main(paramPtr)
   XCmdBlockPtr paramPtr;
{
   int       count, i;
   int       len;
   char      *scanPtr;
   char      separator;
   extended  total;
   extended  value;
   Str255    tempStr;

   if ((count = paramPtr->paramCount) > 16)
      {
         Fail(paramPtr, "Only 16 parameters allowed");
         return;
      }
   /*
      If more than 1 parameter was sent, each parameter can be converted
      to an extended and added to the total.
   */
   total = (extended) 0;
   if (count > 1)
      {
         for (i = 0; i < count; i++)
            {
               HandleToPstr(tempStr, paramPtr->params[i]);
               StrToExt(paramPtr, (Str31 *) &tempStr, &value);
               total += value;
```

continued...

...from previous page

```
            }
        }
/*
    Otherwise the parameter is a list -- either comma-separated or
    carriage return-separated.  Determine which, then sum the list.
*/
else
    {
        /*
            Move the list of global names to the top of heap.
            If there's a comma in the list, assume a comma-separated list,
            otherwise assume a carriage-return separated list.
        */
        MoveHHi(paramPtr->params[0]);
        HLock(paramPtr->params[0]);
        scanPtr = (char *) *(paramPtr->params[0]);
        len = strlen(scanPtr);
        separator = returnChar;
        for (i = 0; i < len; i++ )
            if (scanPtr[i] == commaChar)
                {
                    separator = commaChar;
                    break;
                }
        while (*scanPtr != EOS)
            {
                /*
                    Collect characters until encounter the separator character.
                    Call back to HyperCard to set the value of that global.
                */
                scanPtr = CollectToSpec(scanPtr, (char *) tempStr, separator);
                ToPstr((char *) tempStr);
                StrToExt(paramPtr, (Str31 *) &tempStr, &value);
                total += value;
                /*
                    Must test for end-of-string before & after bumping the
                    pointer, since can't guarantee that the container ends with
                    a separator, followed by a terminating zero byte.  May just
                    end with a zero byte.
                */
                if (*scanPtr == EOS)
                    break;
                ++scanPtr;
            }
        HUnlock(paramPtr->params[0]);
    }
ExtToStr(paramPtr, &total, (Str31 *) &tempStr);
```

continued...

...from previous page

```
   ToCstr((char *) tempStr);
   paramPtr->returnValue = (Handle) CopyStrToHand((char *) tempStr);

   return;
}


/*
   This function copies characters from one string to another until it
   finds the delimiter character "myChar". It returns the pointer into
   the target string.
*/
char *CollectToSpec(targetStr, subStr, myChar)
   char  *targetStr;
   char  *subStr;
   char  myChar;
{
   while ((*targetStr != (char) myChar) && (*targetStr != EOS))
      *subStr++ = *targetStr++;

   *subStr = EOS;
   return(targetStr);
}


/*
   This function gets a handle and copies the error string it receives into the
heap
   for return to HyperCard.
*/
void Fail(paramPtr, str)
   XCmdBlockPtr  paramPtr;
   char          *str;
{
   paramPtr->returnValue = (Handle) CopyStrToHand(str);
   return;
}


/*
   This utility function allocates heapspace and copies a string into it.
*/
Handle CopyStrToHand(str)
   char *str;
{
   Handle  newHndl;
```

continued...

...from previous page

```
    newHndl = (Handle) NewHandle((long) strlen(str) + 1);
    strcpy((char *)(*newHndl), str);
    return(newHndl);
}


/*
   This utility function copies the string pointed to by a handle into
   a character array, then converts the C string to a Pascal string.
   Note that the C string is overwritten by the Pascal string.
*/
void HandleToPstr(str, hndl)
    Str255   str;
    Handle   hndl;
{
    strcpy((char *) str, *hndl);
    ToPstr((char *) str);
}


/*
   This utility function converts a Pascal string to a C string.
   Note that the Pascal string is overwritten in the process.
*/
char *ToCstr(str)
    char *str;
{
    unsigned char length, i;

    length = str[0];
    for (i = 0; i < length; ++i)        /* Shift string 1 byte to the left */
        str[i] = str[i+1];
    str[length] = 0;                    /* Put zero-terminator after string */
    return(str);
}


/*
   This utility function converts a C string to a Pascal string.
   Note that the C string is overwritten in the process.
*/
char *ToPstr(str)
    char *str;
{
    unsigned char length, i;
```

continued...

...from previous page

```
    for (i = 0, length = 0; str[i] != 0; ++i)      /* Find end of string */
        ++length;
    while (i--)                                     /* Shift string 1 byte to right */
        str[i+1] = str[i];
    str[0] = length;                                /* Put string length in 1st byte */
    return(str);
}
```

GetEvent

The GetEvent function returns the next event in the event queue, optionally flushing the event from the queue.

Quick Reference

GetEvent(flushFlag) (flushFlag = true or false)

Parameters

GetEvent takes one parameter:

Parameter 1: a value of true instructs GetEvent to read and flush the next event. A value of false tells GetEvent to read the next event, but leave it in the queue.

The default values for omitted parameters are as follows:

Default for parameter 1: False (don't flush events from the queue)

Examples

GetEvent(TRUE) -- returns and flushes the event
GetEvent(FALSE) -- returns but doesn't flush the event
GetEvent() -- same as GetEvent(FALSE)

Tips

You can use GetEvent to read an event from the event queue before HyperCard gets it, which allows you to decide whether to process the event or pass it on to HyperCard.

For the Pascal Programmer

```
{$R-}
( *
  © 1988 by Gary Bond
  All Rights Reserved

  GetEvent -- a Hypercard XFCN that gets the next event and optionally flushes it

  Form:  GetEvent(flush[true/false])

  Example: IF GetEvent(TRUE) is "KeyDown 65" THEN put "A was pressed"

  Note:  Returns the the event type in word 1 and the Ascii key code in word 2. It
  must be called repeatedly. If the paramter is set to TRUE the event will be flushed
  from the queue. If set to FALSE, it will not.

  _____

  To compile and link this file using MPW Pascal, select the following lines and press
  the ENTER key

  _____


  pascal GetEvent.p
  link -o "HD:Hypercard:Home" -rt XFCN=1514 -sn Main=GetEvent GetEvent.p.o ∂
  {MPW}PLibraries:PasLib.o -m ENTRYPOINT

* )

{$S GetEvent } {Segment name must be the same as the command name}

UNIT DummyUnit;

INTERFACE

USES MemTypes, QuickDraw, OSIntf, ToolIntf, PackIntf, PasLibIntf, HyperXCmd;
```
continued...

...from previous page

PROCEDURE ENTRYPOINT(paramPtr: XCmdPtr);

IMPLEMENTATION

TYPE Str31 = String[31];

PROCEDURE GetEvent(paramPtr: XCmdPtr);   FORWARD;

PROCEDURE ENTRYPOINT(paramPtr: XCmdPtr);

```
BEGIN
  GetEvent(paramPtr);
END;
```

PROCEDURE GetEvent(paramPtr: XCmdPtr);

CONST minParamCount = 1;

```
VAR   eventStr:      Str255;
      tempStr:       Str255;
      flush:         Boolean;
      doCase:        Boolean;
      theEvent:      EventRecord;
```

{$I XCmdGlue.inc } {Includes the glue routines}

PROCEDURE Fail(errStr: Str255); {Exit returning an error message}

```
BEGIN
  paramPtr^.returnValue := PasToZero(errStr); {load  the  result}
  EXIT(GetEvent); {leave the XFCN}
END; {Fail}
```

PROCEDURE CheckParamCount; {checks for the correct parameter count}

VAR numParams: Integer;

```
BEGIN
  numParams := paramPtr^.paramCount; {store the number of parameters passed}
  IF (numParams <> minParamCount)
```

continued...

315

...from previous page

```
      THEN Fail('Form: GetEvent([true|false])');
    END; {CheckParamCount}

BEGIN {main }
  CheckParamCount; {make sure the flush flag is provided}
  eventStr := ''; {initialize the variable}
  ZeroToPas(paramPtr^.params[1]^,tempStr); {get the flush flag}
  flush := StrToBool(tempStr); {convert it to a boolean}
  IF flush THEN doCase := GetNextEvent(everyEvent,theEvent) {flush it}
  ELSE doCase := EventAvail(everyEvent,theEvent); {leave it in the queue}
  IF doCase THEN
    BEGIN
      CASE theEvent.what OF {parse and return the event}
        1: eventStr := 'mouseDown';
        2: eventStr := 'mouseUp';
        3: BEGIN
             tempStr :=
             LongToStr(ORD(CHR(BAnd(theEvent.message,charCodeMask))));
             eventStr := CONCAT('keyDown ',tempStr);
           END;
        5: BEGIN
             tempStr :=
             LongToStr(ORD(CHR(BAnd(theEvent.message,charCodeMask))));
             eventStr := CONCAT('autoKey ',tempStr);
           END;
        6: eventStr := 'update';
        7: eventStr := 'diskEvent';
        8: eventStr := 'activateEvent';
      OTHERWISE
        eventStr := CONCAT('Unknown event: ',LongToStr(theEvent.what));
      END; {case}
    END; {if}
  paramPtr^.returnValue := PasToZero(eventStr); {return the event}
END; {main }

END. {GetEvent}
```

For the C Programmer

```
/*
   © 1988 by Gary Bond
   All Rights Reserved

   Translated to C by Sioux Lacy

   GetEvent:  a Hypercard XFCN that gets the next event and optionally flushes it

   Form:      GetEvent(flush[true/false])

   Example:   if GetEvent(TRUE) is "KeyDown 65" then put "A was pressed"

   Note:      Returns the the event type in word 1 and the Ascii key code
              in word 2. It must be called repeatedly. If the paramter is set
              to TRUE the event will be flushed from the queue. If set to
              FALSE, it will not.
   _____

   Compile and link this file with the MacTraps and string libraries
*/


/*
   Includes
   Note that these header files are for LightspeedC development.
   Substitute the files that are appropriate for your compiler.
*/
#include <MacTypes.h>
#include <EventMgr.h>
#include "HyperXCmd.h"

/*
   LightspeedC Prototypes
*/
pascal   void main(XCmdBlockPtr);
Handle   CatNumToStr(XCmdBlockPtr, char *, int);
short    CheckParamCount(XCmdBlockPtr, char *);
Handle   CopyStrToHand(char *);
Boolean  HandleToBool(XCmdBlockPtr, Handle);
void     HandleToPstr(Str255, Handle);
char     *ToCstr(char *);
char     *ToPstr(char *);


/*
   Defined Constants
*/
```

continued...

...from previous page

```
#define  requiredParamCount  (short)            1
#define  errorFlag           (short)           -1
#define  NIL                 (Handle)           0
#define  EOS                 (unsigned char)    0      /* end of string */


pascal void    main(paramPtr)
   XCmdBlockPtr paramPtr;
{
   Boolean       flush;
   Boolean       wasEvent;
   EventRecord   theEvent;

   if (CheckParamCount(paramPtr, "Form: GetEvent([true|false])") == errorFlag)
      return;

   /*
      Find out whether or not to flush events.
      Get the event, flushing or not as indicated by the flush parameter.
   */
   flush = HandleToBool(paramPtr, paramPtr->params[0]);

   if (flush)
      wasEvent = GetNextEvent((int) everyEvent, &theEvent);
   else
      wasEvent = EventAvail((int) everyEvent, &theEvent);

   /*
      If there was an event,
      Copy a description of the event to the returnValue in the XcmdBlock
   */
   if (wasEvent)
      {
         switch (theEvent.what)
            {
               case 1:
                  paramPtr->returnValue = (Handle) CopyStrToHand ("mouseDown");
                  break;
               case 2:
                  paramPtr->returnValue = (Handle) CopyStrToHand ("mouseUp");
                  break;
               case 3:
```

continued...

...from previous page

```
                    paramPtr->returnValue = (Handle) CatNumToStr(paramPtr,
                        "keyDown ", (theEvent.message & charCodeMask));
                    break;
                case 5:
                    paramPtr->returnValue = (Handle) CatNumToStr(paramPtr,
                        "autoKey ", (theEvent.message & charCodeMask));
                    break;
                case 6:
                    paramPtr->returnValue = (Handle) CopyStrToHand ("update");
                    break;
                case 7:
                    paramPtr->returnValue = (Handle) CopyStrToHand ("diskEvent");
                    break;
                case 8:
                    paramPtr->returnValue = (Handle) CopyStrToHand ("activateEvent");
                    break;
                default:
                    paramPtr->returnValue = (Handle) CatNumToStr(paramPtr,
                        "Unknown event: ", (theEvent.message & charCodeMask));
                    break;
            }
        }
    return;
}


/*
    This function concatenates an integer converted to a string onto a given
    string. For consistency, it returns the handle and allows the caller
    to assign it to paramPtr->returnValue.
*/
Handle CatNumToStr(paramPtr, string, number)
    XCmdBlockPtr    paramPtr;
    char            *string;
    int             number;
{
    Str31    str1, str2;

    strcpy (str1, string);
    LongToStr (paramPtr, (long) number, &str2);
    ToCstr ((char *) str2);
    strcat (str1, str2);
    return ((Handle) CopyStrToHand ((char *) str1));
}
```

continued...

...from previous page

```
/*
   This function checks to see if the correct number of params were received.
   And writes an error message into the returnValue if they were not.
*/
short CheckParamCount(paramPtr, str)
   XCmdBlockPtr paramPtr;
   char         *str;
{
   short    count;

   count = paramPtr->paramCount;
   if (count != requiredParamCount)
      {
         paramPtr->returnValue = (Handle) CopyStrToHand(str);
         return(errorFlag);
      }
   return(count);
}



/*
   This utility function allocates heapspace and copies a string into it.
*/
Handle CopyStrToHand(str)
   char *str;
{
   Handle   newHndl;

   newHndl = (Handle) NewHandle((long) strlen(str) + 1);
   strcpy((char *)(*newHndl), str);
   return(newHndl);
}



/*
   This function makes a callback to HyperCard to convert a string to an
   boolean (true/false).  It takes a handle to a C string as an argument.
*/
Boolean HandleToBool(paramPtr, hndl)
   XCmdBlockPtr  paramPtr;
   Handle        hndl;
{
   Str31    str;

   HandleToPstr(str, hndl);
   return(StrToBool(paramPtr, &str));
}
```

continued...

...from previous page

```
/*
   This utility function copies the string pointed to by a handle into
   a character array, then converts the C string to a Pascal string.
   Note that the C string is overwritten by the Pascal string.
*/
void HandleToPstr(str, hndl)
   Str255   str;
   Handle   hndl;
{
   strcpy((char *) str, *hndl);
   ToPstr((char *) str);
}



/*
   This utility function converts a Pascal string to a C string.
   Note that the Pascal string is overwritten in the process.
*/
char *ToCstr(str)
   char *str;
{
   unsigned char length, i;

   length = str[0];
   for (i = 0; i < length; ++i)        /* Shift string 1 byte to the left */
      str[i] = str[i+1];
   str[length] = 0;                    /* Put zero-terminator after string */
   return(str);
}



/*
   This utility function converts a C string to a Pascal string.
   Note that the C string is overwritten in the process.
*/
char *ToPstr(str)
   char *str;
{
   unsigned char length, i;

   for (i = 0, length = 0; str[i] != 0; ++i)    /* Find end of string */
      ++length;
   while (i--)                                  /* Shift string 1 byte to right */
      str[i+1] = str[i];
   str[0] = length;                             /* Put string length in 1st byte */
   return(str);
}
```

321

QuickSort

The QuickSort function returns the sorted contents of a container (field, variable, or the selection) passed it. QuickSort sorts using either a text or numeric format in low to high (ascending) order.

Quick Reference

QuickSort(container,textNumericFlag)

Parameters

QuickSort takes two parameters:

Parameter 1:   The container to be sorted (the contents of the container aren't changed).
Parameter 2:   Use TEXT here to sort text and NUMERIC to sort numbers.

The default values for omitted parameters are as follows:

Default for parameter 1:   Must be supplied—no default value.
Default for parameter 2:   Sort by text.

Examples

```
put QuickSort(card field 1,text) into card field 1 --sorts that field
put QuickSort(card field 1,text) into card field 2
put QuickSort(the selection,numeric) into the selection
put QuickSort(myVar,numeric) into myOtherVar
```

Tips

If you use a text sort on numeric data, the data will be arranged textually (1.2, 15, 1.9). For an accurate sort, lines or items to be sorted must be separated by carriage returns.

For the Pascal Programmer

```
{$R-}
( *
```

QuickSort -- a Hypercard XFCN that returns the sorted contents of a container.

Form: QuickSort(container,[text|numeric])

Example: QuickSort(card field 1,text)

Note: QuickSort sorts ascending using either text or numeric formats.

To compile and link this file using MPW Pascal, select the following lines and press the ENTER key

---

```
pascal QuickSort.p
link -o "HD:Hypercard:Home" -rt XFCN=1515 -sn Main=QuickSort QuickSort.p.o ∂
{MPW}PLibraries:PasLib.o -m ENTRYPOINT ∂
{MPW}Libraries:Interface.o -m ENTRYPOINT

* )

{$S QuickSort }  {Segment name must be the same as the command name}

UNIT DummyUnit;

INTERFACE

USES MemTypes, QuickDraw, OSIntf, ToolIntf, PasLibIntf, PackIntf, HyperXCmd;

PROCEDURE ENTRYPOINT(paramPtr: XCmdPtr);
```

continued...

...from previous page

IMPLEMENTATION

```
TYPE   Str1   =  String[1];
       Str31  =  String[31];
       Str50  =  String[50];
       Str51  =  String[51];
       TSortArray = ARRAY [1..200] OF Str50;
       NSortArray = ARRAY [1..200] OF Extended;

PROCEDURE QuickSort(paramPtr: XCmdPtr);        FORWARD;

   PROCEDURE ENTRYPOINT(paramPtr: XCmdPtr);

     BEGIN
       QuickSort(paramPtr);
     END;

   PROCEDURE QuickSort(paramPtr: XCmdPtr);

   CONST arrayStart = 1;
         arrayEnd = 200;
         minParamCount = 1;
         maxParamCount = 2;

   VAR    TextStuff:        TSortArray;
          NumbStuff:        NSortArray;
          tempStr:          Str255;
          catString:        Str51;
          return:           Str1;
          scanPtr:          Ptr;
          count:            Integer;
          i:                Integer;
          error:            Integer;
          exitLoop:         Boolean;
          dataType:         Boolean;
          buildFieldHndl:   Handle;

{$I XCmdGlue.inc } {includes the glue routines}
```

continued...

...from previous page

```
PROCEDURE Fail(errStr: Str255); {Exit returning an error message}

  BEGIN
    paramPtr^.returnValue := PasToZero(errStr); {load the result}
    EXIT(QuickSort); {leave the XFCN}
  END; {Fail}


PROCEDURE CheckParamCount; {checks for the correct parameter count}

  VAR numParams: Integer;

  BEGIN
    numParams := paramPtr^.paramCount; {store the number of parameters passed}
    IF ((numParams < minParamCount) OR (numParams > maxParamCount))
    THEN Fail('Form: QuickSort(container,[text|numeric])');
  END; {CheckParamCount}


PROCEDURE TextSort(myStart,myFinish: Integer; VAR  data: TSortArray);

  VAR  starterValue: Str50;
       temp:         Str50;
       left:         Integer;
       right:        Integer;

  BEGIN
    left := myStart;
    right := myFinish;
     {pick center element as start}
    starterValue := data[((myStart + myFinish) DIV 2)];
    REPEAT
      WHILE data[left] < starterValue DO
        left := left + 1; {find a larger value to the left}
      WHILE starterValue < data[right] DO
        right := right - 1; {find a smaller value to the right}
      IF left <= right THEN
```

continued...

...from previous page

```
      BEGIN
        temp := data[left]; {swap them}
        data[left] := data[right];
        data[right] := temp;
        left := left + 1;
        right := right -1;
      END;
  UNTIL right <= left;
  IF (myStart < right) THEN TextSort(myStart,right,data);
  IF (left < myFinish) THEN TextSort(left,myFinish,data);
END; {TextSort}


PROCEDURE NumericSort(myStart,myFinish: Integer; VAR  data: NSortArray);

  VAR starterValue: Extended;
        temp:         Extended;
        left:         Integer;
        right:        Integer;

BEGIN
  left := myStart;
  right := myFinish;
   {pick center element as start}
  starterValue := data[((myStart + myFinish) DIV 2)];
  REPEAT
    WHILE data[left] < starterValue DO
      left := left + 1; {find a larger value to the left}
    WHILE starterValue < data[right] DO
      right := right - 1; {find a smaller value to the right}
    IF left <= right THEN
      BEGIN
        temp := data[left]; {swap them}
        data[left] := data[right];
        data[right] := temp;
        left := left + 1;
        right := right -1;
      END;
  UNTIL right <= left;
  IF (myStart < right) THEN NumericSort(myStart,right,data);
  IF (left < myFinish) THEN NumericSort(left,myFinish,data);
END; {NumericSort}
```

continued...

...from previous page

```
BEGIN {main}
  CheckParamCount; {can take 1 or 2 parameters}
  MoveHHi(paramPtr^.params[1]);
  Hlock(paramPtr^.params[1]);
  HNoPurge(paramPtr^.params[1]);
  return[0] := chr(1); {make a carriage return for the concat}
  return[1] := chr(13);
  count := 1; {initialize the count}
  exitloop := TRUE; {initialize the loop conditional}
  scanPtr := paramPtr^.params[1]^; {initialize the pointer}
  IF paramPtr^.paramCount = 2 THEN {if there's a second parameter - use it}
    BEGIN
      ZeroToPas(paramPtr^.params[2]^,tempStr);
      IF IUEqualString(COPY(tempStr,1,1),'t') = 0
      THEN dataType := StrToBool('TRUE')
      ELSE dataType := StrToBool('FALSE');
    END
  ELSE dataType := StrToBool('TRUE'); {default to text sort}

  WHILE exitLoop DO {get the lines into an array}
    BEGIN
      ReturnToPas(scanPtr,tempStr);
      IF LENGTH(tempStr) > 50 THEN Fail('Can only sort 50 characters per line');
      IF dataType THEN TextStuff[count] := tempStr
      ELSE NumbStuff[count] := StrToExt(tempStr);
      count := count + 1;
      ScanToReturn(scanPtr);
      IF scanPtr^ = 0 THEN exitLoop := FALSE;
      scanPtr := POINTER(ORD(scanPtr)+1);
      IF scanPtr^ = 0 THEN exitLoop := FALSE;
      IF count > arrayEnd THEN exitLoop := FALSE;
    END;

  IF dataType THEN TextSort(arrayStart,(count-1),TextStuff) {do the sort}
  ELSE  NumericSort(arrayStart,(count-1),NumbStuff);
```

continued...

...from previous page

```
   buildFieldHndl := newhandle(0); {build a zero-terminated string in memory}
   FOR i := 1 TO (count -1) DO
     BEGIN
        IF dataType THEN catstring := CONCAT(TextStuff[i],return)
        ELSE catString := CONCAT(ExtToStr(NumbStuff[i]),return);
        error :=
        PtrAndHand(pointer(ORD(@catString)+1),buildFieldHndl,LENGTH(catString));
        {add 1 for > length byte}
     END;
   setHandleSize(buildFieldHndl,(getHandleSize(buildFieldHndl)+1));
   scanPtr := Pointer(ORD(buildFieldHndl^) + getHandleSize(buildFieldHndl)-1);
   scanPtr^ := 0; {stuff a zero at the end of the compiled string}
   HUnlock(paramPtr^.params[1]); {clean-up}
   HPurge(paramPtr^.params[1]);
   paramPtr^.returnValue := buildFieldHndl; {HC disposes the handle}
   END; {main}

END. {QuickSort}
```

For the C Programmer

```
/*
   © 1988 by Gary Bond
   All Rights Reserved

   Translated to C by Sioux Lacy

   QuickSort:    a Hypercard XFCN that returns the sorted contents of a container.

   Form:         QuickSort(container, [text|numeric])

   Example:      QuickSort(card field 1, text)

   Note:         QuickSort sorts ascending using either text or numeric formats.
   _____

   Compile and link this file with the MacTraps and string libraries
*/
```

continued...

...from previous page

```
/*
    Includes
    Note that these header files are for LightspeedC development.
    Substitute the files that are appropriate for your compiler.
*/
#include <MacTypes.h>
#include "HyperXCmd.h"

/*
    Defined Constants and Types
*/
#define  minParamCount  (short)     1
#define  maxParamCount  (short)     2
#define  maxChars                   51
#define  arrayStart                 0
#define  arrayEnd                   200
#define  errorFlag      (short)     -1
#define  returnChar     (char)      0x0d
#define  EOS            (char)      0
#define  NUMERIC        (Boolean)   FALSE
#define  TEXT           (Boolean)   TRUE

typedef char        Str51[maxChars+1];
typedef char        TSortArray[arrayEnd][maxChars+1];
typedef extended    NSortArray[arrayEnd];

/*
    LightspeedC Prototypes
*/
pascal   void main(XCmdBlockPtr);
void     TextSort(int, int, TSortArray);
void     NumericSort(int, int, NSortArray);
char     *CollectToReturn(char *, char *);
short    GetParamCount(XCmdBlockPtr, char *);
void     SortFail(XCmdBlockPtr, char *);
Handle   CopyStrToHand(char *);
void     HandleToPstr(Str255, Handle);
char     *ToCstr(char *);
char     *ToPstr(char *);
```

continued...

...from previous page

```
pascal void    main(paramPtr)
   XCmdBlockPtr paramPtr;
{
   TSortArray  TextStuff;
   NSortArray  NumbStuff;
   Str255      str;
   char        *scanPtr;
   int         count;
   int         i;
   int         len;
   OsErr       error;
   Size        size;
   Boolean     dataType;
   Handle      buildFieldHndl;

   count = GetParamCount(paramPtr, "Form: QuickSort(container, [text|numeric])");
   if (count == errorFlag)
      return;

   /*
      Programming note:
      The handle to the container that will be sorted is moved high on the heap
      and then locked down.  Because it needs to be dereferenced, it must be
      guaranteed not to move.  When a handle is locked, as this one is, care
      must be taken to ensure that it is unlocked before exiting this XFCN.
   */
   MoveHHi(paramPtr->params[0]);
   HLock(paramPtr->params[0]);
   scanPtr = (char *) *(paramPtr->params[0]);

   /*
      Optional 2nd param is "text" or "numeric". Default dataType is "text"
      Just check to see if user passed an "n" as the 1st char of the param
      (This allows some flexibility in parameters)
   */
   dataType = TEXT;
   if (count == 2)
      {
         HandleToPstr(str, paramPtr->params[1]);
         str[0] = 1;
         if (IUEqualString(str,"\1n") == 0)
            dataType = NUMERIC;
      }
```

continued...

...from previous page

```
/*
    Get the lines of the container into an array of strings
    Either finding end-of-string or running out of slots in the
    array will exit from this loop.
*/
count = 0;
while (TRUE)
{
    scanPtr = CollectToReturn(scanPtr, TextStuff[count]);
    if ((len = strlen(TextStuff[count])) == 0)
        --count;                /* Skip over blank lines */
    else
        {
            if (len > maxChars)
                {
                    SortFail(paramPtr, "Can only sort 50 characters per line");
                    return;
                }
            if (dataType == NUMERIC)
                {
                    ToPstr(TextStuff[count]);
                    StrToExt(paramPtr, (Str31 *) &TextStuff[count],
                        &NumbStuff[count]);
                }
        }
    if (*scanPtr++ == EOS) break;          /* Reached end-of-string */
    if (*scanPtr == EOS) break;
    if (count == arrayEnd) break;          /* Can only sort 200 lines */
    ++count;
}
/*
    On exit from loop, count will index the last item copied.
    Sort either the array of strings or the array of numbers.
    Then build a new string in memory of the sorted items.
*/
if (dataType == TEXT)
    TextSort(arrayStart, count, TextStuff);
else
    NumericSort(arrayStart, count, NumbStuff);

buildFieldHndl = NewHandle((long) 0);
for (i = 0; i <= count; i++)
    {
        if (dataType == NUMERIC)
            {
                ExtToStr(paramPtr, &NumbStuff[i], (Str31 *) &TextStuff[i]);
                ToCstr(TextStuff[i]);
            }
```

continued...

...from previous page

```
            len = strlen(TextStuff[i]);
            TextStuff[i][len++] = returnChar;
            TextStuff[i][len] = EOS;

            if ((error = PtrAndHand(TextStuff[i], buildFieldHndl, (long) len)) != noErr
                break;
        }
    str[0] = EOS;
    error = PtrAndHand(str, buildFieldHndl, (long) 1);
    if (error != noErr)
        {
            SortFail(paramPtr, "Couldn't build the sorted list");
            return;
        }

        HUnlock(paramPtr->params[0]);
    paramPtr->returnValue = buildFieldHndl;
    return;
}


/*
    This function will sort a list of string elements.

    It is called recursively to:
        pick a element in the center of the list,
        find a larger one to the left, and a smaller one to the right
        swap the two, and continue until the pointers have crossed.

        Now the function is called again with the start & right pointer,
        and then called with the end & left pointer.
*/
void TextSort(myStart, myFinish, data)
    int        myStart;
    int        myFinish;
    TSortArray data;
{
    Str51      temp;
    Str51      starter;
    int        left;
    int        right;

    left = myStart;
    right = myFinish;
    strcpy(starter, data[((myStart + myFinish) / (int) 2)]);
    do
```

continued...

...from previous page

```
{
    while (strcmp(data[left], starter) < (int) 0)
       ++left;
    while (strcmp(starter, data[right]) < (int) 0)
          --right;
        if (left <= right)
           {
               if (left != right)
                  {
                      strcpy(temp, data[left]);
                      strcpy(data[left], data[right]);
                      strcpy(data[right], temp);
                  }
               ++left;
               --right;
           }
    }
    while (right > left);

    if (myStart < right)
       TextSort(myStart, right, data);
    if (left < myFinish)
       TextSort(left, myFinish, data);
}


void NumericSort(myStart, myFinish, data)
    int          myStart;
    int          myFinish;
    NSortArray data;
{
    extended   temp;
    extended   starter;
    int        left;
    int        right;

    left = myStart;
    right = myFinish;
    starter = data[((myStart + myFinish) / (int) 2)];
    do
       {
           while (data[left] < starter)
              ++left;
           while (starter < data[right])
              --right;
           if (left <= right)
              {
                  if (left != right)
```

continued...

...from previous page

```
                {
                    temp = data[left];
                    data[left] = data[right];
                    data[right] = temp;
                }
            ++left;
            --right;
        }
    }
    while (right > left);

    if (myStart < right)
        NumericSort(myStart, right, data);
    if (left < myFinish)
        NumericSort(left, myFinish, data);
}


/*
    This function fills a 2nd array with the characters from the 1st
    array until it encounters either a carriage return or end-of-string.
    It returns the pointer into the 1st array.
*/
char *CollectToReturn(targetStr, subStr)
    char *targetStr;
    char *subStr;
{
    while ((*targetStr != returnChar) && (*targetStr != EOS))
        *subStr++ = *targetStr++;

    *subStr = EOS;          /* zero-terminate the substring */
    return(targetStr);
}


/*
    This function checks to see if the correct number of params were received.
    And writes an error message into the returnValue if they were not.
*/
short GetParamCount(paramPtr, str)
    XCmdBlockPtr paramPtr;
    char        *str;
{
    short   count;
```

continued...

...from previous page

```
   count = paramPtr->paramCount;
   if ((count > maxParamCount) || (count < minParamCount))
      {
         paramPtr->returnValue = (Handle) CopyStrToHand (str);
         return(errorFlag);
      }
   return(count);
}


/*
   This function gets a handle and copies the error string it receives into the heap
   for return to HyperCard.  It also unlocks the handle to the 1st param.
*/
void SortFail(paramPtr, str)
   XCmdBlockPtr   paramPtr;
   char           *str;
{
   HUnlock(paramPtr->params[0]);
   paramPtr->returnValue = (Handle) CopyStrToHand(str);
   return;
}


/*
   This utility function allocates heapspace and copies a string into it.
*/
Handle CopyStrToHand(str)
   char *str;
{
   Handle   newHndl;

   newHndl = (Handle) NewHandle((long) strlen(str) + 1);
   strcpy((char *)(*newHndl), str);
   return(newHndl);
}


/*
   This utility function copies the string pointed to by a handle into
   a character array, then converts the C string to a Pascal string.
   Note that the C string is overwritten by the Pascal string.
*/
void HandleToPstr(str, hndl)
   Str255   str;
   Handle   hndl;
{
   strcpy((char *) str, *hndl);
   ToPstr((char *) str);
}
```

continued...

...from previous page

```
/*
   This utility function converts a Pascal string to a C string.
   Note that the Pascal string is overwritten in the process.
*/
char *ToCstr(str)
   char *str;
{
   unsigned char length, i;

   length = str[0];
   for (i = 0; i < length; ++i)        /* Shift string 1 byte to the left */
      str[i] = str[i+1];
   str[length] = 0;                     /* Put zero-terminator after string */
   return(str);
}


/*
   This utility function converts a C string to a Pascal string.
   Note that the C string is overwritten in the process.
*/
char *ToPstr(str)
   char *str;
{
   unsigned char length, i;

   for (i = 0, length = 0; str[i] != 0; ++i)    /* Find end of string */
      ++length;
   while (i--)                                   /* Shift string 1 byte to right */
      str[i+1] = str[i];
   str[0] = length;                              /* Put string length in 1st byte */
   return(str);
}
```

CopyRes

The CopyRes command copies a specified resource (such as an XCMD or FONT) from one file or stack to another. Full pathnames must be provided for both the source and destination files.

Quick Reference

CopyRes ResName,ResType,"source path","destination path"

Parameters

CopyRes takes four parameters:

Parameter 1: The name of the resource to be copied.
Parameter 2: The type of resource to be copied (XCMD, FONT, snd, ICON, and so on).
Parameter 3: The full pathname of the stack or file from which to get the resource.
Parameter 4: The full pathname of the stack to attach the copy to.

Examples

CopyRes "Dialog","XCMD","HD:MyStack","HD:Home" --copy XCMD to Home stack
CopyRes "Geneva","FONT","HD:System","HD:Home" --copy font to Home stack

Tips

CopyRes changes the resource number of the copy to prevent the trashing of similarly numbered resources in the destination stack or file. Though CopyRes is recommended for use with stacks, it can be used to copy resources from any Macintosh file or application to any other Macintosh file or application.

For the Pascal Programmer

{$R-}
(*
© 1988 by Gary Bond
All Rights Reserved

CopyRes -- a Hypercard XCMD that copies any resource from one file to another.

Form:
CopyRes "Name of resource", "resource type", "source pathname", "destination pathname"

Example: CopyRes "NewMenuBar","XCMD","HD:Home","HD:Hypercard:Test Stack"

Note: You must supply a full pathname for both the source and destination paths.

To compile and link this file using MPW Pascal, select the following lines and press the ENTER key

---

```
pascal CopyRes.p
link -o "HD:Hypercard:Home" -rt XCMD=1516 -sn Main=CopyRes CopyRes.p.o ∂
{MPW}Libraries:Interface.o -m ENTRYPOINT ∂
{MPW}PLibraries:PasLib.o -m ENTRYPOINT
```

*)

{$S CopyRes } {Segment name must be the same as the command name}

UNIT DummyUnit;

INTERFACE

continued...

...from previous page

```
USES MemTypes, QuickDraw, OSIntf, ToolIntf, HyperXCmd;

PROCEDURE ENTRYPOINT(paramPtr: XCmdPtr);

IMPLEMENTATION

TYPE  Str31 = String[31];

PROCEDURE CopyRes(paramPtr: XCmdPtr);        FORWARD;

  PROCEDURE ENTRYPOINT(paramPtr: XCmdPtr);

  BEGIN
    CopyRes(paramPtr);
  END;

  PROCEDURE CopyRes(paramPtr: XCmdPtr);

  CONST  minParamCount = 4;

  VAR    tempStr:          Str255;
         source:           Str255;
         destination:      Str255;
         resName:          Str255;
         newVol:           Str255;
         oldVol:           Integer;
         attrs:            Integer;
         err:              Integer;
         i:                Integer;
         newResNum:        Integer;
         sourceRefNum:     Integer;
         destRefNum:       Integer;
         myChar:           Integer;
         savedCurResFile:  Integer;
         vRef:             Integer;
         sourceHandle:     Handle;
         theType:          ResType;
         scanPtr:          Ptr;

{$I XCmdGlue.inc } {Includes the glue routines}
```

continued...

...from previous page

```
PROCEDURE Fail(errStr: Str255); {Exit returning an error message}

  BEGIN
    paramPtr^.returnValue := PasToZero(errStr); {load the result}
    EXIT(CopyRes); {leave the XCMD}
  END; {Fail}

PROCEDURE CheckParamCount; {checks for the correct parameter count}

  VAR numParams: Integer;

  BEGIN
    numParams := paramPtr^.paramCount; {store the number of parameters passed}
    IF (numParams <> minParamCount)
    THEN Fail('Form: CopyRes "ResName","ResType","Source path", "Dest path"');
  END; {CheckParamCount}

PROCEDURE CheckResError;

  VAR str:     Str255;
      errVal: Integer;

  BEGIN
    errVal := ResError;
    IF errVal = noErr THEN EXIT(CheckResError); {exit to caller if no error}
    CASE errVal OF
      resNotFound: str := 'Resource not found';
      resFNotFound: str := 'Resource file not found';
      addResFailed: str := 'AddResource failed';
      rmvResFailed: str := 'RmveResource failed';
      resAttrErr:  str := 'Attribute does not permit operation';
      mapReadErr: str := 'Map does not permit operation';
    OTHERWISE
      str := CONCAT('Unknown error: ',NumToStr(errVal));
    END;
    IF sourceHandle <> NIL THEN DisposHandle(sourceHandle); {release the memory}
    Fail('str');
  END;
```

continued...

...from previous page

```
FUNCTION CollectToSpec(VAR scanPtr: Ptr;myChar: Integer): Str255;

  TYPE Str1  =  String[1];

  VAR  exitloop:   BOOLEAN;
       tempStr:    Str1;
       collectStr: Str255;

  BEGIN
    exitloop := FALSE;
    tempStr[0]  :=  chr(1);
    collectStr  :=  '';
    REPEAT
    IF ((scanPtr^ = myChar) OR (scanPtr^ = 0)) THEN exitloop := TRUE
    ELSE
      BEGIN
        tempStr[1]  :=  chr(scanPtr^);
        collectStr  :=  Concat(collectStr,tempStr);
        scanPtr  :=  Pointer(ORD(scanPtr)+1);
        END;
      UNTIL exitloop = TRUE;
      CollectToSpec := collectStr;
  END; {collectToSpec}

BEGIN
  CheckParamCount; {must have all four parameters for this one}

  ZeroToPas(paramPtr^.params[1]^,resName); {get the resource name}
  ZeroToPas(paramPtr^.params[2]^,tempStr); {get resource type}
  FOR i := 1 to 4 DO theType[i] := tempStr[i]; {move string to packed array}
  ZeroToPas(paramPtr^.params[3]^,source); {this is a full pathname}
  ZeroToPas(paramPtr^.params[4]^,destination); {this is a full pathname}

  myChar := 58; {use CollectToSpec to look for a colon}
  scanPtr := paramPtr^.params[3]^; {do preprocessing to get volume name}
  newVol := CollectToSpec(scanPtr,myChar); {get the intended volume name}

  savedCurResFile := CurResFile; {save the current res file so we can restore it later}
  err := GetVol(NIL,oldVol); {get and save the current volume}
  IF err <> noErr THEN Fail('No such Volume');
```

continued...

...from previous page

```
    sourceHandle := GetNamedResource(theType,resName); {handle to res to copy from}
    CheckResError; {check if the call bombed}
    IF sourceHandle = NIL THEN Fail('Unable to allocate new handle');

    attrs := GetResAttrs(sourceHandle); {Get the associated attributes}
    CheckResError; {check to see if the call bombed}
    DetachResource(sourceHandle); {Detach for copying - becomes a relocatable block}

    err := SetVol(@newVol,vRef); {OpenResFile only opens on the default volume}
    {IF err <> noErr THEN Fail('Cannot set source volume');}

    CreateResFile(destination); {create or open the file we are going to copy into}
    destRefNum := OpenResFile(destination); {Open the destination resource fork/file}
    IF destRefNum = -1 THEN CheckResError; {see if the openRes call went ok}
    UseResFile(destRefNum); {This call is needed in case the res file was already open}
    CheckResError; {Check to see if the call bombed}
    newResNum := UniqueID(theType); {get new resNumber for destination copy}
    AddResource(sourceHandle,theType,newResNum,ResName); {attach resource to dest}
    SetResAttrs(sourceHandle,attrs); {set its attributes}
    ChangedResource(sourceHandle); {mark it as changed so it will get written}
    WriteResource(sourceHandle); {make it permanent}

    err := SetVol(NIL,oldVol);  {restore the volume we started with}
    IF err <> noErr THEN Fail('Cannot set original volume');

    UseResFile(SavedCurResFile); {restore the original resFile}
    DisposHandle(sourceHandle); {release the memory}
  END; {main}

END. {CopyRess}
```

For the C Programmer

```
/*
    © 1988 by Gary Bond
    All Rights Reserved

    Translated to C by Sioux Lacy

    CopyRes:    a Hypercard XCMD that copies any resource from one file to another.

    Form:       CopyRes "Name of resource", "resource type", "source pathname",
                "destination pathname"

    Example:    CopyRes "NewMenuBar", "XCMD", "HD:Home", "HD:Hypercard:Test Stack"

    Note:       You must supply a full pathname for both the source and destination
                paths.

    _____

    Compile and link this file with the MacTraps and string libraries
*/


/*
    Includes
    Note that these header files are for LightspeedC development.
    Substitute the files that are appropriate for your compiler.
*/
#include <MacTypes.h>
#include <FileMgr.h>
#include <ResourceMgr.h>
#include "HyperXCmd.h"

/*
    LightspeedC Prototypes
*/
pascal      void main(XCmdBlockPtr);
Boolean     CheckResError(XCmdBlockPtr, char *);
Handle      ConcatErrorStr(XCmdBlockPtr, char *, int);
void        HandleToBytes(char *, Handle);
char        *CollectToSpec(char *, char *, char);
short       CheckParamCount(XCmdBlockPtr, char *);
void        Fail(XCmdBlockPtr, char *);
Handle      CopyStrToHand(char *);
void        HandleToPstr(Str255, Handle);
char        *ToCstr(char *);
char        *ToPstr(char *);
```

continued...

...from previous page

```
/*
   Defined Constants
*/
#define  requiredParamCount  (short)            4
#define  errorFlag           (short)            -1
#define  NIL                 (Handle)           0
#define  EOS                 (unsigned char)    0
#define  colonChar           (char)             0x3a

pascal void    main(paramPtr)
   XCmdBlockPtr paramPtr;
{
   Str255      resName;
   Str255      newVolName;
   ResType     resType;
   int         oldVRefNum;
   int         newVRefNum;
   int         savedCurRefNum;
   int         destRefNum;
   int         newResNum;
   int         attributes;
   char        source[256];
   Str255      destination;
   Handle      sourceHandle;
   OsErr       err;

   if (CheckParamCount(paramPtr,
      "Form: CopyRes \"ResName\", \"ResType\", \"Source pathname\", \"Dest pathname\"
         == errorFlag)
      return;

   HandleToPstr(resName, paramPtr->params[0]);
   HandleToBytes((char *) &resType, paramPtr->params[1]);
   strcpy(source, *(paramPtr->params[2]));           /* full path for source */
   HandleToPstr(destination, paramPtr->params[3]);   /* full path for dest */

   /*
      Get and save the current volume.
      Save the current resource file
      Get handle to resource to copy from.
      Get resource attributes, and detach it (make resource relocable).
   */
   if ((err = GetVol(NIL, &oldVRefNum)) != noErr)
      {
         Fail(paramPtr, "Failed to get volume");
         return;
      }
```

continued...

...from previous page

```
savedCurRefNum = CurResFile();
sourceHandle = GetNamedResource(resType, resName);
if (CheckResError(paramPtr, "GetNamedResource"))
    return;
if (sourceHandle == NIL)
    {
        Fail(paramPtr, "Unable to allocate new handle");
        return;
    }
attributes = GetResAttrs(sourceHandle);
if (CheckResError(paramPtr, "GetResAttrs"))
    return;
DetachResource(sourceHandle);

/*
    Do preprocessing to get volume name of source file.
    Set the volume to the new volume.
    OpenResFile opens only on the default volume.
*/
CollectToSpec(source, (char *) newVolName, colonChar);
ToPstr((char *) newVolName);
newVRefNum = 0;                 /* Don't have a ref num */
if ((err = SetVol(newVolName, newVRefNum)) != noErr)
    {
        Fail(paramPtr, "Cannot set new volume");
        return;
    }

/*
    Create or open the file to copy into. Open resource fork.
    If the ref number is -1, check what went wrong.
    Call UseResFile in case the file was already open.
*/
CreateResFile(destination);
destRefNum = OpenResFile(destination);
if (destRefNum == -1)
    if (CheckResError(paramPtr, "OpenResFile"))
        return;
UseResFile(destRefNum);
if (CheckResError(paramPtr, "UseResFile"))
    return;

newResNum = UniqueID(resType);
AddResource(sourceHandle, resType, newResNum, resName);
SetResAttrs(sourceHandle, attributes);
ChangedResource(sourceHandle);
WriteResource(sourceHandle);
```

continued...

...from previous page

```
    if ((err = SetVol(NIL, oldVRefNum)) != noErr)
        {
            Fail(paramPtr, "Cannot reset original volume");
            return;
        }
    UseResFile(savedCurRefNum);
    DisposHandle(sourceHandle);

    return;
}


/*
    This routine checks for Resource Manager errors.
    If none, it returns FALSE.  Otherwise, it sets up returnValue & returns TRUE.
*/
Boolean CheckResError(paramPtr, resCall)
    XCmdBlockPtr paramPtr;
    char         *resCall;
{
    OsErr    err;
    char  str[256];

    strcpy(str, resCall);  /* Tell user which Resource Mgr call failed */
    err = ResError();
    switch (err)
        {
        case noErr:
            return(FALSE);        /* No error occurred */
            break;
        case mapReadErr:
            strcat(str, ": Map does not permit operation");
            paramPtr->returnValue = (Handle) CopyStrToHand(str);
            break;
        case resAttrErr:
            strcat(str, ": Attribute does not permit operation");
            paramPtr->returnValue = (Handle) CopyStrToHand(str);
            break;
        case rmvResFailed:
            strcat(str, ": RmveResource failed");
            paramPtr->returnValue = (Handle) CopyStrToHand(str);
            break;
        case addResFailed:
            strcat(str, ": AddResource failed");
            paramPtr->returnValue = (Handle) CopyStrToHand(str);
            break;
        case resFNotFound:
            strcat(str, ": Resource file not found");
```

continued...

...from previous page

```
            paramPtr->returnValue = (Handle) CopyStrToHand(str);
            break;
        case resNotFound:
            strcat(str, ": Resource not found");
            paramPtr->returnValue = (Handle) CopyStrToHand(str);
            break;
        default:
            strcat(str, ": Unknown Error = ");
            paramPtr->returnValue = (Handle) ConcatErrorStr(paramPtr, str, err);
            break;
    }
    return(TRUE);
}


/*
    This function concatenates an integer converted to a string onto a given
    error message. For consistency, it returns the handle and allows the caller
    to assign it to paramPtr->returnValue.
*/
Handle ConcatErrorStr(paramPtr, errorString, errorNumber)
    XCmdBlockPtr   paramPtr;
    char           *errorString;
    int            errorNumber;
{
    Str31    str1, str2;

    strcpy(str1, errorString);
    LongToStr(paramPtr, (long) errorNumber, &str2);
    ToCstr((char *) str2);
    strcat(str1, str2);
    return((Handle) CopyStrToHand((char *) str1));
}


/*
    This function copies the string pointed to by a handle into an array
    of bytes.  It does not copy the terminating 0.
*/
void HandleToBytes(array, hndl)
    char     *array;
    Handle   hndl;
```

continued...

...from previous page

```
{
    char  *ptr;

    HLock(hndl);
    ptr = *hndl;
    while (*ptr != EOS)
        *array++ = *ptr++;
    HUnlock(hndl);
}


/*
    This function copies characters from one string to another until it
    finds the delimiter character "myChar". It returns the pointer into
    the target string.
*/
char *CollectToSpec(targetStr, subStr, myChar)
    char  *targetStr;
    char  *subStr;
    char  myChar;
{
    while ((*targetStr != (char) myChar) && (*targetStr != EOS))
        *subStr++ = *targetStr++;

    *subStr = EOS;
    return(targetStr);
}


/*
    This function checks to see if the correct number of params were received.
    And writes an error message into the returnValue if they were not.
*/
short CheckParamCount(paramPtr, str)
    XCmdBlockPtr paramPtr;
    char         *str;
{
    short    count;

    count = paramPtr->paramCount;
    if (count != requiredParamCount)
        {
            paramPtr->returnValue = (Handle) CopyStrToHand(str);
            return(errorFlag);
        }
    return(count);
}
```

continued...

...from previous page

```
/*
   This function gets a handle and copies the error string it receives into the
heap
   for return to HyperCard.
*/
void Fail(paramPtr, str)
   XCmdBlockPtr   paramPtr;
   char          *str;
{
   paramPtr->returnValue = (Handle) CopyStrToHand(str);
   return;
}


/*
   This utility function allocates heapspace and copies a string into it.
*/
Handle CopyStrToHand(str)
   char *str;
{
   Handle   newHndl;

   newHndl = (Handle) NewHandle((long) strlen(str) + 1);
   strcpy((char *)(*newHndl), str);
   return(newHndl);
}


/*
   This utility function copies the string pointed to by a handle into
   a character array, then converts the C string to a Pascal string.
   Note that the C string is overwritten by the Pascal string.
*/
void HandleToPstr(str, hndl)
   Str255   str;
   Handle   hndl;
{
   strcpy((char *) str, *hndl);
   ToPstr((char *) str);
}
```

continued...

...from previous page

```
/*
   This utility function converts a Pascal string to a C string.
   Note that the Pascal string is overwritten in the process.
*/
char *ToCstr(str)
   char *str;
{
   unsigned char length, i;

   length = str[0];
   for (i = 0; i < length; ++i)        /* Shift string 1 byte to the left */
      str[i] = str[i+1];
   str[length] = 0;                    /* Put zero-terminator after string */
   return(str);
}


/*
   This utility function converts a C string to a Pascal string.
   Note that the C string is overwritten in the process.
*/
char *ToPstr(str)
   char *str;
{
   unsigned char length, i;

   for (i = 0, length = 0; str[i] != 0; ++i)    /* Find end of string */
      ++length;
   while (i--)                                  /* Shift string 1 byte to right */
      str[i+1] = str[i];
   str[0] = length;                             /* Put string length in 1st byte */
   return(str);
}
```

GetDiskVol

The GetDiskVol function returns the name of the start-up volume (the disk you booted from).

Quick Reference

GetDiskVol()

Parameters

GetDiskVol takes no parameters.

Examples

```
put GetDislVol() into myVar
IF GetDiskVol() = "HD" THEN DeleteFile "HD:Junk"
```

Tips

You can use GetDiskVol to determine the volume when trying to build a pathname from scratch.

For the Pascal Programmer

```
{$R-}
( *
  © 1988 by Gary Bond
  All Rights Reserved

  GetDiskVol -- a Hypercard XFCN that returns the name of the currently mounted
              volume.

  Form: GetDiskVol()

  Example: GetDiskVol()

  Note: The call to GetDiskVol() doesn't take any parameters.

  ─────────────────────────────────────────────

  To compile and link this file using MPW Pascal, select the following lines and press
  the ENTER key
  ─────────────────────────────────────────────
```

continued...

...from previous page

```
pascal GetDiskVol.p
link -o "HD:Hypercard:Home" -rt XFCN=1517 -sn Main=GetDiskVol GetDiskVol.p.o ∂
{MPW}Libraries:Interface.o -m ENTRYPOINT

* )

{$S GetDiskVol } {Segment name must be the same as the command name}

UNIT DummyUnit;

INTERFACE

USES MemTypes, QuickDraw, OSIntf, ToolIntf, PasLibIntf, PackIntf, HyperXCmd;

PROCEDURE ENTRYPOINT(paramPtr: XCmdPtr);

IMPLEMENTATION

TYPE Str31 = String[31];

PROCEDURE GetDiskVol(paramPtr: XCmdPtr);        FORWARD;

PROCEDURE ENTRYPOINT(paramPtr: XCmdPtr);

  BEGIN
    GetDiskVol(paramPtr);
  END;
  PROCEDURE GetDiskVol(paramPtr: XCmdPtr);

    CONST minParamCount = 0;

    VAR  volName:   Str255;
         err:       Integer;
         vRefNum:   Integer;

{$I XCmdGlue.inc } {includes glue routines}

    PROCEDURE Fail(errStr: Str255); {Exit returning an error message}
```

continued...

...from previous page

```
    BEGIN
      paramPtr^.returnValue := PasToZero(errStr); {load the result}
      EXIT(GetDiskVol); {Leave the XCMD}
    END; {Fail}

  PROCEDURE CheckParamCount; {checks for the correct parameter count}

    VAR numParams: Integer;

    BEGIN
      numParams := paramPtr^.paramCount; {store the number of parameters passed}
      IF (numParams <> minParamCount)
      THEN Fail('Form: GetDiskVol()');
    END; {CheckParamCount}

  BEGIN {main}
    err := GetVol(@volName,vRefNum);
    IF err <> noErr THEN Fail('File system error - cannot get volume name');
    paramPtr^.returnValue := PasToZero(volName);
  END; {main}

END. {GetDiskVol}
```

For the C Programmer

```
/*
  © 1988 by Gary Bond
  All Rights Reserved

  Translated to C by Sioux Lacy

  GetDiskVol:   a Hypercard XFCN that returns the name of the currently mounted
                volume.

  Form:         GetDiskVol()

  Example:      GetDiskVol()

  Note:         The call to GetDiskVol() doesn't take any parameters.
```

continued...

...from previous page

```
   Compile and link this file with the MacTraps and string libraries
*/


/*
   Includes
   Note that these header files are for LightspeedC development.
   Substitute the files that are appropriate for your compiler.
*/
#include <MacTypes.h>
#include <FileMgr.h>
#include "HyperXCmd.h"

/*
   LightspeedC Prototypes
*/
pascal   void main(XCmdBlockPtr);
short    CheckParamCount(XCmdBlockPtr, char *);
void     Fail(XCmdBlockPtr, char *);
Handle   CopyStrToHand(char *);
char     *ToCstr(char *);


/*
   Defined Constants
*/
#define requiredParamCount  (short) 0
#define errorFlag           (short) -1


pascal   void  main(paramPtr)
   XCmdBlockPtr   paramPtr;
{
     Str255       volName;
   int          vRefNum;

   if (GetParamCount(paramPtr, "Form: GetDiskVol()") == errorFlag)
      return;

   if (GetVol((StringPtr) volName, &vRefNum) != noErr)
      {
        Fail(paramPtr, "File system error: cannot get volume name");
        return;
      }
   ToCstr((char *) volName);
   paramPtr->returnValue = (Handle) CopyStrToHand((char *) volName);
   return;
}
```

continued...

...from previous page

```
/*
   This function checks to see if the correct number of params were received.
   And writes an error message into the returnValue if they were not.
*/
short CheckParamCount(paramPtr, str)
   XCmdBlockPtr paramPtr;
   char         *str;
{
   short    count;

   count = paramPtr->paramCount;
   if (count != requiredParamCount)
      {
         paramPtr->returnValue = (Handle) CopyStrToHand(str);
         return(errorFlag);
      }
   return(count);
}


/*
   This function gets a handle and copies the error string it receives into the heap
   for return to HyperCard.
*/
void Fail(paramPtr, str)
   XCmdBlockPtr  paramPtr;
   char          *str;
{
   paramPtr->returnValue = (Handle) CopyStrToHand(str);
   return;
}


/*
   This utility function allocates heapspace and copies a string into it.
*/
Handle CopyStrToHand(str)
   char *str;
{
   Handle   newHndl;

   newHndl = (Handle) NewHandle((long) strlen(str) + 1);
   strcpy((char *)(*newHndl), str);
   return(newHndl);
}
```

continued...

...from previous page

```
/*
   This utility function converts a Pascal string to a C string.
   Note that the Pascal string is overwritten in the process.
*/
char *ToCstr(str)
   char *str;
{
   unsigned char length, i;

   length = str[0];
   for (i = 0; i < length; ++i)        /* Shift string 1 byte to the left */
      str[i] = str[i+1];
   str[length] = 0;                    /* Put zero-terminator after string */
   return(str);
}
```

TalkString

The TalkString command uses the MacinTalk speech drivers to interpret and speak the string or container you pass into it. The speech is in a robotic-sounding male voice. You must have the MacinTalk speech driver in your system folder for TalkString to work.

Quick Reference

TalkString "String to be spoken"

Parameters

TalkString takes one parameter:

Parameter 1: any string, container, or string expression (field, variable, the selection, the message box)

Examples

TalkString "Hello, I am an apple computer"
TalkString card field 1
TalkString myVar
TalkString the selection

Tips

Try different spellings if some words do not sound right when spoken. For example, you might spell the name "Gary" as "Gary," "Gairy," or "Gaire" to obtain the best pronunciation.

For the Pascal Programmer

```
{$R-}
( *
  © 1988 by Gary Bond
  All Rights Reserved

  TalkString -- a Hypercard XCMD that uses the MacinTalk speech driver to speak the
               string passed.

  Form: TalkString "String to be spoken"

  Example: TalkString "I am an Apple Computer"

  Note: The user must have MacinTalk installed in their system folder.
  _____

  To compile and link this file using MPW Pascal, select the following lines and press
  the ENTER key
  _____

  pascal TalkString.p
  link -o "HD:Hypercard:Home" -rt XCMD=1518 -sn Main=TalkString TalkString.p.o ∂
  {MPW}Libraries:Interface.o -m ENTRYPOINT∂
  {MPW}Libraries:SpeechIntf.o -m ENTRYPOINT

* )
```

continued...

...from previous page

{$S TalkString } {Segment name must be the same as the command name}

UNIT DummyUnit;

INTERFACE

USES MemTypes, QuickDraw, OSIntf, ToolIntf, SpeechIntf, HyperXCmd;

PROCEDURE ENTRYPOINT(paramPtr: XCmdPtr);

IMPLEMENTATION

TYPE Str31 = String[31];

PROCEDURE TalkString(paramPtr: XCmdPtr);   FORWARD;

PROCEDURE ENTRYPOINT(paramPtr: XCmdPtr);

```
  BEGIN
    TalkString(paramPtr);
  END;
```

  PROCEDURE TalkString(paramPtr: XCmdPtr);

  CONST minParamCount = 1;

```
  VAR  temp:          Integer;
       myHSize:       LongInt;
       myHandle:      Handle;
       speakHandle:   SpeechHandle;
```

{$I XCmdGlue.inc } {Includes the glue routines}

  PROCEDURE Fail(errStr: Str255); {Exit returning an error message}

```
    BEGIN
      paramPtr^.returnValue := PasToZero(errStr); {load the result}
      EXIT(TalkString); {Leave the XCMD}
    END; {Fail}
```

continued...

...from previous page

```
PROCEDURE CheckParamCount; {checks for the correct parameter count}

  VAR numParams: Integer;
  BEGIN
    numParams := paramPtr^.paramCount; {store the number of parameters passed}
    IF (numParams <> minParamCount)
    THEN Fail('Form: TalkString "String To Be Spoken"');
  END; {CheckParamCount}

BEGIN {main}
  CheckParamCount; {make sure there's a string to speak}
  IF (SpeechOn('',speakHandle) = noErr) THEN {check if the driver is present}
    BEGIN
      myHandle := NewHandle(0); {create for a later call}
      HLock(paramPtr^.params[1]);
      HNoPurge(paramPtr^.params[1]); {don't want these going anywhere}
      myHSize := GetHandleSize(paramPtr^.params[1])-1; {size of text to speak}
      IF Reader(speakHandle,paramPtr^.params[1]^,myHSize,myHandle) = noErr
      THEN temp := MacinTalk(speakHandle,myHandle)
      ELSE Fail('MacinTalk reader error'); {fail if reader can't interpret text}
      HUnlock(paramPtr^.params[1]); {clean-up}
      HPurge(paramPtr^.params[1]);
      DisposHandle(myHandle);
      SpeechOff(speakHandle); {speechOff disposes the handle}
      DisposHandle (Handle(speakHandle));
    END {if}
  ELSE Fail('Cannot find MacinTalk speech driver');
END; {main}

END. {TalkString}
```

For the C Programmer

```
/*
   © 1988 by Gary Bond
   All Rights Reserved

   Translated to C by Sioux Lacy

   TalkString:     a Hypercard XCMD that uses the MacinTalk speech driver
                   to speak the string passed.

   Form:           TalkString "String to be spoken"

   Example:        TalkString "I am an Apple Computer"

   Note:           The user must have MacinTalk installed in the system
                   folder, or this XCMD may crash.


   ─────────────────────────────────────────────────────────────

   Compile and link this file with the MacTraps and string libraries
*/


/*
   Includes
   Note that these header files are for LightspeedC development.
   Substitute the files that are appropriate for your compiler.
*/
#include <MacTypes.h>
#include <Macintalk.h>
#include "HyperXCmd.h"

/*
   LightspeedC Prototypes
*/
pascal    void main(XCmdBlockPtr);
short     CheckParamCount(XCmdBlockPtr, char *);
void      Fail(XCmdBlockPtr, char *);
Handle    CopyStrToHand(char *);


/*
   Defined Constants
*/
#define  requiredParamCount  (short)    1
#define  errorFlag           (short)    -1
#define  NIL                 (Handle)   0
```

continued...

...from previous page

```
pascal void    main(paramPtr)
    XCmdBlockPtr paramPtr;
{
    Size          hndlSize;
    Handle        myHandle;
    SpeechHandle  speakHandle;
    Str255        exceptions;
    /*
        Verify that one parameter was received.
        Then initialize the MacinTalk driver.
    */
    if (CheckParamCount(paramPtr, "Form: TalkString \"String To Be Spoken\"") ==
        errorFlag)
        return;

    exceptions[0] = 0;              /* There are no exceptions */
    if (SpeechOn(exceptions, &speakHandle) == noErr)
        {
        /*
            Get a handle in reserve.
            Lock down the handle to the speak string.
            Figure out how long the string is.
            Have Macintalk reader interpret the text.
        */
        myHandle = NewHandle((Size) 0);
        HLock(paramPtr->params[0]);
        hndlSize = GetHandleSize(paramPtr->params[0]) - 1;

        if (Reader(speakHandle, *(paramPtr->params[0]), hndlSize, myHandle) ==
            noErr)
            MacinTalk(speakHandle, myHandle);
        else
            Fail(paramPtr, "MacinTalk reader error");

        /*
            Clean up by unlocking the param handle, making it purgeable,
            disposing the reserved handle, and turning speech off.
            (SpeechOff disposes the speakHandle.)
        */
        HUnlock(paramPtr->params[0]);
        DisposHandle(myHandle);
        SpeechOff(speakHandle);
        }
    else
        Fail(paramPtr, "Cannot find MacinTalk speech driver");
        HUnlock(speakHandle);
        DisposHandle (speakHandle);

    return;
}
```

continued...

...from previous page

```
/*
   This function checks to see if the correct number of params were received.
   And writes an error message into the returnValue if they were not.
*/
short CheckParamCount(paramPtr, str)
   XCmdBlockPtr paramPtr;
   char         *str;
{
   short   count;

   count = paramPtr->paramCount;
   if (count != requiredParamCount)
      {
         paramPtr->returnValue = (Handle) CopyStrToHand (str);
         return(errorFlag);
      }
   return(count);
}


/*
   This function gets a handle and copies the error string it receives into the
      heap
   for return to HyperCard.
*/
void Fail(paramPtr, str)
   XCmdBlockPtr  paramPtr;
   char          *str;
{
   paramPtr->returnValue = (Handle) CopyStrToHand(str);
   return;
}


/*
   This utility function allocates heapspace and copies a string into it.
*/
Handle CopyStrToHand(str)
   char *str;
{
   Handle  newHndl;

   newHndl = (Handle) NewHandle((long) strlen(str) + 1);
   strcpy((char *)(*newHndl), str);
   return(newHndl);
}
```

GetPathName

The GetPathName function displays the standard file dialog window and returns the full pathname of the item you choose. You can limit the types of files you see by providing a file type (APPL for applications, STAK for stacks, and so on) before calling GetPathName. GetPathName returns empty if the user clicks the Cancel button in the standard field dialog window.

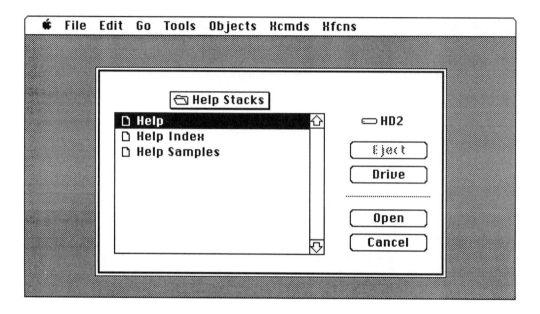

Figure 6.8

The StandardFile dialog window

Quick Reference

GetPathName("STAK")

Parameters

GetPathName takes one parameter:

Parameter 1: The file type of the files you want to view.

The default values for omitted parameters are as follows:

Default for parameter 1:   If you leave the parameter blank, GetPathName shows you all file types.

Examples

```
put GetPathName("STAK") into myVar -- HyperCard stacks
put GetPathName("TEXT") into the message box -- Text files
put GetPathName("WORD") into myVar -- MacWrite files
put GetPathName("APPL") into the message box -- Applications

on mouseUp -- see DeleteFile in this section
  answer "Click OK to delete a file"
  if it is "OK" then DeleteFIle(GetPathName())
end mouseUp
```

Tips

You can use GetPathName to launch any application from the standard file dialog. Following is a scipt that shows you one way to do this:

```
on mouseUp
  put GetPathName("APPL") into tempVar
  if tempVar is not empty then open tempVar
end mouseUp
```

For the Pascal Programmer

```
{$R-}
( *
    © 1988 by Gary Bond
    All Rights Reserved

    GetPathName -- a Hypercard XFCN that returns the pathname of the file using the
                    standard file dialog window.

    Form: GetPathName "File type to display in standard file window"

    Example: GetPathName("TEXT")

    Note:  If the user doesn't supply a file type, all file types are displayed.
```

To compile and link this file using MPW Pascal, select the following lines and press the ENTER key

---

```
pascal GetPathName.p
link -o "HD:Hypercard:Home" -rt XFCN=1519 ∂
-sn Main=GetPathName GetPathName.p.o ∂
{MPW}Libraries:Interface.o -m ENTRYPOINT∂
{MPW}PLibraries:PasLib.o -m ENTRYPOINT

* )

{$S GetPathName } {Segment name must be the same as the command name}

UNIT DummyUnit;

INTERFACE

USES MemTypes, QuickDraw, OSIntf, ToolIntf, PackIntf, PasLibIntf, HyperXCmd;

PROCEDURE ENTRYPOINT(paramPtr: XCmdPtr);

IMPLEMENTATION

TYPE Str31 = String[31];
```

continued...

...from previous page

```
PROCEDURE GetPathName(paramPtr: XCmdPtr);        FORWARD;

  PROCEDURE ENTRYPOINT(paramPtr: XCmdPtr);

    BEGIN
      GetPathName(paramPtr);
    END;

  PROCEDURE GetPathName(paramPtr: XCmdPtr);

    CONST  centerTop = 60;
           centerLeft = 82;
           rootDirID = 2;
           maxParamCount = 1;

    VAR  tempStr:        Str255;
         fileName:       Str255;
         numTypes:       Integer;
         windLeft:       Integer;
         windTop:        Integer;
         err:            OSErr;
         displayPt:      Point;
         theTypeList:    SFTypeList;
         theReply:       SFReply;
         myWDPBPtr:      WDPBPtr;
         myWDPBRec:      WDPBRec;
         cInfoPBBlock:   CInfoPBRec;

{$I XCmdGlue.inc } {includes the glue routines}

  PROCEDURE Fail(errStr: Str255); {Exit returning an error message}

    BEGIN
      paramPtr^.returnValue := PasToZero(errStr); {load the result}
      EXIT(GetPathName); {leave the XFCN}
    END; {Fail}

  PROCEDURE CheckParamCount; {checks for the correct parameter count}

    VAR numParams: Integer;
```

continued...

...from previous page

```
BEGIN
    numParams := paramPtr^.paramCount; {store the number of parameters passed}
    IF (numParams > maxParamCount)
    THEN Fail('Form: GetPathName "File type to display in standard file window"');
END; {CheckParamCount}

PROCEDURE GetLocOfCardWindow; {gets the left and top edges of the card window}

    VAR  tempStr: Str255;
         tempHandle: Handle;

    BEGIN {use call backs to get current window loc}
        tempHandle := EvalExpr('Item 1 of rect of card window'); {left edge}
        ZeroToPas(tempHandle^,tempStr); {convert to a string and then an integer}
        windLeft := StrToNum(tempStr); {now have left edge of card window}
        disposHandle(tempHandle); {don't need this any longer}
        tempHandle := EvalExpr('Item 2 of rect of card window'); {top edge}
        ZeroToPas(tempHandle^,tempStr); {convert to a string and then an integer}
        windTop := StrToNum(tempStr); {now have top edge of card window}
        disposHandle(tempHandle); {don't need this any longer}
    END; {GetLocOfCardWindow}

BEGIN {main}
    CheckParamCount;
    GetLocOfCardWindow; {for centering the dialog}

    SetPt(displayPt,windLeft+centerLeft,windTop+centerTop); {to show SFGetFile}
    numTypes := -1; {display all types as the default}
    fileName := 'Pathname not found'; {initialize this variable}
    myWDPBPtr := @myWDPBRec; {make a local pointer so don't destroy original}

    IF paramPtr^.paramCount <> 0 THEN {set the type supplied}
      BEGIN
        numTypes := 1; {display only one type}
        BlockMove(paramPtr^.params[1]^,@theTypeList[0],4);
      END;

    SFGetFile(displayPt,'',NIL,numTypes,theTypeList,NIL,theReply); {show SFGetFile}
```

    continued...

...from previous page

```
IF theReply.good THEN {if they click OK from SFGetFile}
  BEGIN
    fileName := theReply.fName; {Get the filename}
    tempStr := ''; {initialize so no left over garbage}
    myWDPBPtr^.ioNamePtr := @tempStr; {set up the parameter block}
    myWDPBPtr^.ioVrefNum := theReply.vRefNum; {to get working directory ID}
    myWDPBPtr^.ioWDIndex := 0;
    IF PBGetWDInfo(myWDPBPtr,FALSE) <> noErr THEN Fail('No such volume');

    CInfoPBBlock.ioCompletion := NIL; {set parameter block to loop to the root}
    CInfoPBBlock.ioNamePtr := @tempStr;
    CInfoPBBlock.ioVRefNum := myWDPBPtr^.ioVRefNum;
    CInfoPBBlock.ioFDirIndex := -1;
    CInfoPBBlock.ioDrParID := myWDPBPtr^.ioWDDirID;

    REPEAT {Loop upwards adding each folder name you pass through}
      CInfoPBBlock.ioDrDirID := CInfoPBBlock.ioDrParID;
      err := PBGetCatInfo(@CInfoPBBlock,FALSE);
      IF err <> noErr THEN Fail('Cannot read disk catalog');
      fileName := CONCAT(CInfoPBBlock.ioNamePtr^,':',fileName); {build pathname}
    UNTIL ((CInfoPBBlock.ioDrDirID = rootDirID) OR (err <> noErr));

    IF err <> noErr THEN Fail('I/O error');

  END {if theReply}
  ELSE fileName := ''; {return empty if they click cancel}
  paramPtr^.returnValue := PasToZero(fileName); {return the complete path name}
END; {main}

END. {GetPathName}
```

SetWindowName

The SetWindowName command changes the name of the card window to the passed string or container. The string is limited to 255 characters. (This command is most useful with a MAC II.)

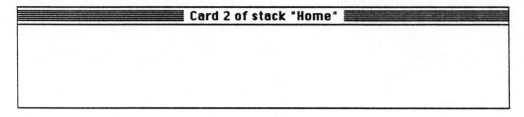

Figure 6.9

The result of the SetWindowName command.

Quick Reference

SetWindowName "New window name"

Parameters

SetWindowName takes one parameter:

Parameter 1:   A string, string expression, or container representing the new name for the window.

Examples

```
SetWindowName "Don't Do That!"
SetWindowName field id 9
SetWindowName the selection
SetWindowName myVar

on openCard
  SetWindowName "Card:" && number of this card && "of" && ¬
  name of this stack
end openCard
```

Tips

Use a larger monitor (such as a Mac II monitor) to see the window's title, or show the card window at 0,100.

For the Pascal Programmer

```
{$R-}
( *
    © 1988 by Gary Bond
    All Rights Reserved

    SetWindowName -- a Hypercard XCMD that sets the name of the top most window to
                     the specified string

    Form: SetWindowName "String Expression"

    Example: SetWindowName "Card" && number of this card

    Note:  SetWindowName tricks the FindWindow ROM routine by passing it a point inside
    the card window.  This lets you set the name of the card window name even though the
    card window isn't the top-most window.  You might need to move your card window to
    0,50 to see the title change.

    _____

    To compile and link this file using MPW Pascal, select the following lines and press
    the ENTER key

    _____


    pascal SetWindowName.p
    link -o "HD:Hypercard:Home" -rt XCMD=1520 -sn ∂
    Main=SetWindowName SetWindowName.p.o ∂
    {MPW}Libraries:Interface.o -m ENTRYPOINT

* )

{$S SetWindowName } {Segment name must be the same as the command name}

UNIT DummyUnit;

INTERFACE
```

continued...

...from previous page

```
USES MemTypes, QuickDraw, OSIntf, ToolIntf, HyperXCmd;

PROCEDURE ENTRYPOINT(paramPtr: XCmdPtr);

IMPLEMENTATION

TYPE  Str31  =  String[31];

PROCEDURE SetWindowName(paramPtr: XCmdPtr);        FORWARD;

PROCEDURE ENTRYPOINT(paramPtr: XCmdPtr);

  BEGIN
    SetWindowName(paramPtr);
  END;

PROCEDURE SetWindowName(paramPtr: XCmdPtr);

  CONST  minParamCount = 1;
         clearMenuBar = 50; {need to get below the menu bar on Plus or SE}

    VAR  newName:        Str255;
         errStr:         Str255;
         str:            Str255;
         numParams:      Integer;
         top:            Integer;
         left:           Integer;
         locNum:         Integer;
         windLoc:        Point;
         myHandle:       Handle;
         currentWindow:  WindowPtr;

  {$I XCmdGlue.inc } {Includes the glue routines}
```

continued...

...from previous page

```
PROCEDURE Fail(errStr: Str255); {Exit returning an error message}

  BEGIN
    paramPtr^.returnValue := PasToZero(errStr); {load the result}
    EXIT(SetWindowName); {Leave the XCMD}
  END; {Fail}

PROCEDURE CheckParamCount; {checks for the correct parameter count}

  BEGIN
    numParams := paramPtr^.paramCount; {store the number of parameters passed}
    IF (numParams <> minParamCount)
    THEN Fail('Form: SetWindowName "String Expression"');
  END; {CheckParamCount}

BEGIN {main}
  CheckParamCount; {verify the correct number of parameters}
  ZeroToPas(paramPtr^.params[1]^,newName); {convert and store the name}
  myHandle := EvalExpr('item 1 of loc of card window');
  {IF (paramPtr^.result <> noErr) THEN Fail('Cannot find the card window');
  ZeroToPas(myHandle^,str); {convert and store horz coord of card window}
  left := StrToNum(str);
  disposHandle(myHandle);
  myHandle := EvalExpr('item 2 of loc of card window');
  {IF (paramPtr^.result <> noErr) THEN Fail('Cannot find the card window');
  ZeroToPas(myHandle^,str); {convert and store vert coord of card window}
  top := StrToNum(str) + clearMenuBar;
  disposHandle(myHandle);
  SetPt(windLoc,left,top); {fake a point inside the card window}
  locNum := FindWindow(windLoc,currentWindow); {don't need contents of locNum}
  IF currentWindow = NIL THEN Fail('Card window partially hidden');
  SetWTitle(currentWindow,newName); {set name of the card window}
END; {main}

END. {SetWindowName}
```

For the C Programmer

```
/*
   © 1988 by Gary Bond
   All Rights Reserved
   Translated to C by Sioux Lacy

   SetWindowName:        a Hypercard XCMD that sets the name of the topmost window to
                         the specified string

   Form:                 SetWindowName "String Expression"

   Example:              SetWindowName "Card" && number of this card

   Note:                 SetWindowName tricks the FindWindow ROM routine by passing
                         it a point inside the card window.  This lets you set the
                         name of the card window name even though the card window
                         isn't the top-most window.  You might need to move your card
                         window to 0,50 to see the title change.
```

```
   Compile and link this file with the MacTraps and string libraries
*/


/*
   Includes
   Note that these header files are for LightspeedC development.
   Substitute the files that are appropriate for your compiler.
*/
#include <MacTypes.h>
#include <DialogMgr.h>
#include <EventMgr.h>
#include <QuickDraw.h>
#include "HyperXCmd.h"

/*
   LightspeedC Prototypes
*/
pascal   void main(XCmdBlockPtr);
int      GetLocOfCardWindow(XCmdBlockPtr, Point *);
short    CheckParamCount(XCmdBlockPtr, char *);
void     Fail(XCmdBlockPtr, char *);
Handle   CopyStrToHand(char *);
long     HandleToNum(XCmdBlockPtr, Handle);
void     HandleToPstr(Str255, Handle);
char     *ToPstr(char *);
```

continued...

...from previous page

```
/*
   Defined Constants
*/
#define  requiredParamCount  (short)    1
#define  errorFlag           (short)   -1
#define  clearMenuBar        (int)     50   /* to position window below the menu bar
#define  NIL                 (Handle)   0


pascal void    main(paramPtr)
   XCmdBlockPtr paramPtr;
{
   Str255      newName;
   Handle      myHandle;
   Point       cardWindowLoc;
   WindowPtr   currentWindow;

   if (CheckParamCount(paramPtr, "Form: SetWindowName \"String Expression\"") ==
errorFlag)
      return;

   /*
      Get the 1st param: the new name for the window
      Get the upper left corner of the card window.
      Offset the upper coordinate in order to clear the menuBar
   */
   HandleToPstr(newName, paramPtr->params[0]);
   if ((GetLocOfCardWindow(paramPtr, &cardWindowLoc)) == errorFlag)
      return;
   cardWindowLoc.v += clearMenuBar;

   /*
      Fake a point inside the card window.
      Get the current window from that point.
      Set its title to the new name.
   */
   SetPt(&cardWindowLoc, cardWindowLoc.h, cardWindowLoc.v);
   FindWindow(cardWindowLoc, &currentWindow);
   if (currentWindow == (WindowPtr) NIL)
      Fail(paramPtr, "Card window partially hidden");
   SetWTitle(currentWindow, newName);

   return;
}
```

continued...

...from previous page

```
/*
   This function uses a callback to get the location (upper, left) of HyperCard's
   window.  It fills in the values in the loc argument sent to it.
*/
int GetLocOfCardWindow(paramPtr, loc)
   XCmdBlockPtr   paramPtr;
   Point          *loc;
{
   Handle   hndl;
   char     str[256];

   strcpy(str, "item 1 of rect of card window");
   hndl = EvalExpr(paramPtr, (StringPtr) ToPstr(str));
   if (paramPtr->result == noErr)
      {
         loc->h = HandleToNum(paramPtr, hndl);
         DisposHandle(hndl);

         strcpy(str, "item 2 of rect of card window");
         hndl = EvalExpr(paramPtr, (StringPtr) ToPstr(str));
         if (paramPtr->result == noErr)
            {
               loc->v = HandleToNum(paramPtr, hndl);
               DisposHandle(hndl);
               return(noErr);
            }
      }
   paramPtr->returnValue = (Handle) CopyStrToHand("Can't get rect of card window");
   return((int) errorFlag);
}


/*
   This function checks to see if the correct number of params were received.
   And writes an error message into the returnValue if they were not.
*/
short CheckParamCount(paramPtr, str)
   XCmdBlockPtr paramPtr;
   char         *str;
{
   short    count;
```

continued...

...from previous page

```
      count = paramPtr->paramCount;
      if (count != requiredParamCount)
          {
              paramPtr->returnValue = (Handle) CopyStrToHand (str);
              return(errorFlag);
          }
      return(count);
}



/*
   This function gets a handle and copies the error string it receives into the
   heap for return to HyperCard.
*/
void Fail(paramPtr, str)
   XCmdBlockPtr   paramPtr;
   char           *str;
{
   paramPtr->returnValue = (Handle) CopyStrToHand(str);
   return;
}



/*
   This utility function allocates heapspace and copies a string into it.
*/
Handle CopyStrToHand(str)
   char *str;
{
   Handle   newHndl;

   newHndl = (Handle) NewHandle((long) strlen(str) + 1);
   strcpy((char *)(*newHndl), str);
   return(newHndl);
}



/*
   This function makes a callback to HyperCard to convert a string to an
   unsigned long integer.  It takes a handle to a C string as an argument.
*/
long HandleToNum(paramPtr, hndl)
   XCmdBlockPtr   paramPtr;
   Handle         hndl;
{
   char   str[32];
   long   num;
```

continued...

...from previous page

```
   strcpy(str, *hndl);
   num = StrToLong(paramPtr, (Str31 *) ToPstr(str));
   return(num);
}


/*
   This utility function copies the string pointed to by a handle into
   a character array, then converts the C string to a Pascal string.
   Note that the C string is overwritten by the Pascal string.
*/
void HandleToPstr(str, hndl)
   Str255   str;
   Handle   hndl;
{
   strcpy((char *) str, *hndl);
   ToPstr((char *) str);
}


/*
   This utility function converts a C string to a Pascal string.
   Note that the C string is overwritten in the process.
*/
char *ToPstr(str)
   char *str;
{
   unsigned char length, i;

   for (i = 0, length = 0; str[i] != 0; ++i)      /* Find end of string */
      ++length;
   while (i--)                                     /* Shift string 1 byte to right */
      str[i+1] = str[i];
   str[0] = length;                                /* Put string length in 1st byte */
   return(str);
}
```

FontReal

The FontReal function returns TRUE if the font name and font size you pass it can be found in any open resource file. Open resource files include the resource file of the system, HyperCard, the Home stack, and the current stack (if it is different from the Home stack). If the font name and size cannot be found, FontReal returns FALSE.

Quick Reference

FontReal("fontName",fontSize)

Parameters

FontReal takes two parameters:

Parameter 1: The name of the font to look for.
Parameter 2: The point size of the font to look for.

Examples

FontReal("Arabic-12",12)

if FontReal("future",12) then
    set textFont of card field 3 to "future"
    set textSize of card field 3 to 12
end if

if FontReal("Cairo",12) then CopyRes "Cairo","FONT","HD:source","HD:dest"

Tips

You can put FontReal in a loop to check for all the point sizes of a given font. Following is a script that shows one way to do this:

```
on mouseUp
    put "9,10,12,14,18,20,24,48" into fontSizes
    put "times" into fontType
    repeat with i = 1 to the number of items in fontSizes
        if not FontReal(fontType,item i of fontSizes) then
            put item i of fontSizes && "point" && fontType & return after var
        end if
    end repeat
    put var into card field 1
end mouseUp
```

For the Pascal Programmer

```
{$R-}
( *
    © 1988 by Gary Bond
    All Rights Reserved

    FontReal -- a Hypercard XFCN that returns TRUE if the font and font size you pass it
                can be found in any of the currently open resource files.

    Form:  FontReal(fontname,fontsize)

    Example:  FontReal(geneva,48)

    Note: This function is set up so that the fontname can be supplied as either the first or
    second parameter.
    _____

    To compile and link this file using MPW Pascal, select the following lines and press
    the ENTER key
    _____
```

continued...

...from previous page

```
pascal FontReal.p
link -o "HD:Hypercard:Home" -rt XFCN=1521∂
-sn Main=FontReal FontReal.p.o -m ENTRYPOINT
```

` * )`

`{$S FontReal }  {Segment name must be the same as the command name}`

`UNIT DummyUnit;`

`INTERFACE`

`USES MemTypes, QuickDraw, OSIntf, ToolIntf, PasLibIntf, HyperXCmd;`

`PROCEDURE ENTRYPOINT(paramPtr: XCmdPtr);`

`IMPLEMENTATION`

`TYPE  Str31 = String[31];`

`PROCEDURE FontReal(paramPtr: XCmdPtr);      FORWARD;`

`PROCEDURE ENTRYPOINT(paramPtr: XCmdPtr);`

```
  BEGIN
   FontReal(paramPtr);
  END;
```

`PROCEDURE FontReal(paramPtr: XCmdPtr);`

`  CONST minParamCount = 2;`

```
    VAR  nameFont:      Str255;
         param1:        Str255;
         param2:        Str255;
         fontResult:    Boolean;
         sizeFont:      Integer;
         fontNum:       Integer;
```

`{$I XCmdGlue.inc }  {Includes the glue routines}`

continued...

continued...

```
    PROCEDURE Fail(errStr: Str255); {Exit returning an error message}

      BEGIN
        paramPtr^.returnValue := PasToZero(errStr); {load the result}
        EXIT(FontReal); {leave the XFCN}
      END; {Fail}

    PROCEDURE CheckParamCount; {checks for the correct parameter count}
    VAR numParams: Integer;

    BEGIN
        numParams := paramPtr^.paramCount; {store the number of parameters passed}
        IF (numParams <> minParamCount)
        THEN Fail('Form: FontReal("fontname",fontsize)');
      END; {CheckParamCount}

  BEGIN {main}
      CheckParamCount; {make sure both parameters are there}
      ZeroToPas(paramPtr^.params[1]^,param1); {both parameters for font size check}
      ZeroToPas(paramPtr^.params[2]^,param2);
      IF ((StrToNum(param1) <= 0) AND (StrToNum(param2) <= 0)) {not supplied}
      THEN Fail('Form: FontReal("fontname",fontsize)');
      IF StrToNum(param2) > 0 THEN {the second parameter is the fontsize}
        BEGIN
          sizeFont := StrToNum(param2); {store the fontsize}
          nameFont := param1;
        END;
      IF StrToNum(param1) > 0 THEN {the first parameter is the fontsize}
        BEGIN
          sizeFont := StrToNum(param1); {store the fontsize}
          nameFont := param2;
        END;
      GetFNum(nameFont,fontNum); {convert the fontname to a font number for RealFont}
      IF fontNum = 0 THEN fontResult := StrToBool('FALSE') {err or fontname not found}
      ELSE fontResult := RealFont(fontNum,sizeFont); {check for name and point size}
      paramPtr^.returnValue := PasToZero(BoolToStr(fontResult)); {the function result}
    END; {main}

END. {FontReal}
```

For the C Programmer

```
/*
    © 1988 by Gary Bond
    All Rights Reserved

    Translated to C by Sioux Lacy

    FontReal:   a Hypercard XFCN that returns TRUE if the font and font size you
                pass it can be found in any of the currently open resource files.

    Form:       FontReal(fontname, fontsize)

    Example:    FontReal(Geneva, 48)

    Note:       This function is set up so that the fontname can be supplied as
                either the first or second parameter.

    ─────────────────────────────────────────────────────────────

    Compile and link this file with the MacTraps and string libraries
*/


/*
    Includes
    Note that these header files are for LightspeedC development.
    Substitute the files that are appropriate for your compiler.
*/
#include <MacTypes.h>
#include <MenuMgr.h>
#include "HyperXCmd.h"

/*
    LightspeedC Prototypes
*/
pascal   void main(XCmdBlockPtr);
short    CheckParamCount(XCmdBlockPtr, char *);
void     Fail(XCmdBlockPtr, char *);
Handle   CopyStrToHand(char *);
long     HandleToNum(XCmdBlockPtr, Handle);
void     HandleToPstr(Str255, Handle);
Boolean  isNumber(Handle);
char     *ToCstr(char *);
char     *ToPstr(char *);


/*
    Defined Constants
*/
```

continued...

...from previous page

```
#define  requiredParamCount  (short)          2
#define  errorFlag           (short)         -1
#define  NIL                 (Handle)         0
#define  EOS                 (unsigned char)  0     /* end of string */


pascal void    main(paramPtr)
   XCmdBlockPtr paramPtr;
{
   Str255  nameFont;
   Str31   str;
   int     sizeFont;
   int     fontNum;
   Boolean fontResult;

   if (CheckParamCount(paramPtr, "Form: FontReal(\"fontname\", fontsize)") ==
         errorFlag)
      return;

   if (isNumber(paramPtr->params[0]))
      {
         sizeFont = (int) HandleToNum(paramPtr, paramPtr->params[0]);
         HandleToPstr(nameFont, paramPtr->params[1]);
      }
   else if (isNumber(paramPtr->params[1]))
      {
         HandleToPstr(nameFont, paramPtr->params[0]);
         sizeFont = (int) HandleToNum(paramPtr, paramPtr->params[1]);
      }
   else
      {
         Fail(paramPtr, "Form: FontReal(\"fontname\",fontsize)");
         return;
      }
   /*
      Convert the fontname to a font number for RealFont
      Check for invalid font number
      Check if font in this point size is available
   */
   GetFNum(nameFont, &fontNum);
   if (fontNum == 0)
      fontResult = FALSE;
   else
      fontResult = RealFont(fontNum, sizeFont);
   BoolToStr(paramPtr, fontResult, &str);
   paramPtr->returnValue = (Handle) CopyStrToHand(ToCstr((char *) str));

   return;
}
```

continued...

...from previous page

```
/*
   This function checks to see if the correct number of params were received.
   And writes an error message into the returnValue if they were not.
*/
short CheckParamCount(paramPtr, str)
   XCmdBlockPtr paramPtr;
   char         *str;
{
   short    count;

   count = paramPtr->paramCount;
   if (count != requiredParamCount)
      {
         paramPtr->returnValue = (Handle) CopyStrToHand(str);
         return(errorFlag);
      }
   return(count);
}


/*
   This function gets a handle and copies the error string it receives into the
heap
   for return to HyperCard.
*/
void Fail(paramPtr, str)
   XCmdBlockPtr  paramPtr;
   char          *str;
{
   paramPtr->returnValue = (Handle) CopyStrToHand(str);
   return;
}


/*
   This utility function allocates heapspace and copies a string into it.
*/
Handle CopyStrToHand(str)
   char *str;
{
   Handle   newHndl;

   newHndl = (Handle) NewHandle((long) strlen(str) + 1);
   strcpy((char *)(*newHndl), str);
   return(newHndl);
}
```

continued...

...from previous page

```
/*
   This function makes a callback to HyperCard to convert a string to an
   unsigned long integer.  It takes a handle to a C string as an argument.
*/
long HandleToNum(paramPtr, hndl)
   XCmdBlockPtr  paramPtr;
   Handle        hndl;
{
   char  str[32];
   long  num;

   strcpy(str, *hndl);
   num = StrToLong(paramPtr, (Str31 *) ToPstr(str));
   return(num);
}


/*
   This utility function copies the string pointed to by a handle into
   a character array, then converts the C string to a Pascal string.
   Note that the C string is overwritten by the Pascal string.
*/
void HandleToPstr(str, hndl)
   Str255  str;
   Handle  hndl;
{
   strcpy((char *) str, *hndl);
   ToPstr((char *) str);
}


/*
   This utility function evaluates whether the string pointed to by the
   handle is a number (contains only digits). Negative numbers will fail.
*/
Boolean isNumber(hndl)
   Handle hndl;
{
   char *ptr;

   HLock(hndl);
   ptr = *hndl;
   while (*ptr != EOS)
      {
         if ((*ptr >= '0') && (*ptr <= '9'))
            ++ptr;
         else
```

continued...

...from previous page

```
              {
                 HUnlock(hndl);
                 return(FALSE);
              }
        }
     HUnlock(hndl);
     return(TRUE);
}


/*
   This utility function converts a Pascal string to a C string.
   Note that the Pascal string is overwritten in the process.
*/
char *ToCstr(str)
   char *str;
{
   unsigned char length, i;

   length = str[0];
   for (i = 0; i < length; ++i)      /* Shift string 1 byte to the left */
      str[i] = str[i+1];
   str[length] = 0;                  /* Put zero-terminator after string */
   return(str);
}


/*
   This utility function converts a C string to a Pascal string.
   Note that the C string is overwritten in the process.
*/
char *ToPstr(str)
   char *str;
{
   unsigned char length, i;

   for (i = 0, length = 0; str[i] != 0; ++i)    /* Find end of string */
      ++length;
   while (i--)                                   /* Shift string 1 byte to right */
      str[i+1] = str[i];
   str[0] = length;                              /* Put string length in 1st byte */
   return(str);
}
```

DeleteFile

The DeleteFile command deletes any stack, text file, application, or other disk file from the disk you specify.

Quick Reference

DeleteFile "path name"

Parameters

DeleteFile takes one parameter:

Parameter 1: Pathname to the file to be deleted. (You do not need to supply a full pathname if you are deleting a file in the current directory.)

Examples

DeleteFile "HD:Junk Stack"
DeleteFile fileName
DeleteFile the selection
DeleteFile the message box
DeleteFile GetPathName("TEXT") -- see GetPathName above.

Tips

You can use DeleteFile to clean up those empty text files that sometimes get created with HyperCard's open, read, and write commands.

For the Pascal Programmer

```
{$R-}
( *
  © 1988 by Gary Bond
  All Rights Reserved

  DeleteFile -- a Hypercard XCMD that deletes the specified file

  Form: DeleteFile filename

  Example: DeleteFile "HD:MyFolder:MyFile"

  Note: Pathnames are allowed and are necessary if the file is not on the root level
```

To compile and link this file using MPW Pascal, select the following lines and press the ENTER key

---

```
pascal DeleteFile.p
link -o "HD:Hypercard:Home" -rt XCMD=1522 -sn Main=DeleteFile DeleteFile.p.o ∂
{MPW}Libraries:Interface.o -m ENTRYPOINT ∂
{MPW}PLibraries:PasLib.o -m ENTRYPOINT

* )

{$S DeleteFile }  {Segment name must be the same as the command name}

UNIT DummyUnit;

INTERFACE {Must include the HyperXCmd file in the uses clause}

USES MemTypes, QuickDraw, OSIntf, ToolIntf, PasLibIntf, HyperXCmd;

PROCEDURE ENTRYPOINT(paramPtr: XCmdPtr);

IMPLEMENTATION

TYPE Str31 = String[31];

PROCEDURE DeleteFile(paramPtr: XCmdPtr);  FORWARD;
```

continued...

...from previous page

```
PROCEDURE ENTRYPOINT(paramPtr: XCmdPtr);

  BEGIN
  DeleteFile(paramPtr);
  END;


PROCEDURE DeleteFile(paramPtr: XCmdPtr);

CONST maxParamCount = 1;

  VAR  str:        Str255;
       fileName:   Str255;
       err:        Integer;
       vRefNum:    Integer;
```

{$I XCmdGlue.inc } {Includes the glue routines}

```
  BEGIN {main}
    IF (paramPtr^.paramcount <> maxParamCount) THEN
      BEGIN {Exit loading the result if no filename or incorrect parameters supplied}
        IF paramPtr^.paramcount = 0 THEN str := 'Filename Parameter Missing'
        ELSE str := 'Incorrect Parameter Count';
        paramPtr^.returnValue := PasToZero(str); {This call loads the result}
        EXIT(DeleteFile); {Leave the XCMD}
      END;
    ZeroToPas(paramPtr^.params[1]^,fileName); {Get the filename from user}
    {** vRefNum is used as a place holder in the FSDelete call below **}
    err := FSDelete(fileName,vRefNum); {delete the specified file}
    IF err <> noErr THEN {Look for file system errors - noErr is a file system const}
      BEGIN
        {** The strings here are our error msgs - they get loaded into the result **}
        CASE err OF {These following are file system constants}
          bdNamErr: str := 'Bad File Name';
          extFSErr: str := 'External File System';
          fBsyErr: str := 'File Busy';
          fLckdErr: str := 'File Locked';
          fnfErr: str := 'File Not Found';
          ioErr: str := 'I/O Error';
          nsvErr: str := 'No Such Volume';
          vLckdErr: str := 'Software Volume Lock';
          wPrErr:  str := 'Disk Is Locked';
```

continued...

...from previous page

```
        OTHERWISE str := CONCAT('Unknown Error: ',NumToStr(err));
        END; {Case}
        paramPtr^.returnValue := PasToZero(str);   {Load the result}
      END; {If err begin}
   END; {main}

END. {DeleteFile}
```

For the C Programmer

```
/*
  © 1988 by Gary Bond
  All Rights Reserved

  Translated to C by Sioux Lacy

  DeleteFile --    a Hypercard XCMD that deletes the specified file

  Form:            DeleteFile filename

  Example:         DeleteFile "HD:MyFolder:MyFile"

  Note:            Pathnames are allowed and are necessary if the file is not on the
                   root level


  ─────────────────────────────────────────────────────────────

  Compile and link this file with the MacTraps and string libraries
*/


/*
  Includes
  Note that these header files are for LightspeedC development.
  Substitute the files that are appropriate for your compiler.
*/
#include <MacTypes.h>
#include <FileMgr.h>
#include "HyperXCmd.h"
```

continued...

...from previous page

```
/*
  LightspeedC Prototypes
*/
pascal void main(XCmdBlockPtr);
Handle ConcatErrorStr(XCmdBlockPtr, char *, int);
Handle CopyStrToHand(char *);
void    HandleToPstr(Str255, Handle);
char    *ToCstr(char *);
char    *ToPstr(char *);


/*
  Defined Constants
*/
#define   requiredParamCount    (short) 1


pascal void  main(paramPtr)
  XCmdBlockPtr paramPtr;
{
  Str255 str;
  Str255 fileName;
  int    err;
  int    vRefNum;

  if (paramPtr->paramCount != requiredParamCount)        /* Right number of params? */
    {
      if (paramPtr->paramCount == 0)
        paramPtr->returnValue = (Handle) CopyStrToHand("Filename Parameter Missing");
      else
        paramPtr->returnValue = (Handle) CopyStrToHand("Incorrect Parameter Count");
      return;
    }
  /*
    Get the filename from the parameter block
  */
  HandleToPstr(fileName, paramPtr->params[0]);

  /*
    Delete the specified file.
    0 is used as a place holder for vRefNum in the FSDelete call.
  */
  err = FSDelete(fileName, (int) 0);
```

continued...

...from previous page

```
switch (err)
  {
    case noErr:
    /* No error occurrred */
    break;
    case bdNamErr:
    paramPtr->returnValue = (Handle) CopyStrToHand("Bad File Name");
    break;
    case extFSErr:
    paramPtr->returnValue = (Handle) CopyStrToHand("External File System");
    break;
    case fBsyErr:
    paramPtr->returnValue = (Handle) CopyStrToHand("File Busy");
    break;
    case fLckdErr:
    paramPtr->returnValue = (Handle) CopyStrToHand("File Locked");
    break;
    case fnfErr:
    paramPtr->returnValue = (Handle) CopyStrToHand("File Not Found");
    break;
    case ioErr:
    paramPtr->returnValue = (Handle) CopyStrToHand("I/O Error");
    break;
    case nsvErr:
    paramPtr->returnValue = (Handle) CopyStrToHand("No Such Volume");
    break;
    case vLckdErr:
    paramPtr->returnValue = (Handle) CopyStrToHand("Software Volume Lock");
    break;
    case wPrErr:
    paramPtr->returnValue = (Handle) CopyStrToHand("Disk Is Locked");
    break;
    default:
    paramPtr->returnValue = (Handle) ConcatErrorStr(paramPtr, "Unknown Error:",
      err);
    break;
  }
}
```

continued...

...from previous page

```
/*
  This function concatenates an integer converted to a string onto a given
  error message. For consistency, it returns the handle and allows the caller
  to assign it to paramPtr->returnValue.
*/
Handle ConcatErrorStr(paramPtr, errorString, errorNumber)
  XCmdBlockPtr  paramPtr;
  char          *errorString;
  int           errorNumber;
{
  Str31   str1, str2;

  strcpy(str1, errorString);
  LongToStr(paramPtr, (long) errorNumber, &str2);
  ToCstr((char *) str2);
  strcat(str1, str2);
  return((Handle) CopyStrToHand((char *) str1));
}


/*
  This utility function allocates heapspace and copies a string into it.
*/
Handle CopyStrToHand(str)
  char *str;
{
  Handle newHndl;

  newHndl = (Handle) NewHandle((long) strlen(str) + 1);
  strcpy((char *)(*newHndl), str);
  return(newHndl);
}


/*
  This utility function copies the string pointed to by a handle into
  a character array, then converts the C string to a Pascal string.
  Note that the C string is overwritten by the Pascal string.
*/
void HandleToPstr(str, hndl)
  Str255 str;
  Handle hndl;
{
  strcpy((char *) str, *hndl);
  ToPstr((char *) str);
}
```

continued...

...from previous page

```
/*
  This utility function converts a Pascal string to a C string.
  Note that the Pascal string is overwritten in the process.
*/
char *ToCstr(str)
  char *str;
{
  unsigned char length, i;

  length = str[0];
  for (i = 0; i < length; ++i)      /* Shift string 1 byte to the left */
    str[i] = str[i+1];
  str[length] = 0;                  /* Put zero-terminator after string */
  return(str);
}


/*
  This utility function converts a C string to a Pascal string.
  Note that the C string is overwritten in the process.
*/
char *ToPstr(str)
  char *str;
{
  unsigned char length, i;

  for (i = 0, length = 0; str[i] != 0; ++i)     /* Find end of string */
    ++length;
  while (i--)                                   /* Shift string 1 byte to right */
    str[i+1] = str[i];
  str[0] = length;                              /* Put string length in 1st byte */
  return(str);
}
```

WHERE TO FIND OTHER XCMD'S AND XFCN'S

During the first few months after HyperCard shipped, several XCMD's and XFCN's appeared in the public domain. One of those XCMD's is called Deprotect; its only purpose is to strip password protection from a stack. (When Bill Atkinson found out, he said, "I knew it would happen sooner or later. I just didn't think it would be *this* soon!")

Looking at other people's XCMD's and XFCN's will give you ideas of your own and will help you learn tips and tricks discovered by others. A good place to start looking for XCMD's and XFCN's is your local user group. Talk to members who are XCMD/ XFCN programmers, and ask them for a copy of their source code. You will find that most members are eager to share their experiences with you.

Another place to look for XCMD's and XFCN's is the resource fork of any public domain stacks you have. (If you do not have any public domain stacks, you can obtain some from your local user group or from on-line services such as CompuServe.)

You will find that public domain stacks often contain the name and address of the author. When you write to ask for a copy of the author's source code, be sure to explain what you want the source code for.

HINTS AND TIPS

- If you want to maintain the copyright on your XCMD's and XFCN's with a minimum of legal hassle, it is a good idea to have your XCMD's and XFCN's display a copyright message on the screen when they are first called.

- Because many people use Command-H to move to the Home stack, you should include a menu item with that command key equivalent in any stack you create that replaces HyperCard's menu bar.

SUMMARY

In this chapter, you learned how to create 20 different XCMD's and XFCN's and how they might be used from HyperTalk.

XCMD's and XFCN's allow you to extend HyperCard beyond its boundaries. With XCMD's and XFCN's, you can add almost any feature you can think of.

You are free to use the XCMD's and XFCN's shown in this book in your own non-commercial stacks.

APPENDICES

APPENDIX A: THE XCmdBlock RECORD

The XCmdBlock record consists of a record definition that contains nine fields. Each field has its own data type and either passes information into HyperCard or receives information back from HyperCard. The data type and size of each field are "hard-wired" so you cannot change them.

For the Pascal Programmer

```
XCmdPtr = ^XCmdBlock;
XCmdBlock =
   RECORD
      paramCount:    Integer;
      params:        ARRAY[1..16] OF Handle;
      returnValue:   Handle;
      passFlag:      Boolean;

      entryPoint:    ProcPtr;
      request:       Integer;
      result:        Integer;
      inArgs:        ARRAY[1..8] OF LongInt;
      outArgs:       ARRAY[1..4] OF LongInt;
   END;
```

For the C Programmer

```
typedef struct
   {
      short      paramCount;
      Handle     params[16];
      Handle     returnValue;
      Boolean    passFlag;

      void       (*entryPoint)();
      short      request;
      short      result;
      long       inArgs[8];
      long       outArgs[4];
   } XCmdBlock, *XCmdBlockPtr;
```

A Summary of the XCmdBlock Record's Fields

parmCount: contains the number of parameters sent with the XCMD or XFCN (1-16).

params: contains 16 handles that point to the data passed in each parameter.

returnValue: used to send information back to HyperCard. When used inside an XCMD, the HyperTalk function *the result* is sent the contents of the passed handle. When used inside an XFCN, this field returns the result of the XFCN.

passFlag: used to pass the message that invoked your XCMD or XFCN along the inheritance path. Set this field to TRUE to pass the message. The default value for this field is FALSE.

entryPoint: contains a jump address used to access HyperCard's internal routines.

request: used to return errors made by the EvalExpr and StrToBool glue routines in versions of HyperCard through 1.1, and for all glue routines in versions greater than 1.1.

InArgs: used to pass parameters for glue routines into HyperCard.

OutArgs: used to receive parameters for glue routines back from HyperCard.

APPENDIX B: A QUICK REFERENCE TO THE GLUE ROUTINES

The following 29 glue routines are a collection of procedures and functions providing access to some of the routines and data inside HyperCard. Using the glue routines is the only method by which you can set and get the contents of a HyperCard field, set and get the contents of a HyperTalk global variable, evaluate a HyperTalk expression, or send a HyperCard message.

BoolToStr

FUNCTION BoolToStr(bool: Boolean): Str31;

EvalExpr

FUNCTION EvalExpr(expr: Str255): Handle;

ExtToStr

FUNCTION ExtToStr(num: Extended): Str31;

GetFieldByID

FUNCTION GetFieldByID(cardFieldFlag: Boolean; fieldID: Integer): Handle;

GetFieldByName

FUNCTION GetFieldByName(cardFieldFlag: Boolean; fieldName: Str255): Handle;

GetFieldByNum

FUNCTION GetFieldByNum(cardFieldFlag: Boolean; fieldNum: Integer): Handle;

GetGlobal

FUNCTION GetGlobal(globName: Str255): Handle;

LongToStr

FUNCTION LongToStr(posNum: LongInt): Str31;

NumToHex

FUNCTION NumToHex(num: LongInt): Str31;

NumToStr

FUNCTION NumToStr(num: LongInt): Str31:

PasToZero

FUNCTION PasToZero(str: Str255): Handle;

ReturnToPas

PROCEDURE ReturnToPas(zeroStr: Ptr;   VAR pasStr: Str255);

ScanToReturn

PROCEDURE ScanToReturn(VAR scanPtr: Ptr);

ScanToZero

PROCEDURE ScanToZero(VAR scaPtr: Ptr);

SendCardMessage

PROCEDURE SendCardMessage(msg: Str255);

SendHCMessage

PROCEDURE SendHCMessage(msg: Str255);

SetFieldByID

PROCEDURE SetFieldByID(cardFieldFlag: Boolean; fieldID: Integer: fieldVal: Handle);

SetFieldByName

PROCEDURE SetFieldByName(cardFieldFlag: Boolean; fieldName: Str255: fieldVal: Handle);

SetFieldByNum

PROCEDURE SetFieldByNum(cardFieldFlag: Boolean; fieldNum: Integer: fieldVal: Handle);

SetGlobal

PROCEDURE SetGlobal(globName: Str255; globValue: Handle);

StringEqual

FUNCTION StringEqual(str1,str2: Str255): Boolean;

StringLength

FUNCTION StringLength(strPtr: Ptr): LongInt;

StringMatch

FUNCTION StringMatch(pattern: Str255; target: Ptr): Ptr;

StrToBool

FUNCTION StrToBool(str: Str31): Boolean;

StrToExt

FUNCTION StrToExt(str: Str31): Extended;

StrToLong

FUNCTION StrToLong(str: Str31): LongInt;

StrToNum

FUNCTION StrToNum(str: Str31): LongInt;

ZeroToPas

PROCEDURE ZeroToPas(zeroStr: Ptr; VAR pasStr: Str255);

ZeroBytes

PROCEDURE ZeroBytes(dstPtr: Ptr; longCount: longInt);

APPENDIX C: THE GLUE ROUTINES FOR MPW PASCAL

The glue routines for MPW Pascal are shown in the following section. To use the routines, enter them into your compiler's editor and save the file using the file name XCmdGlue.inc.

```
{ XCmdGlue.inc -- Sample glue routines to call back to HyperCard.
  See example use in Peek.p and Flash.p
  By Dan Winkler.  DO NOT call the author!  Contact Apple Developer
  Support on AppleLink "MacDTS" or on MCI "MacTech".

  ©Apple Computer, Inc. 1987
  All Rights Reserved.
}

{ The Pascal code for the XCMD or XFCN should include HyperXCmd.p at
  the beginning in the USES clause and this file at the end with the $I
  directive.  There must be a variable named "paramPtr" that is the argument
  that was passed into the XCMD or XFCN. All strings are Pascal strings
  unless noted as zero-terminated strings (no length byte and the string
  goes until a zero byte is encountered). }


PROCEDURE DoJsr(addr: ProcPtr); INLINE $205F,$4E90;
{ Jump subroutine to a procedure.   Pop address into A0, JSR (A0) }


PROCEDURE SendCardMessage(msg: Str255);
{ Send a HyperCard message (a command with arguments) to the current card. }
BEGIN
  WITH paramPtr^ DO
  BEGIN
    inArgs[1] := ORD(@msg);
    request := xreqSendCardMessage;
    DoJsr(entryPoint);
  END;
END;
```

continued...

...from previous page

```
FUNCTION EvalExpr(expr: Str255): Handle;
{ Evaluate a HyperCard expression and return the answer.  The answer is
   a handle to a zero-terminated string. }
BEGIN
  WITH paramPtr^ DO
   BEGIN
      inArgs[1] := ORD(@expr);
      request := xreqEvalExpr;
      DoJsr(entryPoint);
      EvalExpr := Handle(outArgs[1]);
   END;
END;


FUNCTION StringLength(strPtr: Ptr): LongInt;
{ Count the characters from where strPtr points until the next zero byte.
   Does not count the zero itself.  strPtr must be a zero-terminated string. }
BEGIN
  WITH paramPtr^ DO
   BEGIN
      inArgs[1] := ORD(strPtr);
      request := xreqStringLength;
      DoJsr(entryPoint);
      StringLength := outArgs[1];
   END;
END;


FUNCTION StringMatch(pattern: Str255; target: Ptr): Ptr;
{ Perform case-insensitive match looking for pattern anywhere in
   target, returning a pointer to first character of the first match,
   in target or NIL if no match found.  pattern is a Pascal string,
   and target is a zero-terminated string. }
BEGIN
  WITH paramPtr^ DO
   BEGIN
      inArgs[1] := ORD(@pattern);
      inArgs[2] := ORD(target);
      request := xreqStringMatch;
      DoJsr(entryPoint);
      StringMatch := Ptr(outArgs[1]);
   END;
END;
```

continued...

406

...from previous page

```
PROCEDURE SendHCMessage(msg: Str255);
{ Send a HyperCard message (a command with arguments) to HyperCard. }
BEGIN
  WITH paramPtr^ DO
   BEGIN
      inArgs[1] := ORD(@msg);
      request := xreqSendHCMessage;
      DoJsr(entryPoint);
   END;
END;


PROCEDURE ZeroBytes(dstPtr: Ptr; longCount: LongInt);
{ Write zeros into memory starting at dstPtr and going for longCount
  number of bytes. }
BEGIN
  WITH paramPtr^ DO
   BEGIN
      inArgs[1] := ORD(dstPtr);
      inArgs[2] := longCount;
      request := xreqZeroBytes;
      DoJsr(entryPoint);
   END;
END;


FUNCTION PasToZero(str: Str255): Handle;
{ Convert a Pascal string to a zero-terminated string.  Returns a handle
  to a new zero-terminated string.  The caller must dispose the handle. }
BEGIN
  WITH paramPtr^ DO
   BEGIN
      inArgs[1] := ORD(@str);
      request := xreqPasToZero;
      DoJsr(entryPoint);
      PasToZero := Handle(outArgs[1]);
   END;
END;
```

continued...

...from previous page

```
PROCEDURE ZeroToPas(zeroStr: Ptr; VAR pasStr: Str255);
{  Fill the Pascal string with the contents of the zero-terminated
   string.  You create the Pascal string and pass it in as a VAR
   parameter.  Useful for converting the arguments of any XCMD to
   Pascal strings.}
BEGIN
  WITH paramPtr^ DO
   BEGIN
      inArgs[1] := ORD(zeroStr);
      inArgs[2] := ORD(@pasStr);
      request := xreqZeroToPas;
      DoJsr(entryPoint);
   END;
END;


FUNCTION StrToLong(str: Str31): LongInt;
{  Convert a string of ASCII decimal digits to an unsigned long integer. }
BEGIN
  WITH paramPtr^ DO
   BEGIN
      inArgs[1] := ORD(@str);
      request := xreqStrToLong;
      DoJsr(entryPoint);
      StrToLong := outArgs[1];
   END;
END;


FUNCTION StrToNum(str: Str31): LongInt;
{  Convert a string of ASCII decimal digits to a signed long integer.
   Negative sign is allowed.  }
BEGIN
  WITH paramPtr^ DO
   BEGIN
      inArgs[1] := ORD(@str);
      request := xreqStrToNum;
      DoJsr(entryPoint);
      StrToNum := outArgs[1];
   END;
END;
```

continued...

...from previous page

```
FUNCTION StrToBool(str: Str31): BOOLEAN;
{  Convert the Pascal strings 'true' and 'false' to booleans. }
BEGIN
  WITH paramPtr^ DO
   BEGIN
      inArgs[1] := ORD(@str);
      request := xreqStrToBool;
      DoJsr(entryPoint);
      StrToBool := BOOLEAN(outArgs[1]);
   END;
END;


FUNCTION StrToExt(str: Str31): Extended;
{  Convert a string of ASCII decimal digits to a floating point number. }
VAR x: Extended;
BEGIN
  WITH paramPtr^ DO
   BEGIN
      inArgs[1] := ORD(@str);
      inArgs[2] := ORD(@x);
      request := xreqStrToExt;
      DoJsr(entryPoint);
      StrToExt := x;
   END;
END;


FUNCTION LongToStr(posNum: LongInt): Str31;
{  Convert an unsigned long integer to a Pascal string.  }
VAR  str: Str31;
BEGIN
  WITH paramPtr^ DO
   BEGIN
      inArgs[1] := posNum;
      inArgs[2] := ORD(@str);
      request := xreqLongToStr;
      DoJsr(entryPoint);
      LongToStr := str;
   END;
END;
```

continued...

...from previous page

```
FUNCTION NumToStr(num: LongInt): Str31;
{  Convert a signed long integer to a Pascal string.  }
VAR  str: Str31;
BEGIN
  WITH paramPtr^ DO
   BEGIN
      inArgs[1] := num;
      inArgs[2] := ORD(@str);
      request := xreqNumToStr;
      DoJsr(entryPoint);
      NumToStr := str;
   END;
END;


FUNCTION NumToHex(num: LongInt; nDigits: INTEGER): Str31;
{  Convert an unsigned long integer to a hexadecimal number and put it
   into a Pascal string.  }
VAR  str: Str31;
BEGIN
  WITH paramPtr^ DO
   BEGIN
      inArgs[1] := num;
      inArgs[2] := nDigits;
      inArgs[3] := ORD(@str);
      request := xreqNumToHex;
      DoJsr(entryPoint);
      NumToHex := str;
   END;
END;
```

continued...

...from previous page

```
FUNCTION BoolToStr(bool: BOOLEAN): Str31;
{  Convert a boolean to 'true' or 'false'.  }
VAR  str: Str31;
BEGIN
  WITH paramPtr^ DO
   BEGIN
      inArgs[1] := LongInt(bool);
      inArgs[2] := ORD(@str);
      request := xreqBoolToStr;
      DoJsr(entryPoint);
      BoolToStr := str;
   END;
END;


FUNCTION ExtToStr(num: Extended): Str31;
{  Convert a floating point number to decimal digits in a string.  }
VAR  str: Str31;
BEGIN
  WITH paramPtr^ DO
   BEGIN
      inArgs[1] := ORD(@num);
      inArgs[2] := ORD(@str);
      request := xreqExtToStr;
      DoJsr(entryPoint);
      ExtToStr := str;
   END;
END;


FUNCTION GetGlobal(globName: Str255): Handle;
{  Return a handle to a zero-terminated string containing the value of
   the specified HyperTalk global variable.  }
BEGIN
  WITH paramPtr^ DO
   BEGIN
      inArgs[1] := ORD(@globName);
      request := xreqGetGlobal;
      DoJsr(entryPoint);
      GetGlobal := Handle(outArgs[1]);
   END;
END;
```

continued...

...from previous page

```
PROCEDURE SetGlobal(globName: Str255; globValue: Handle);
{  Set the value of the specified HyperTalk global variable to be
   the zero-terminated string in globValue.  The contents of the
   Handle are copied, so you must still dispose it afterwards.  }
BEGIN
  WITH paramPtr^ DO
   BEGIN
      inArgs[1] := ORD(@globName);
      inArgs[2] := ORD(globValue);
      request := xreqSetGlobal;
      DoJsr(entryPoint);
   END;
END;



FUNCTION GetFieldByName(cardFieldFlag: BOOLEAN; fieldName: Str255): Handle;
{  Return a handle to a zero-terminated string containing the value of
   field fieldName on the current card.  You must dispose the handle.  }
BEGIN
  WITH paramPtr^ DO
   BEGIN
      inArgs[1] := ORD(cardFieldFlag);
      inArgs[2] := ORD(@fieldName);
      request := xreqGetFieldByName;
      DoJsr(entryPoint);
      GetFieldByName := Handle(outArgs[1]);
   END;
END;
```

continued...

...from previous page

```
FUNCTION GetFieldByNum(cardFieldFlag: BOOLEAN; fieldNum: INTEGER): Handle;
{  Return a handle to a zero-terminated string containing the value of
   field fieldNum on the current card.  You must dispose the handle.  }
BEGIN
  WITH paramPtr^ DO
  BEGIN
     inArgs[1] := ORD(cardFieldFlag);
     inArgs[2] := fieldNum;
     request := xreqGetFieldByNum;
     DoJsr(entryPoint);
     GetFieldByNum := Handle(outArgs[1]);
  END;
END;


FUNCTION GetFieldByID(cardFieldFlag: BOOLEAN; fieldID: INTEGER): Handle;
{  Return a handle to a zero-terminated string containing the value of
   the field whise ID is fieldID.  You must dispose the handle.  }
BEGIN
  WITH paramPtr^ DO
  BEGIN
     inArgs[1] := ORD(cardFieldFlag);
     inArgs[2] := fieldID;
     request := xreqGetFieldByID;
     DoJsr(entryPoint);
     GetFieldByID := Handle(outArgs[1]);
  END;
END;
```

continued...

...from previous page

```
PROCEDURE SetFieldByName(cardFieldFlag: BOOLEAN; fieldName: Str255; fieldVal: Handle);
{  Set the value of field fieldName to be the zero-terminated string
   in fieldVal.  The contents of the Handle are copied, so you must
   still dispose it afterwards.  }
BEGIN
  WITH paramPtr^ DO
   BEGIN
      inArgs[1] := ORD(cardFieldFlag);
      inArgs[2] := ORD(@fieldName);
      inArgs[3] := ORD(fieldVal);
      request := xreqSetFieldByName;
      DoJsr(entryPoint);
   END;
END;


PROCEDURE SetFieldByNum(cardFieldFlag: BOOLEAN; fieldNum: INTEGER; fieldVal: Handle);
{  Set the value of field fieldNum to be the zero-terminated string
   in fieldVal.  The contents of the Handle are copied, so you must
   still dispose it afterwards.  }
BEGIN
  WITH paramPtr^ DO
   BEGIN
      inArgs[1] := ORD(cardFieldFlag);
      inArgs[2] := fieldNum;
      inArgs[3] := ORD(fieldVal);
      request := xreqSetFieldByNum;
      DoJsr(entryPoint);
   END;
END;
```

continued...

...from previous page

```
PROCEDURE SetFieldByID(cardFieldFlag: BOOLEAN; fieldID: INTEGER; fieldVal: Handle);
{  Set the value of the field whose ID is fieldID to be the zero-
   terminated string in fieldVal.  The contents of the Handle are
   copied, so you must still dispose it afterwards.  }
BEGIN
  WITH paramPtr^ DO
   BEGIN
      inArgs[1] := ORD(cardFieldFlag);
      inArgs[2] := fieldID;
      inArgs[3] := ORD(fieldVal);
      request := xreqSetFieldByID;
      DoJsr(entryPoint);
   END;
END;


FUNCTION StringEqual(str1,str2: Str255): BOOLEAN;
{  Return true if the two strings have the same characters.
   Case insensitive compare of the strings.  }
BEGIN
  WITH paramPtr^ DO
   BEGIN
      inArgs[1] := ORD(@str1);
      inArgs[2] := ORD(@str2);
      request := xreqStringEqual;
      DoJsr(entryPoint);
      StringEqual := BOOLEAN(outArgs[1]);
   END;
END;
```

continued...

...from previous page

```
PROCEDURE ReturnToPas(zeroStr: Ptr; VAR pasStr: Str255);
{  zeroStr points into a zero-terminated string.  Collect the
   characters from there to the next carriage Return and return
   them in the Pascal string pasStr.  If a Return is not found,
   collect chars until the end of the string. }
BEGIN
  WITH paramPtr^ DO
  BEGIN
      inArgs[1] := ORD(zeroStr);
      inArgs[2] := ORD(@pasStr);
      request := xreqReturnToPas;
      DoJsr(entryPoint);
  END;
END;



PROCEDURE ScanToReturn(VAR scanPtr: Ptr);
{  Move the pointer scanPtr along a zero-terminated
   string until it points at a Return character
   or a zero byte.  }
BEGIN
  WITH paramPtr^ DO
  BEGIN
      inArgs[1] := ORD(@scanPtr);
      request := xreqScanToReturn;
      DoJsr(entryPoint);
  END;
END;



PROCEDURE ScanToZero(VAR scanPtr: Ptr);
{  Move the pointer scanPtr along a zero-terminated
   string until it points at a zero byte.  }
BEGIN
  WITH paramPtr^ DO
  BEGIN
      inArgs[1] := ORD(@scanPtr);
      request := xreqScanToZero;
      DoJsr(entryPoint);
  END;
END;
```

416

APPENDIX D: THE GLUE ROUTINES FOR LIGHTSPEEDC™

The following is a complete listing of the glue routines for LightspeedC™. To use these routines, enter them into your compiler's editor and save the file using the name XCmdGlue.c.

The individual glue routines are discussed in Chapter 3.

```
/*
    XCmdGlue.c  Functions for calling all standard HyperCard callback
    routines from C.  This file derived from the Pascal interface.

    Note that the arguments are slightly different than Pascal. The first
    argument is always a pointer to the parameter block that HyperCard
    passed to the XCMD or XFCN.


    ©Apple Computer, Inc. 1987
    All Rights Reserved.
*/


/*
    Includes
    Note that these header files are for LightspeedC development.
    Substitute the files that are appropriate for your compiler.
*/
#include <MacTypes.h>
#include "HyperXCmd.h"


pascal void SendCardMessage (paramPtr, msg)
    XCmdBlockPtr  paramPtr;
    StringPtr  msg;
{
    paramPtr->inArgs[0] = (long) msg;
    paramPtr->request = xreqSendCardMessage;
    DoJsr (paramPtr);
}
```

continued...

...from previous page

```
pascal Handle EvalExpr (paramPtr, expr)
   XCmdBlockPtr   paramPtr;
   StringPtr      expr;
{
   paramPtr->inArgs[0] = (long) expr;
   paramPtr->request = xreqEvalExpr;
   DoJsr (paramPtr);
   return (Handle) paramPtr->outArgs[0];
}


pascal long StringLength (paramPtr, strPtr)
   XCmdBlockPtr   paramPtr;
   StringPtr      strPtr;
{
   paramPtr->inArgs[0] = (long) strPtr;
   paramPtr->request = xreqStringLength;
   DoJsr (paramPtr);
   return (long) paramPtr->outArgs[0];
}


pascal Ptr StringMatch (paramPtr, pattern, target)
   XCmdBlockPtr   paramPtr;
   StringPtr      pattern;
   Ptr            target;
{
   paramPtr->inArgs[0] = (long) pattern;
   paramPtr->inArgs[1] = (long) target;
   paramPtr->request = xreqStringMatch;
   DoJsr (paramPtr);
   return (Ptr)paramPtr->outArgs[0];
}


pascal void SendHCMessage (paramPtr, msg)
   XCmdBlockPtr   paramPtr;
   StringPtr      msg;
{
   paramPtr->inArgs[0] = (long) msg;
   paramPtr->request = xreqSendHCMessage;
   DoJsr (paramPtr);
}
```

continued...

...from previous page

```
pascal void ZeroBytes (paramPtr, dstPtr, longCount)
   XCmdBlockPtr   paramPtr;
   Ptr            dstPtr;
   long           longCount;
{
   paramPtr->inArgs[0] = (long) dstPtr;
   paramPtr->inArgs[1] = longCount;
   paramPtr->request = xreqZeroBytes;
   DoJsr (paramPtr);
}


pascal Handle PasToZero (paramPtr, pasStr)
   XCmdBlockPtr   paramPtr;
   StringPtr      pasStr;
{
   paramPtr->inArgs[0] = (long) pasStr;
   paramPtr->request = xreqPasToZero;
   DoJsr (paramPtr);
   return (Handle) paramPtr->outArgs[0];
}


pascal void ZeroToPas (paramPtr, zeroStr, pasStr)
   XCmdBlockPtr   paramPtr;
   char           *zeroStr;
   StringPtr      pasStr;
{
   paramPtr->inArgs[0] = (long) zeroStr;
   paramPtr->inArgs[1] = (long) pasStr;
   paramPtr->request = xreqZeroToPas;
   DoJsr (paramPtr);
}


pascal long StrToLong (paramPtr, strPtr)
   XCmdBlockPtr   paramPtr;
   Str31          *strPtr;
{
   paramPtr->inArgs[0] = (long) strPtr;
   paramPtr->request = xreqStrToLong;
   DoJsr (paramPtr);
   return (long) paramPtr->outArgs[0];
}
```

continued...

...from previous page

```
pascal long StrToNum (paramPtr, str)
   XCmdBlockPtr   paramPtr;
   Str31          *str;
{
   paramPtr->inArgs[0] = (long) str;
   paramPtr->request = xreqStrToNum;
   DoJsr (paramPtr);
   return (long) paramPtr->outArgs[0];
}


pascal Boolean StrToBool (paramPtr, str)
   XCmdBlockPtr   paramPtr;
   Str31          *str;
{
   paramPtr->inArgs[0] = (long) str;
   paramPtr->request = xreqStrToBool;
   DoJsr (paramPtr);
   return (Boolean) paramPtr->outArgs[0];
}


pascal void StrToExt (paramPtr, str, myext)
   XCmdBlockPtr   paramPtr;
   Str31          *str;
   extended       *myext;
{
   paramPtr->inArgs[0] = (long) str;
   paramPtr->inArgs[1] = (long) myext;
   paramPtr->request = xreqStrToExt;
   DoJsr (paramPtr);
}


pascal void LongToStr (paramPtr, posNum, mystr)
   XCmdBlockPtr   paramPtr;
   long           posNum;
   Str31          *mystr;
{
   paramPtr->inArgs[0] = (long) posNum;
   paramPtr->inArgs[1] = (long) mystr;
   paramPtr->request = xreqLongToStr;
   DoJsr (paramPtr);
}
```

continued...

...from previous page

```
pascal void NumToStr (paramPtr, num, mystr)
   XCmdBlockPtr  paramPtr;
   long          num;
   Str31         *mystr;
{
   paramPtr->inArgs[0] = num;
   paramPtr->inArgs[1] = (long) mystr;
   paramPtr->request = xreqNumToStr;
   DoJsr (paramPtr);
}


pascal void NumToHex (paramPtr, num, nDigits, mystr)
   XCmdBlockPtr  paramPtr;
   long          num;
   short int     nDigits;
   Str31         *mystr;
{
   paramPtr->inArgs[0] = num;
   paramPtr->inArgs[1] = nDigits;
   paramPtr->inArgs[2] = (long) mystr;
   paramPtr->request = xreqNumToHex;
   DoJsr (paramPtr);
}


pascal void BoolToStr (paramPtr, bool, mystr)
   XCmdBlockPtr  paramPtr;
   Boolean       bool;
   Str31         *mystr;
{
   paramPtr->inArgs[0] = (long) bool;
   paramPtr->inArgs[1] = (long) mystr;
   paramPtr->request = xreqBoolToStr;
   DoJsr (paramPtr);
}


pascal void ExtToStr (paramPtr, myext, mystr)
   XCmdBlockPtr  paramPtr;
   extended      *myext;
   Str31         *mystr;
{
   paramPtr->inArgs[0] = (long) myext;
   paramPtr->inArgs[1] = (long) mystr;
   paramPtr->request = xreqExtToStr;
   DoJsr (paramPtr);
}
```

continued...

...from previous page

```
pascal Handle GetGlobal (paramPtr,globName)
   XCmdBlockPtr   paramPtr;
   StringPtr      globName;
{
   paramPtr->inArgs[0] = (long) globName;
   paramPtr->request = xreqGetGlobal;
   DoJsr (paramPtr);
   return (Handle) paramPtr->outArgs[0];
}


pascal void SetGlobal (paramPtr, globName, globValue)
   XCmdBlockPtr   paramPtr;
   StringPtr      globName;
   Handle         globValue;
{
   paramPtr->inArgs[0] = (long)globName;
   paramPtr->inArgs[1] = (long)globValue;
   paramPtr->request = xreqSetGlobal;
   DoJsr (paramPtr);
}


pascal Handle GetFieldByName (paramPtr, cardFieldFlag, fieldName)
   XCmdBlockPtr   paramPtr;
   Boolean        cardFieldFlag;
   StringPtr      fieldName;
{
   paramPtr->inArgs[0] = (long) cardFieldFlag;
   paramPtr->inArgs[1] = (long) fieldName;
   paramPtr->request = xreqGetFieldByName;
   DoJsr (paramPtr);
   return (Handle) paramPtr->outArgs[0];
}


pascal Handle GetFieldByNum (paramPtr, cardFieldFlag, fieldNum)
   XCmdBlockPtr   paramPtr;
   Boolean        cardFieldFlag;
   short int      fieldNum;
{
   paramPtr->inArgs[0] = (long) cardFieldFlag;
   paramPtr->inArgs[1] = fieldNum;
   paramPtr->request = xreqGetFieldByNum;
   DoJsr (paramPtr);
   return (Handle) paramPtr->outArgs[0];
}
```

continued...

...from previous page

```
pascal Handle GetFieldByID (paramPtr, cardFieldFlag, fieldID)
   XCmdBlockPtr  paramPtr;
   Boolean       cardFieldFlag;
   short int     fieldID;
{
   paramPtr->inArgs[0] = (long) cardFieldFlag;
   paramPtr->inArgs[1] = fieldID;
   paramPtr->request = xreqGetFieldByID;
   DoJsr (paramPtr);
   return (Handle) paramPtr->outArgs[0];
}


pascal void SetFieldByName (paramPtr, cardFieldFlag, fieldName, fieldVal)
   XCmdBlockPtr  paramPtr;
   Boolean       cardFieldFlag;
   StringPtr     fieldName;
   Handle        fieldVal;
{
   paramPtr->inArgs[0] = (long) cardFieldFlag;
   paramPtr->inArgs[1] = (long) fieldName;
   paramPtr->inArgs[2] = (long) fieldVal;
   paramPtr->request = xreqSetFieldByName;
   DoJsr (paramPtr);
}


pascal void SetFieldByNum (paramPtr, cardFieldFlag, fieldNum, fieldVal)
   XCmdBlockPtr  paramPtr;
   Boolean       cardFieldFlag;
   short int     fieldNum;
   Handle        fieldVal;
{
   paramPtr->inArgs[0] = (long) cardFieldFlag;
   paramPtr->inArgs[1] = fieldNum;
   paramPtr->inArgs[2] = (long) fieldVal;
   paramPtr->request = xreqSetFieldByNum;
   DoJsr (paramPtr);
}
```

continued...

...from previous page

```
pascal void SetFieldByID (paramPtr, cardFieldFlag, fieldID, fieldVal)
   XCmdBlockPtr   paramPtr;
   Boolean        cardFieldFlag;
   short int      fieldID;
   Handle         fieldVal;
{
   paramPtr->inArgs[0] = (long) cardFieldFlag;
   paramPtr->inArgs[1] = fieldID;
   paramPtr->inArgs[2] = (long) fieldVal;
   paramPtr->request = xreqSetFieldByID;
   DoJsr (paramPtr);
}


pascal Boolean StringEqual (paramPtr, str1, str2)
   XCmdBlockPtr   paramPtr;
   Str31          *str1, *str2;
{
   paramPtr->inArgs[0] = (long) str1;
   paramPtr->inArgs[1] = (long) str2;
   paramPtr->request = xreqStringEqual;
   DoJsr (paramPtr);
   return (Boolean) paramPtr->outArgs[0];
}


pascal void ReturnToPas (paramPtr, zeroStr, pasStr)
   XCmdBlockPtr   paramPtr;
   Ptr            zeroStr;
   StringPtr      pasStr;
{
   paramPtr->inArgs[0] = (long)zeroStr;
   paramPtr->inArgs[1] = (long)pasStr;
   paramPtr->request = xreqReturnToPas;
   DoJsr (paramPtr);
}


pascal void ScanToReturn (paramPtr, scanHndl)
   XCmdBlockPtr   paramPtr;
   Ptr            *scanHndl;
{
   paramPtr->inArgs[0] = (long) scanHndl;
   paramPtr->request = xreqScanToReturn;
   DoJsr (paramPtr);
}
```

continued...

...from previous page

```
pascal void ScanToZero (paramPtr, scanHndl)
   XCmdBlockPtr   paramPtr;
   Ptr            *scanHndl;
{
   paramPtr->inArgs[0] = (long) scanHndl;
   paramPtr->request = xreqScanToZero;
   DoJsr (paramPtr);
}


pascal   void  DoJsr (paramPtr)
   XCmdBlockPtr   paramPtr;
{
   /* This is the LightspeedC implementation for this function */

   CallPascal (paramPtr->entryPoint);

   /*
      Other compilers will probably accept this syntax:
      (*paramPtr->entryPoint)();
   */

}
```

APPENDIX E: MPW C HEADER FILE

Following is the HyperXCmd.h file for MPW C. To use this file with the MPW C compiler, type it into MPW and save it with the name HyperXCmd.h.

```
/*
 *      HyperXCmd.h - Interfaces for HyperTalk callback routines
 *      - Copyright Apple Computer, Inc. 1987,1988.
 *      - All Rights Reserved.
 *
 *      #include this file before your program.
 *      #include "XCmdGlue.c" after your code.
 *
 */

#include <Types.h>
#include <Memory.h>

pascal void Debugger() extern 0xA9FF;

typedef struct XCmdBlock {
    short       paramCount;
    Handle      params[16];
    Handle      returnValue;
    Boolean     passFlag;

    void        (*entryPoint)();
    short       request;
    short       result;
    long        inArgs[8];
    long        outArgs[4];
} XCmdBlock,   *XCmdBlockPtr;

typedef struct Str31 {
    char      guts[32];
} Str31,    *Str31Ptr;

/* result codes */
#define xresSucc    0
#define xresFail    1
#define xresNotImp  2
```

continued...

...from previous page

```
/* request codes */
#define  xreqSendCardMessage     1
#define  xreqEvalExpr             2
#define  xreqStringLength         3
#define  xreqStringMatch          4
#define  xreqSendHCMessage        5
#define  xreqZeroBytes            6
#define  xreqPasToZero            7
#define  xreqZeroToPas            8
#define  xreqStrToLong            9
#define  xreqStrToNum            10
#define  xreqStrToBool           11
#define  xreqStrToExt            12
#define  xreqLongToStr           13
#define  xreqNumToStr            14
#define  xreqNumToHex            15
#define  xreqBoolToStr           16
#define  xreqExtToStr            17
#define  xreqGetGlobal           18
#define  xreqSetGlobal           19
#define  xreqGetFieldByName      20
#define  xreqGetFieldByNum       21
#define  xreqGetFieldByID        22
#define  xreqSetFieldByName      23
#define  xreqSetFieldByNum       24
#define  xreqSetFieldByID        25
#define  xreqStringEqual         26
#define  xreqReturnToPas         27
#define  xreqScanToReturn        28
#define  xreqScanToZero          39

/* Forward definitions of glue routines.  Main program
   must include XCmdGlue.c after its routines.   */

pascal void SendCardMessage(paramPtr,msg)
   XCmdBlockPtr  paramPtr;   StringPtr  msg; extern;
pascal Handle EvalExpr(paramPtr,expr)
   XCmdBlockPtr  paramPtr;   StringPtr  expr;   extern;
pascal long StringLength(paramPtr,strPtr)
   XCmdBlockPtr  paramPtr;   StringPtr  strPtr; extern;
pascal Ptr StringMatch(paramPtr,pattern,target)
   XCmdBlockPtr  paramPtr;   StringPtr  pattern;
   Ptr   target; extern;
pascal void SendHCMessage(paramPtr,msg)
   XCmdBlockPtr  paramPtr;   StringPtr  msg; extern;
pascal void ZeroBytes(paramPtr,dstPtr,longCount)
   XCmdBlockPtr  paramPtr;   Ptr   dstPtr;
   long  longCount; extern;
```

continued...

428

...from previous page

```
pascal Handle PasToZero(paramPtr,pasStr)
   XCmdBlockPtr  paramPtr;  StringPtr  pasStr; extern;
pascal void ZeroToPas(paramPtr,zeroStr,pasStr)
   XCmdBlockPtr  paramPtr;  char *zeroStr;
   StringPtr  pasStr; extern;
pascal long StrToLong(paramPtr,strPtr)
   XCmdBlockPtr  paramPtr;  Str31 * strPtr; extern;
pascal long StrToNum(paramPtr,str)
   XCmdBlockPtr  paramPtr;  Str31 *  str; extern;
pascal Boolean StrToBool(paramPtr,str)
   XCmdBlockPtr  paramPtr;  Str31 *  str; extern;
pascal void StrToExt(paramPtr,str,myext)
   XCmdBlockPtr  paramPtr;  Str31 *  str;
   extended * myext;  extern;
pascal void LongToStr(paramPtr,posNum,mystr)
   XCmdBlockPtr  paramPtr;  long  posNum;
   Str31 * mystr;  extern;
pascal void NumToStr(paramPtr,num,mystr)
   XCmdBlockPtr  paramPtr;  long  num;
   Str31 * mystr;  extern;
pascal void NumToHex(paramPtr,num,nDigits,mystr)
   XCmdBlockPtr  paramPtr;  long  num;
   short  nDigits;  Str31 * mystr;  extern;
pascal void BoolToStr(paramPtr,bool,mystr)
   XCmdBlockPtr  paramPtr;  Boolean bool;
   Str31 * mystr;  extern;
pascal void ExtToStr(paramPtr,myext,mystr)
   XCmdBlockPtr  paramPtr;  extended * myext;
   Str31 * mystr;  extern;
pascal Handle GetGlobal(paramPtr,globName)
   XCmdBlockPtr  paramPtr;  StringPtr  globName;  extern;
pascal void SetGlobal(paramPtr,globName,globValue)
   XCmdBlockPtr  paramPtr;  StringPtr  globName;
   Handle  globValue; extern;
pascal Handle GetFieldByName(paramPtr,cardFieldFlag,fieldName)
   XCmdBlockPtr  paramPtr;  Boolean cardFieldFlag;
   StringPtr  fieldName; extern;
pascal Handle GetFieldByNum(paramPtr,cardFieldFlag,fieldNum)
   XCmdBlockPtr  paramPtr;  Boolean cardFieldFlag;
   short  fieldNum; extern;
pascal Handle GetFieldByID(paramPtr,cardFieldFlag,fieldID)
   XCmdBlockPtr  paramPtr;  Boolean cardFieldFlag;
   short  fieldID;  extern;
pascal void SetFieldByName(paramPtr,cardFieldFlag,fieldName,fieldVal)
   XCmdBlockPtr  paramPtr;  Boolean cardFieldFlag;
   StringPtr  fieldName; Handle  fieldVal;  extern;
pascal void SetFieldByNum(paramPtr,cardFieldFlag,fieldNum,fieldVal)
   XCmdBlockPtr  paramPtr;  Boolean cardFieldFlag;
   short  fieldNum;  Handle  fieldVal;  extern;
```

continued...

...from previous page

```
pascal void SetFieldByID(paramPtr,cardFieldFlag,fieldID,fieldVal)
   XCmdBlockPtr  paramPtr;  Boolean cardFieldFlag;
   short   fieldID;          Handle  fieldVal;  extern;
pascal Boolean StringEqual(paramPtr,str1,str2)
   XCmdBlockPtr  paramPtr;  Str31 *    str1;
   Str31 *    str2;  extern;
pascal void ReturnToPas(paramPtr,zeroStr,pasStr)
   XCmdBlockPtr  paramPtr;  Ptr    zeroStr;
   StringPtr  pasStr;  extern;
pascal void ScanToReturn(paramPtr,scanHndl)
   XCmdBlockPtr  paramPtr;  Ptr *    scanHndl;  extern;
pascal void ScanToZero(paramPtr,scanHndl)
   XCmdBlockPtr  paramPtr;  Ptr *    scanHndl;  extern;
```

APPENDIX F: GLUE ROUTINES FOR MPW C

```
/*
 *      XCmdGlue.c      - Implementation of HyperTalk callback routines
 *                      - Copyright Apple Computer, Inc. 1987,1988.
 *                      - All Rights Reserved.
 *
 *      #include "HyperXCmd.h" before your program.
 *      #include this file after your code.
 *
 */

pascal void SendCardMessage(paramPtr,msg)
   XCmdBlockPtr   paramPtr;   StringPtr   msg;
   /* Send a HyperCard message (a command with arguments) to the current card.
      msg is a pointer to a Pascal format string.  */
{
   paramPtr->inArgs[0] = (long)msg;
   paramPtr->request = xreqSendCardMessage;
   paramPtr->entryPoint();
}


pascal Handle EvalExpr(paramPtr,expr)
   XCmdBlockPtr   paramPtr;   StringPtr   expr;
   /* Evaluate a HyperCard expression and return the answer.  The answer is
      a handle to a zero-terminated string. */
{
   paramPtr->inArgs[0] = (long)expr;
   paramPtr->request = xreqEvalExpr;
   paramPtr->entryPoint();
   return (Handle)paramPtr->outArgs[0];
}


pascal long StringLength(paramPtr,strPtr)
   XCmdBlockPtr   paramPtr;   StringPtr   strPtr;
/* Count the characters from where strPtr points until the next zero byte.
   Does not count the zero itself.  strPtr must be a zero-terminated string. */
{
   paramPtr->inArgs[0] = (long)strPtr;
   paramPtr->request = xreqStringLength;
   paramPtr->entryPoint();
   return (long)paramPtr->outArgs[0];
}


pascal Ptr StringMatch(paramPtr,pattern,target)
   XCmdBlockPtr   paramPtr;   StringPtr   pattern;   Ptr   target;
```

continued...

...from previous page

```
/* Perform case-insensitive match looking for pattern anywhere in
   target, returning a pointer to first character of the first match,
   in target or NIL if no match found.  pattern is a Pascal string,
   and target is a zero-terminated string. */
{
   paramPtr->inArgs[0] = (long)pattern;
   paramPtr->inArgs[1] = (long)target;
   paramPtr->request = xreqStringMatch;
   paramPtr->entryPoint();
   return (Ptr)paramPtr->outArgs[0];
}


pascal void SendHCMessage(paramPtr,msg)
   XCmdBlockPtr  paramPtr;  StringPtr  msg;
   /* Send a HyperCard message (a command with arguments) to HyperCard.
      msg is a pointer to a Pascal format string.  */
{
   paramPtr->inArgs[0] = (long)msg;
   paramPtr->request = xreqSendHCMessage;
   paramPtr->entryPoint();
}


pascal void ZeroBytes(paramPtr,dstPtr,longCount)
   XCmdBlockPtr  paramPtr;  Ptr  dstPtr; long longCount;
/* Write zeros into memory starting at destPtr and going for longCount
   number of bytes. */
{
   paramPtr->inArgs[0] = (long)dstPtr;
   paramPtr->inArgs[1] = longCount;
   paramPtr->request = xreqZeroBytes;
   paramPtr->entryPoint();
}


pascal Handle PasToZero(paramPtr,pasStr)
   XCmdBlockPtr  paramPtr;  StringPtr  pasStr;
/* Convert a Pascal string to a zero-terminated string.  Returns a handle
   to a new zero-terminated string.  The caller must dispose the handle.
   You'll need to do this for any result or argument you send from
   your XCMD to HyperTalk. */
{
   paramPtr->inArgs[0] = (long)pasStr;
   paramPtr->request = xreqPasToZero;
   paramPtr->entryPoint();
   return (Handle)paramPtr->outArgs[0];
}
```

continued...

...from previous page

```
pascal void ZeroToPas(paramPtr,zeroStr,passtr)
   XCmdBlockPtr  paramPtr;   char *zeroStr;   StringPtr  passtr;
/* Fill the Pascal string with the contents of the zero-terminated
   string.  You create the Pascal string and pass it in as a VAR
   parameter.  Useful for converting the arguments of any XCMD to
   Pascal strings. */
{
   paramPtr->inArgs[0] = (long)zeroStr;
   paramPtr->inArgs[1] = (long)passtr;
   paramPtr->request = xreqZeroToPas;
   paramPtr->entryPoint();
}


pascal long StrToLong(paramPtr,strPtr)
   XCmdBlockPtr  paramPtr;   Str31 * strPtr;
/* Convert a string of ASCII decimal digits to an unsigned long integer. */
{
   paramPtr->inArgs[0] = (long)strPtr;
   paramPtr->request = xreqStrToLong;
   paramPtr->entryPoint();
   return (long)paramPtr->outArgs[0];
}


pascal long StrToNum(paramPtr,str)
   XCmdBlockPtr  paramPtr;   Str31 *     str;
/* Convert a string of ASCII decimal digits to a signed long integer.
   Negative sign is allowed. */
{
   paramPtr->inArgs[0] = (long)str;
   paramPtr->request = xreqStrToNum;
   paramPtr->entryPoint();
   return paramPtr->outArgs[0];
}


pascal Boolean StrToBool(paramPtr,str)
   XCmdBlockPtr  paramPtr;   Str31 *     str;
/* Convert the Pascal strings 'true' and 'false' to booleans. */
{
   paramPtr->inArgs[0] = (long)str;
   paramPtr->request = xreqStrToBool;
   paramPtr->entryPoint();
   return (Boolean)paramPtr->outArgs[0];
}
```

continued...

...from previous page

```
pascal void StrToExt (paramPtr, str, myext)
   XCmdBlockPtr  paramPtr;  Str31 *    str;  extended * myext;
 /* Convert a string of ASCII decimal digits to an extended long integer.
    Instead of returning a new extended, as Pascal does, it expects you
    to create myext and pass it in to be filled. */
{
   paramPtr->inArgs[0] = (long) str;
   paramPtr->inArgs[1] = (long) myext;
   paramPtr->request = xreqStrToExt;
   paramPtr->entryPoint ();
}


pascal void LongToStr (paramPtr, posNum, mystr)
   XCmdBlockPtr  paramPtr;  long     posNum;  Str31 * mystr;
 /* Convert an unsigned long integer to a Pascal string.  Instead of
    returning a new string, as Pascal does, it expects you to
    create mystr and pass it in to be filled. */
{
   paramPtr->inArgs[0] = (long) posNum;
   paramPtr->inArgs[1] = (long) mystr;
   paramPtr->request = xreqLongToStr;
   paramPtr->entryPoint ();
}


pascal void NumToStr (paramPtr, num, mystr)
   XCmdBlockPtr  paramPtr;  long     num;  Str31 * mystr;
 /* Convert a signed long integer to a Pascal string.  Instead of
    returning a new string, as Pascal does, it expects you to
    create mystr and pass it in to be filled. */
{
   paramPtr->inArgs[0] = num;
   paramPtr->inArgs[1] = (long) mystr;
   paramPtr->request = xreqNumToStr;
   paramPtr->entryPoint ();
}


pascal void NumToHex (paramPtr, num, nDigits, mystr)
   XCmdBlockPtr  paramPtr;  long     num;
   short    nDigits;           Str31 * mystr;
 /* Convert an unsigned long integer to a hexadecimal number and put it
    into a Pascal string.  Instead of returning a new string, as
    Pascal does, it expects you to create mystr and pass it in to be filled. */
{
   paramPtr->inArgs[0] = num;
```

continued...

...from previous page

```
   paramPtr->inArgs[1] = nDigits;
   paramPtr->inArgs[2] = (long)mystr;
   paramPtr->request = xreqNumToHex;
   paramPtr->entryPoint();
}


pascal void BoolToStr(paramPtr,bool,mystr)
   XCmdBlockPtr  paramPtr;  Boolean bool;   Str31 * mystr;
 /* Convert a boolean to 'true' or 'false'.  Instead of returning
    a new string, as Pascal does, it expects you to create mystr
    and pass it in to be filled. */
{
   paramPtr->inArgs[0] = (long)bool;
   paramPtr->inArgs[1] = (long)mystr;
   paramPtr->request = xreqBoolToStr;
   paramPtr->entryPoint();
}


pascal void ExtToStr(paramPtr,myext,mystr)
   XCmdBlockPtr  paramPtr;  extended * myext;   Str31 * mystr;
 /* Convert an extended long integer to decimal digits in a string.
    Instead of returning a new string, as Pascal does, it expects
    you to create mystr and pass it in to be filled. */
{
   paramPtr->inArgs[0] = (long)myext;
   paramPtr->inArgs[1] = (long)mystr;
   paramPtr->request = xreqExtToStr;
   paramPtr->entryPoint();
}


pascal Handle GetGlobal(paramPtr,globName)
   XCmdBlockPtr  paramPtr;  StringPtr  globName;
/* Return a handle to a zero-terminated string containing the value of
   the specified HyperTalk global variable. */
{
   paramPtr->inArgs[0] = (long)globName;
   paramPtr->request = xreqGetGlobal;
   paramPtr->entryPoint();
   return (Handle)paramPtr->outArgs[0];
}
```

continued...

...from previous page

```
pascal void SetGlobal(paramPtr,globName,globValue)
   XCmdBlockPtr paramPtr;  StringPtr globName;  Handle  globValue;
/* Set the value of the specified HyperTalk global variable to be
   the zero-terminated string in globValue.  The contents of the
   Handle are copied, so you must still dispose it afterwards.  */
{
   paramPtr->inArgs[0] = (long)globName;
   paramPtr->inArgs[1] = (long)globValue;
   paramPtr->request = xreqSetGlobal;
   paramPtr->entryPoint();
}


pascal Handle GetFieldByName(paramPtr,cardFieldFlag,fieldName)
   XCmdBlockPtr paramPtr;  Boolean cardFieldFlag;
   StringPtr  fieldName;
/* Return a handle to a zero-terminated string containing the value of
   field fieldName on the current card.  You must dispose the handle. */
{
   paramPtr->inArgs[0] = (long)cardFieldFlag;
   paramPtr->inArgs[1] = (long)fieldName;
   paramPtr->request = xreqGetFieldByName;
   paramPtr->entryPoint();
   return (Handle)paramPtr->outArgs[0];
}


pascal Handle GetFieldByNum(paramPtr,cardFieldFlag,fieldNum)
   XCmdBlockPtr paramPtr;  Boolean cardFieldFlag;
   short    fieldNum;
/* Return a handle to a zero-terminated string containing the value of
   field fieldNum on the current card.  You must dispose the handle. */
{
   paramPtr->inArgs[0] = (long)cardFieldFlag;
   paramPtr->inArgs[1] = fieldNum;
   paramPtr->request = xreqGetFieldByNum;
   paramPtr->entryPoint();
   return (Handle)paramPtr->outArgs[0];
}


pascal Handle GetFieldByID(paramPtr,cardFieldFlag,fieldID)
   XCmdBlockPtr paramPtr;  Boolean cardFieldFlag;
   short    fieldID;
/* Return a handle to a zero-terminated string containing the value of
   the field whise ID is fieldID.  You must dispose the handle. */
{
   paramPtr->inArgs[0] = (long)cardFieldFlag;
```

continued...

...from previous page

```
    paramPtr->inArgs[1] = fieldID;
    paramPtr->request = xreqGetFieldByID;
    paramPtr->entryPoint();
    return (Handle)paramPtr->outArgs[0];
}


pascal void SetFieldByName(paramPtr,cardFieldFlag,fieldName,fieldVal)
    XCmdBlockPtr  paramPtr;  Boolean cardFieldFlag;
    StringPtr  fieldName; Handle  fieldVal;
/* Set the value of field fieldName to be the zero-terminated string
   in fieldVal.  The contents of the Handle are copied, so you must
   still dispose it afterwards. */
{
    paramPtr->inArgs[0] = (long)cardFieldFlag;
    paramPtr->inArgs[1] = (long)fieldName;
    paramPtr->inArgs[2] = (long)fieldVal;
    paramPtr->request = xreqSetFieldByName;
    paramPtr->entryPoint();
}


pascal void SetFieldByNum(paramPtr,cardFieldFlag,fieldNum,fieldVal)
    XCmdBlockPtr  paramPtr;  Boolean cardFieldFlag;
    short    fieldNum;       Handle  fieldVal;
/* Set the value of field fieldNum to be the zero-terminated string
   in fieldVal.  The contents of the Handle are copied, so you must
   still dispose it afterwards. */
{
    paramPtr->inArgs[0] = (long)cardFieldFlag;
    paramPtr->inArgs[1] = fieldNum;
    paramPtr->inArgs[2] = (long)fieldVal;
    paramPtr->request = xreqSetFieldByNum;
    paramPtr->entryPoint();
}


pascal void SetFieldByID(paramPtr,cardFieldFlag,fieldID,fieldVal)
    XCmdBlockPtr  paramPtr;  Boolean cardFieldFlag;
    short    fieldID;        Handle  fieldVal;
/* Set the value of the field whose ID is fieldID to be the zero-
   terminated string in fieldVal.  The contents of the Handle are
   copied, so you must still dispose it afterwards. */
{
    paramPtr->inArgs[0] = (long)cardFieldFlag;
    paramPtr->inArgs[1] = fieldID;
    paramPtr->inArgs[2] = (long)fieldVal;
    paramPtr->request = xreqSetFieldByID;
    paramPtr->entryPoint();
}
```

continued...

...from previous page

```
}


pascal Boolean StringEqual(paramPtr,str1,str2)
   XCmdBlockPtr  paramPtr;  Str31 *    str1;    Str31 *    str2;
/* Return true if the two strings have the same characters.
   Case insensitive compare of the strings. */
{
   paramPtr->inArgs[0] = (long)str1;
   paramPtr->inArgs[1] = (long)str2;
   paramPtr->request = xreqStringEqual;
   paramPtr->entryPoint();
   return (Boolean)paramPtr->outArgs[0];
}


pascal void ReturnToPas(paramPtr,zeroStr,pasStr)
   XCmdBlockPtr  paramPtr;  Ptr    zeroStr;    StringPtr  pasStr;
/* zeroStr points into a zero-terminated string.  Collect the
   characters from there to the next carriage Return and return
   them in the Pascal string pasStr.  If a Return is not found,
   collect chars until the end of the string. */
{
   paramPtr->inArgs[0] = (long)zeroStr;
   paramPtr->inArgs[1] = (long)pasStr;
   paramPtr->request = xreqReturnToPas;
   paramPtr->entryPoint();
}


pascal void ScanToReturn(paramPtr,scanHndl)
   XCmdBlockPtr  paramPtr;  Ptr *    scanHndl;
/* Move the pointer scanPtr along a zero-terminated
   string until it points at a Return character
   or a zero byte.  */
{
   paramPtr->inArgs[0] = (long)scanHndl;
   paramPtr->request = xreqScanToReturn;
   paramPtr->entryPoint();
}


pascal void ScanToZero(paramPtr,scanHndl)
   XCmdBlockPtr  paramPtr;  Ptr *    scanHndl;
/* Move the pointer scanPtr along a zero-terminated
   string until it points at a zero byte.  */
{
   paramPtr->inArgs[0] = (long)scanHndl;
   paramPtr->request = xreqScanToZero;
      paramPtr->entryPoint();
}
```

APPENDIX G: ADDITIONAL GLUE ROUTINES

Following are some additional glue routines you can add to the end of your XCmdGlue file. Most of these routines are discussed in Chapters 2, 3, and 5.

For the Pascal Programmer

```
PROCEDURE IncrementPointer(VAR scanPtr: Ptr; count: LongInt);
{Increments the specified pointer by the number of
bytes passed in count}

  BEGIN
     scanPtr := Pointer(ORD(scanPtr)+count);
  END;

PROCEDURE ScanToSpace(VAR scanPtr: Ptr);
{Move the pointer represented by scanPtr along a zero-terminated
   string until it points at a space or if none found, a zero byte.}

  VAR  exitloop: BOOLEAN;

  BEGIN
     exitloop := FALSE;
     REPEAT
     IF ((scanPtr^ = $20) OR (scanPtr^ = 0)) THEN exitloop := TRUE
     ELSE scanPtr := Pointer(ORD(scanPtr)+1);
     UNTIL exitloop = TRUE;
  END;
```

continued...

...from previous page

```
PROCEDURE ScanToComma(VAR scanPtr: Ptr);
{Move the pointer represented by scanPtr along a zero-terminated
   string until it points at a comma or if none found, a zero byte.}

   VAR  exitloop: BOOLEAN;

   BEGIN
      exitloop := FALSE;
      REPEAT
      IF ((scanPtr^ = $2C) OR (scanPtr^ = 0)) THEN exitloop := TRUE
      ELSE scanPtr := Pointer(ORD(scanPtr)+1);
      UNTIL exitloop = TRUE;
   END;



PROCEDURE ScanToSpec(VAR scanPtr: Ptr; myChar: Integer);
{Move the pointer represented by scanPtr along a zero-terminated
   string until it points at the specified delimiter or if none found, a zero byte.  The
   value passed in myChar is the Ascii value of the character}

   VAR  exitloop: BOOLEAN;

   BEGIN
      exitloop := FALSE;
      REPEAT
      IF ((scanPtr^ = myChar) OR (scanPtr^ = 0)) THEN exitloop := TRUE
      ELSE scanPtr := Pointer(ORD(scanPtr)+1);
      UNTIL exitloop = TRUE;
   END;

( *
FUNCTION CollectToComma(VAR scanPtr: Ptr): Str255;
{Move the pointer scanPtr along a zero-terminated
   string collecting characters until a comma or zero byte.}

   TYPE Str1  =  String[1];
```

continued...

...from previous page

```
VAR  exitloop:  BOOLEAN;
     tempStr: Str1;
        collectStr: Str255;

BEGIN
   exitloop := FALSE;
   tempStr[0]  :=  chr(1);
   collectStr  :=  '';
   REPEAT
   IF ((scanPtr^ = $2C) OR (scanPtr^ = 0)) THEN exitloop := TRUE
   ELSE
      BEGIN
         tempStr[1]  :=  chr(scanPtr^);
         collectStr  :=  Concat(collectStr,tempStr);
         scanPtr  :=  Pointer(ORD(scanPtr)+1);
         END;
   UNTIL exitloop = TRUE;
   CollectToComma := collectStr;
  END;
* )
```

```
FUNCTION CollectToSpace(VAR scanPtr: Ptr): Str255;
{Move the pointer scanPtr along a zero-terminated
  string collecting characters until a space or zero byte.}

TYPE Str1  =  String[1];

VAR  exitloop:  BOOLEAN;
     tempStr: Str1;
        collectStr: Str255;

BEGIN
   exitloop := FALSE;
   tempStr[0]  :=  chr(1);
   collectStr  :=  '';
   REPEAT
   IF ((scanPtr^ = $20) OR (scanPtr^ = 0)) THEN exitloop := TRUE
   ELSE
```

continued...

...from previous page

```
      BEGIN
      tempStr[1]  :=  chr(scanPtr^);
      collectStr  :=  Concat(collectStr,tempStr);
      scanPtr  :=  Pointer(ORD(scanPtr)+1);
        END;
    UNTIL exitloop = TRUE;
    CollectToSpace := collectStr;
  END;

FUNCTION CollectToSpec(VAR scanPtr: Ptr;myChar: Integer): Str255;
{Move the pointer scanPtr along a zero-terminated
   string collecting characters until a comma or zero byte.}

TYPE Str1  =  String[1];

VAR  exitloop:   BOOLEAN;
     tempStr: Str1;
       collectStr: Str255;

  BEGIN
    exitloop := FALSE;
    tempStr[0]  :=  chr(1);
    collectStr  :=  '';
    REPEAT
    IF ((scanPtr^ = myChar) OR (scanPtr^ = 0)) THEN exitloop := TRUE
    ELSE
      BEGIN
        tempStr[1]  :=  chr(scanPtr^);
        collectStr  :=  Concat(collectStr,tempStr);
        scanPtr  :=  Pointer(ORD(scanPtr)+1);
        END;
    UNTIL exitloop = TRUE;
    CollectToSpec := collectStr;
  END;

FUNCTION Rnd(Range: Integer): Integer;
{Generates a positive random integer from 1 to the number passed in Range.}

VAR   GetRand:   Integer;
```

continued...

...from previous page

```
BEGIN
  GetRand := ABS(RANDOM);
  Rnd := (GetRand-(TRUNC(GetRand/Range)*Range))+1;
END;


PROCEDURE Display(displayStr: Str255);
{displays the Dialog XCMD's dialog window with the string you pass it}

  BEGIN
    SendCardMessage(CONCAT('Dialog ',displayStr));
  END;

PROCEDURE MakeGlobal(myGlobName: Str255);
{creates one or more HyperTalk global variables - to create more than one global, pass a
comma separated list of global names in myGlobName}
  BEGIN
    SendCardMessage('set lockscreen to true');
    SendCardMessage('domenu "new field"');
    SendCardMessage('put "on makeglobal" & return into last card field');
    SendCardMessage(CONCAT('put "global ',myGlobName,'" after last card field'));
    SendCardMessage('put return & "end makeglobal" after last card field');
    SendCardMessage('set script of last card field to last card field');
    SendCardMessage('send "makeglobal" to last card field');
    SendCardMessage('click at loc of last card field');
    SendCardMessage('domenu "clear field"');
    SendCardMessage('choose browse tool');
    SendCardMessage('set lockscreen to false');
  END; {MakeGlobal}

PROCEDURE Fail(errNumber: Integer); {call Fail with your own error code}

  CONST RomError = 1; {Use appropriate names for your constants}
        O/S Error = 2 ;
        MyError = 3 ;
```

continued...

...from previous page

```
BEGIN {Fail}
   CASE errNumber OF
      RomError: str := 'Error message 1'; {Use appropriate error messages}
      O/SError: str := 'Error message 2';
      MyyError: str := 'Error message 3';
   OTHERWISE {If none found, return a generic error message}
      str := CONCAT('Unknown error: ', NumToStr(errNumber));
   END; {Case}
   paramPtr^.returnValue := PasToZero(str); {Load 'the result'}
   EXIT(myXCMD); {replace myXCMD with the name of your XCMD}
END; {Fail}
```

For the C Programmer

```c
char *ScanToSpace(str)
   char *str;
{
   while ((*str != ' ') && (*str != 0))
      ++str;
   return(str);
}

/*
   Example:

   myPointer = *(paramPtr->params[0]);
   myPointer = ScanToSpace(myPointer);
*/


char *ScanToComma(str)
   char *str;
{
   while ((*str != ',') && (*str != 0))
      ++str;
   return(str);
}
```

continued...

...from previous page

```
/*
   Example:

   myPointer = * (paramPtr->params[0]);
   myPointer = ScanToComma (myPointer);
*/


char *ScanToSpec(str, myChar)
   char  *str;
   char  myChar;
{
   while ((*str != myChar) && (*str != 0))
      ++str;
   return(str);
}

/*
   Example (scan until $):

   myPointer = * (paramPtr->params[0]);
   myPointer = ScanToSpec(myPointer, '$');
*/


char *CollectToComma(targetStr, subStr)
   char  *targetStr;
   char  *subStr;
{
   while ((*targetStr != ',') && (*targetStr != 0))
      *subStr++ = *targetStr++;

   return(targetStr);
}

/*
   Example: (Note that the subStr does not get 0 terminated)

   Str255  mySubstring;

   myPointer = * (paramPtr->params[0]);
   myPointer = CollectToComma(myPointer, (char *) mySubstring);
*/
```

continued...

...from previous page

```
char *CollectToSpace(targetStr, subStr)
   char *targetStr;
   char *subStr;
{
   while ((*targetStr != ' ') && (*targetStr != 0))
      *subStr++ = *targetStr++;

   return(targetStr);
}

/*
   Example: (Note that the subStr does not get 0 terminated)

   Str255  mySubstring;
   myPointer = * (paramPtr->params[0]);
   myPointer = CollectToSpace(myPointer, (char *) mySubstring);
*/


char *CollectToSpec(targetStr, subStr, myChar)
   char *targetStr;
   char *subStr;
   char myChar;
{
   while ((*targetStr != myChar) && (*targetStr != 0))
      *subStr++ = *targetStr++;

   return(targetStr);
}

/*
   Example: (Note that the subStr does not get 0 terminated)

   Str255  mySubstring;

   myPointer = * (paramPtr->params[0]);
   myPointer = CollectToSpace(myPointer, (char *) mySubstring, '$');
*/
```

continued...

446

...from previous page

```
/*
    This function, via a series of SendCardMessage callbacks,
    creates a global variable with the specified name.
*/
void MakeGlobal(paramPtr, name)
    XCmdBlockPtr  paramPtr;
    char          *name;
{
    Str255   message;

    mySendCardMessage(paramPtr, "set lockScreen to true");
    mySendCardMessage(paramPtr, "doMenu \"New Field\"");
    mySendCardMessage(paramPtr,
        "put \"on makeglobal\" & return into last card field");
    strcpy(message, "put \"global ");
    strcat(message, name);
    strcat(message, "\" & return after last card field");
    mySendCardMessage(paramPtr, (char *) message);
    mySendCardMessage(paramPtr,
        "put return & \"end makeglobal\" & return after last card field");
    mySendCardMessage(paramPtr, "set script of last card field to last card field");
    mySendCardMessage(paramPtr, "send \"makeglobal\" to last card field");
    mySendCardMessage(paramPtr, "click at the loc of last card field");
    mySendCardMessage(paramPtr, "doMenu \"Clear Field\"");
    mySendCardMessage(paramPtr, "choose browse tool");
    mySendCardMessage(paramPtr, "set lockScreen to false");
}


/*
    This cover routine does the conversion to a pascal string and calls
    SendCardMessage with the message.
*/
void mySendCardMessage(paramPtr, str)
    XCmdBlockPtr paramPtr;
    char          *str;
{
    Str255 message;
    strcpy(message, str);
    ToPstr((char *) message);
    SendCardMessage(paramPtr, message);
}
```

continued...

...from previous page

```
#define RomError    1
#define OSError     2
#define MyError     3

void Fail(paramPtr, errorNumber)
   XCmdBlockPtr    paramPtr;
   int             errorNumber;
{
   switch (errorNumber)
      {
         case RomError:
            paramPtr->returnValue = (Handle) CopyStrToHand("Error message 1");
            break;
         case OSError:
            paramPtr->returnValue = (Handle) CopyStrToHand("Error message 2");
            break;
         case MyError:
            paramPtr->returnValue = (Handle) CopyStrToHand("Error message 3");
            break;
         default:
            paramPtr->returnValue = (Handle) ConcatErrorStr(paramPtr,
            "Unknown Error:", errorNumber);
            break;
      }
}

Handle ConcatErrorStr(paramPtr, errorString, errorNumber)
   XCmdBlockPtr   paramPtr;
   char           *errorString;
   int            errorNumber;
{
   Str31    str1, str2;

   strcpy(str1, errorString);
   LongToStr(paramPtr, (long) errorNumber, &str2);
   ToCstr((char *) str2);
   strcat(str1, str2);
   return((Handle) CopyStrToHand((char *) str1));
}

Handle CopyStrToHand(str)
   char *str;
{
   Handle   newHndl;

   newHndl = (Handle) NewHandle((long) strlen(str) + 1);
   strcpy((char *) (*newHndl), str);
   return(newHndl);
}
```

APPENDIX H: THE STARTER FILES

XCMD and XFCN starter files are files that contain the minimum code necessary to create an XCMD or XFCN, using either MPW Pascal or LightspeedC. You should enter the code for the appropriate file into your compiler and save it as a template for future use. (See the end of Chapter 3 for more details.)

For the Pascal Programmer

(*

© Add appropriate copyright information
All Rights Reserved

myXCMDName-- Describe what your XCMD or XFCN does

Form: Describe the parameters your XCMD or XFCN takes

Example: Give an exact example of your XCMD or XFCN is use

Note: Put any notes about your XCMD or XFCN here

To compile and link this file using MPW Pascal, select the following lines and press ENTER

```
pascal myXCMDName.p
link -o "HD:HyperCard:Home" -rt XCMD=2000 -sn Main=myXCMDName myXCMDName.p.o ∂
{MPW}Libraries:Interface.o -m ENTRYPOINT ∂
{MPW}PLibraries:PasLib.o -m ENTRYPOINT
```

Note: Include other link files as necessary. Use option-D in MPW to continue the line.

*)

{$R-} {Dollar sign R and S are MPW compiler directives}

{$S myXCMDName} {The name of the segment must be the same as the name of your XCMD or XFCN}

UNIT DummyUnit;

continued...

...from previous page

```
INTERFACE

USES MemTypes, QuickDraw, OSIntf, ToolIntf, PasLibIntf, HyperXCmd;
{HyperXCmd is the interface file}

PROCEDURE EntryPoint(paramPtr: XCmdPtr);

IMPLEMENTATION

TYPE Str31 = String[31];

{Put other type definitions here}

PROCEDURE myXCMDName(paramPtr: XCmdPtr); FORWARD;

   PROCEDURE EntryPoint(paramPtr: XCmdPtr);

   BEGIN
      myXCMDName(paramPtr);
   END;

   PROCEDURE myXCMDName(paramPtr: XCmdPtr);

   CONST {Constant declarations for your main procedure - eliminate if not necessary}

   VAR {Variable declarations for your main procedure - eliminate if not necessary}

   {Put any sub-procedures or sub-functions that are called by your main procedure here}

   {$I XCmdGlue.inc } {This is an MPW directive which includes the glue routines}

   BEGIN {main}

      {Your main procedure goes here}

   END; {main}

END. {myXCMDName}
```

For the C Programmer

```
/*
   © Add appropriate copyright information
   All Rights Reserved

   myXCMDName -- Describe what your XCMD or XFCN does

   Form: Describe the parameters your XCMD or XFCN takes

   Example: Give an exact example of your XCMD or XFCN in use

   Note: Put any notes about your XCMD or XFCN here

   _____

   Compile and link this file with the MacTraps and string libraries
*/


/*
   Includes:
   Substitute the header files that are appropriate for your compiler.
*/
#include <MacTypes.h>
#include "HyperXCmd.h"    /* This header file appears earlier in this chapter */

pascal  void main(XCmdBlockPtr);

/* Define your constants here */


/* Include type definitions here */


pascal void main(paramPtr)
   XCmdBlockPtr paramPtr;
{
   /* Insert the main body of your XCMD here */
}


/* Put your subroutines here */
```

APPENDIX I: THE ASCII TABLE

Non-Printing Characters

0	Null (NUL)
1	Start of Heading (SOH)
2	Start of Text (STX)
3	End of Text (ETX)
4	End of Transmission (EOT)
5	Enquiry (ENQ)
6	Acknowledge (ACK)
7	Bell (BEL)
8	Backspace (BS)
9	Horizontal Tab (HT)
10	Line Feed (LF)
11	Vertical Tab (VT)
12	Form Feed (FF)
13	Carriage Return (CR)
14	Shift Out (SO)
15	Shift In (SI)
16	Data Line Escape (DLE)
17	Device Control 1 (DC1)
18	Device Control 2 (DC2)
19	Device Control 3 (DC3)
20	Device Control 4 (DC4)
21	Negative Acknowledge (NAK)
22	Synchronous (SYN)
23	End of Transmission Block (ETB)
24	Cancel (CAN)
25	End of Medium (EM)
26	Substitute (SUB)
27	Escape (ESC)
28	File Separator (FS)
29	Group Separator (GS)
30	Record Separator (RS)
31	Unit Separator (US)

Printing Characters

32	space	64	@	96	`
33	!	65	A	97	a
34	"	66	B	98	b
35	#	67	C	99	c
36	$	68	D	100	d
37	%	69	E	101	e
38	&	70	F	102	f
39	'	71	G	103	g
40	(	72	H	104	h
41	)	73	I	105	i
42	*	74	J	106	j
43	+	75	K	107	k
44	,	76	L	108	l
45	-	77	M	109	m
46	.	78	N	110	n
47	/	79	O	111	o
48	0	80	P	112	p
49	1	81	Q	113	q
50	2	82	R	114	r
51	3	83	S	115	s
52	4	84	T	116	t
53	5	85	U	117	u
54	6	86	V	118	v
55	7	87	W	119	w
56	8	88	X	120	x
57	9	89	Y	121	y
58	:	90	Z	122	z
59	;	91	[	123	{
60	<	92	\	124	|
61	=	93	]	125	}
62	>	94	^	126	~
63	?	95	_		

APPENDIX J: CONTACTING A USER GROUP

Both user groups listed below have extensive libraries of public domain stacks, many of which contain XCMD's and XFCN's:

Berkeley Macintosh Users Group (BMUG)
1442A Walnut Street, Suite 153
Berkeley, California 94709

(415) 849-9114 (announcement number)
(415) 849-BMUG (bulletin board number)

Boston Computer Society
1 Center Plaza
Boston, Mass. 02108

(617) 367-8080